About the author

Lise Garon is Professor of Political Communication at Laval University, Quebec, Canada. She chairs the International Political Science Association's Political Research Committee on Contemporary North Africa. A close observer of political change in North Africa, she has conducted fieldwork there over many years. Her research has focused on democratization processes, public debates and the media in that region. She is the author of two books: *L'obsession unitaire et la Nation trompée: La fin de l'Algérie socialiste* (Presses de l'Université Laval, 1993), and *Le Silence Tunisien: Les alliances dangereuses au Maghreb* (L'Harmattan, 1998).

Zed Books: Selected Titles on the Middle East

Marwan Bishara, *Palestine/Israel: Peace or Apartheid*

Habib Boulares, *Islam: The Fear and the Hope*

Gérard Chaliand, *The Kurdish Tragedy*

Levon Chorbajian, Patrick Donabedian and Claude Mutafian, *The Caucasian Knot: The History and Politics of Nagorno-Karabagh*

Nicholas Guyatt, *The Absence of Peace: Understanding the Israeli-Palestinian Conflict*

Pervez Hoodbhoy, *Islam and Science*

Dietrich Jung with Wolfango Piccoli, *Modern-day Turkey in the Greater Middle East: Kemalism Faced with its Ottoman Legacy*

Nabil Khoury and Valentine Moghadam (eds), *Gender and Development in the Arab World*

Sheri Laizer, *Martyrs, Traitors and Patriots: Kurdistan after the Gulf War*

Julie Marcus, *A World of Difference: Islam and Gender Hierarchy in Turkey*

Fatima Mernissi, *Women's Rebellion and Islamic Memory*

Haideh Moghissi, *Feminism and Islamic Fundamentalism: Limits of Postmodern Analysis*

Ephraim Nimni (ed.), *The Challenge of Post-Zionism*

Mariam Poya, *Women, Work and Islamism: Ideology and Resistance in Iran*

Ali Rahnema (ed.), *Pioneers of Islamic Revival*

Ali Rahnema and Farhad Nomani, *The Secular Miracle: Religion, Politics and Economic Policy in Iran*

Nawal el Saadawi, *The Hidden Face of Eve: Women in the Arab World*

Nawal el Saadawi, *The Nawal El Saadawi Reader*

Rosemary Sayigh, *Too Many Enemies: The Palestinian Experience in Lebanon*

S. Sayyid, *A Fundamental Fear: Eurocentrism and the Emergence of Islamism*

Martin van Bruinessen, *Agha, Shaikh and State: The Social and Political Structures of Kurdistan*

Paul J. White, *Primitive Rebels or Revolutionary Modernisers? The Kurdish Nationalist Movement in Turkey*

For full details of this list and Zed's other subject and general catalogues, please write to: The Marketing Department, Zed Books, 7 Cynthia Street, London N1 9JF, UK or email Sales@zedbooks.demon.co.uk

Visit our website at: http://www.zedbooks.demon.co.uk

Dangerous Alliances

CIVIL SOCIETY, THE MEDIA AND
DEMOCRATIC TRANSITION IN NORTH AFRICA

LISE GARON

Foreword by
CLOVIS DEMERS
President of Human Rights Internet

Zed Books
London & New York

Dangerous Alliances was first published by
Zed Books Ltd, 7 Cynthia Street, London N1 9JF, UK and
Room 400, 175 Fifth Avenue, New York, NY 10010, USA.

www.zedbooks.demon.co.uk

Cover designed by Andrew Corbett
Typeset in 9½/12 pt Palatino by Long House, Cumbria, UK
Printed and bound in Malaysia

Distributed in the USA exclusively by Palgrave, a division of
St Martin's Press, LLC,175 Fifth Avenue, New York, NY 10010

A catalogue record for this book
is available from the British Library

US Cataloging-in-Publication Data is available from the Library of Congress

ISBN   Hb 1 84277 160 4 Hb
        Pb 1 84277 161 2 Pb

Contents

Abbreviations

AFP	Agence France-Presse	LTDH	Tunisian League of Human Rights
AJT	Tunisian Journalists' Association	MAOL	Algerian Free Officers' Movement
ANEP	National Editing and Publishing Agency (Algeria)	MDS	Socialist Democrats' Movement (Tunisia)
ATCE	Tunisian External Communication Agency	NGO	non-governmental organization
ATFD	Tunisian Women's Association for Democracy	OMDH	Moroccan Human Rights Organization
ATTAC	Association for the Taxation of Financial Transactions for the Aid of Citizens (anti-globalization movement)	PAGS	Socialist Vanguard Party (Algeria)
		PCOT	Tunisian Communist Labour Party
CDT	Democratic Confederation of Labour (affiliated to the Moroccan USFP)	PPS	Party of Progress and Socialism
CNLT	National Council for Freedoms in Tunisia	RAID	Rally for an Alternative International Development (Tunisia – affiliated to ATTAC)
CPJ	Committee to Protect Journalists	RAJ	Algerian Gathering of Youth
CRLDHT	Committee for the Defence of Liberties and Human Rights in Tunisia	RCD	Assembly for Culture and Democracy (Algeria)
		RCD	Constitutional Democratic Rally (Tunisian ruling party)
EMHRN	Euro-Mediterranean Human Rights Movement	RSF	Reporters sans frontières
FFS	Front of Socialist Forces (Algeria)	TAP	Tunis Afrique Presse
		UGET	General Union of Tunisian Students
FIS	Islamic Salvation Front (Algeria)	UGTA	General Union of Algerian Workers
FLN	National Liberation Front, formerly the sole political party in Algeria	UGTM	General Union of Moroccan Workers
GDS	Socialist Democrats' Group (Tunisia)	UGTT	Tunisian General Union of Labour
GIA	Armed Islamic Group (Algeria)	UN	United Nations
		UNEM	National Union of Moroccan Students
HAMAS	Movement for the Islamic Society (Algeria)	UNJM	National Union of Moroccan Journalists
IFHR	International Federation for Human Rights	USFP	Socialist Union of Popular Forces (Morocco)
IMF	International Monetary Fund		
IOC	International Olympic Committee	WAAC	World Algeria Action Committee (www.waac.org)
LADDH	Algerian League for the Defence of Human Rights	WOAT	World Organization Against Torture

Foreword

CLOVIS DEMERS
President of Human Rights Internet

All is quiet on the Tunisian front ... nothing but the comforting buzz of government ads about a small, hospitable land blessed with sunshine and white beaches for European and North American tourists to enjoy, South Pacific on the Med. It is a no-problem country: orchestrated presidential utterings, imaginative legislation, cultural stage-shows and folkloric evenings celebrating tradition, democracy and human rights, casual reports by casual foreign reporters and laundered articles by a co-opted Tunisian press. All this is 'white noise' to mask unwanted noises and give light sleepers a sense of calm. Using her own sources inside and outside Tunisia, Garon has broken through this sound screen and given voice to the courageous few who, from the inside, have a different story to tell and are reaching out, at their peril, to tell it.

Garon meticulously documents the Tunisian regime's uninhibited violations of the fundamental rights and freedoms of its people, the state police's record of torture, the kangaroo courts and the trials presided over by government-controlled judges with accommodating consciences, the harassment and imprisonment of dissidents and their families and friends, and the intimidation of the inquisitors. To this day, Garon's findings are confirmed again and again by international bodies (the UN Committee against Torture, the US State Department, Human Rights Watch, Reporters without Borders, Amnesty International, the International Federation for Human Rights and others) and, increasingly, by those inside who are prepared to face the enormous risks involved (the National Council for Freedoms in Tunisia, the Tunisian Women's Association for Democracy, the Young Lawyers' Association, the General Union of Tunisian Students). They bring confirmation and added immediacy to Garon's analysis of Tunisia's fake democracy and to her sad description of a civil society subdued, controlled and muzzled by lies, empty promises and intimidation. In a book published by La Découverte in Paris in October 1999, *Notre ami, Ben Ali,* investigative reporters Nicolas Beau and Jean-Pierre Turquoi provide further illustration of the 'unwanted noise'. Garon heard behind the screen of propaganda. Bringing together all the components of this sordid story, Garon enlightens those who are unfamiliar with the evolution of Tunisia and Tunisian society and those who, unwittingly or otherwise, have fallen victim to this police state's successful misinformation and propaganda machine.

Garon's most important contribution, however, the one that will pass the test of time, is her analysis of the 'how' and 'why' of President Ben Ali's success (and also the success of his predecessor Bourguiba) in locking in his power and of the failure of a sophisticated society to resist and demand accountability for his actions. Her methodical examination of the coming together of a power-hungry leader and a civil society content to let him wield power gives Garon's work much of its originality and importance. In 1987, when Ben Ali deposed an ageing and discredited Bourguiba, he found himself in a strong position: he had a powerful police force under his orders and, to legitimize his assumption of power, the democratic yearnings that Tunisians society had developed over the previous decade. Moreover, Ben Ali was dealing with a society accustomed to expect everything from the state, delighted to hear his discourse on democracy, freedom and pluralism, inclined, by reflex it seems, to 'bring together all points of view, to limit disagreement and to deepen points of agreement'; a society with, by nature, a 'preference for democracy granted by the Prince', as King Hassan II of Morocco once said, 'rather than for that which must be fought for'.

History can in part explain this attitude and, in this regard, Garon brings new insights that, interestingly enough, have relevance to Algeria and Morocco as well. In Algeria, she points out, before the 1988 riots, civil society had been held under tight control for more than two centuries, first by the colonial system and later by the militaristic rule of the FLN. In Morocco, a unique case in the Maghreb, civil society – and the labour movement in particular – had long been accustomed, even under French colonial rule, to group its institutions around political parties. Garon's references to history are not exhaustive. Undoubtedly, they could be expanded into another book. However, they still provide useful lighting for the well-defined path she chose for her research: the theme of 'les liaisons dangereuses', that is, those hazardous deals sometimes struck between state and society, power and opposition.

'The domination of those who govern', she coldly points out, 'finds some of its explanation in the submissiveness of the governed,' and she concludes, 'tyranny cannot easily take root without the consent of its victims, at least some of its victims'. This may please the postgame quarterbacks who, from afar, deplore the 'inaction' of the victims and get annoyed when they ask the outside world to come and scold their president … But, of course, there is more to it than that and Garon goes on to explain that 'the first instrument for the consolidation of tyranny, the one which substantiates and explains the others, is inherent to independent Tunisia's political culture and history. It is a patriarchal view of power based on the interest of the nation and on consensus around the leader who personifies it.'

Then how is it that with all power in his hands and a society willing to leave them there, President Ben Ali, so adept at making speeches on democracy, human rights and modernity, has not been capable of delivering the model of democratic transition that Tunisians, and indeed the world, had reason to expect in that small country blessed with a high degree of literacy? Garon's answer – in the form of questions – is disarmingly simple and graced with great common sense: 'For democratic reforms to survive,' she asks, 'is it sufficient for those governing to have a desire to help civic society develop? But then, why would they want that? Why would they need to nurture the growth of a competing political force? Since when have politicians become angels?'

This reality-check type of response, tinged with a bit of cynicism, carries into the other side of the equation. Indeed, the complicity involved in those hazardous deals struck in the Maghreb between the state and civil society was accepted by the elite 'in the hope that they could thus accede to political power'. Except that, in this case, the deals had the opposite effect. The elite was isolated and reduced to muteness as soon as the network of civil institutions capable of promoting and feeding public debate had been neutralized. Patriarchal moral order, a police state, a cowed judiciary, and unavailable political alternatives were the resources that the new regime put to work to consolidate its tyranny.

In Chapter 10, entitled 'Islam: Dismantling a Cliché', Garon guides her reader through a painstaking analysis of references to Islam in the Maghrebi press which, summarily but very convincingly, disproves preconceived ideas about the inevitability of tyranny in Arab (or Muslim, or Maghrebi or 'underdeveloped') societies. One wishes that Garon would, perhaps in a future book, expand on this subject and examine at length the transition to modernity in countries with a tradition of authoritarian regimes. Current conventional wisdom and hasty analyses, which are all too common around the issue of Islam and Islamic fundamentalism, beg to be challenged by Garon's type of research.

Dangerous Alliances is the work of a seasoned academic. The painstaking research, the rigorous analysis and the clearly defined application of the conclusions, as well as the care with which the methodology is explained, make this book an excellent teaching tool, widely relevant beyond Tunisia and the Maghreb. The importance given to analysis of the press and to the mechanics and impact of the media on civil society gives it a degree of immediacy and relevance which is bound to please the teacher as well as the general reader.

Acknowledgements

Authors are not alone in writing books. They are supported by unexpected encounters and collaborators.

Such are Tesnim, Mourad and their friends who have benevolently translated into English the original French version of this book, thus hoping to help their loved ones unfairly thrown into jail.

Introduction

Tunis, 1987: Habib Bourguiba and the *Neo-Destour*, a one-party state in all but the name, have presided over the country's destiny since independence. Tunisian civil society courageously struggles against social annihilation, into which the ageing Supreme Warrior's entourage would like to plunge it. For more than a decade through multiplying pamphlets, strikes, demonstrations, and riots, the trade unions and students have been trying to establish themselves as actors with full rights in the political arena. Independent newspapers and opposition parties support the struggle for freedom. The periodic confrontations with the government are violent and violently repressed.

On the morning of 7 November, prime minister Zin Al-Abidin Ben Ali announces the overthow of the dictator and the advent of human rights. All civil actors applaud their new ally and protector who invites them to join him in the building of a 'responsible democracy'. The National Pact, signed some time afterwards, seals the alliance of the civil actors with the new president. The Tunisian political sky would never again be as blue: two elections later, in April 1994, corruption, rigged trials, torture, denunciations and censorship had become more and more widespread under the pretext of warding off the 'fundamentalist' threat; the young Tunisian democracy had reached a level of terror comparable to Stalin's democracy. How could this happen? And why?

Algiers, 1989: after a quarter of a century of catastrophic management, euphemistically called 'independent development', the country has just been rocked by a wave of riots. Popular anger has dealt such a blow to the legitimacy of the regime that President Chadli Ben Jadid and his entourage have undertaken democratic reforms. With multipartyism, freedom of the press, the rule of law and elections, Algerian democracy is born just a few months before the fall of the Berlin Wall.

After the collapse of single-party rule in Algeria, the freedom to speak out and to act reaches a level unparalleled in the Arab world. Algerians proudly repeat among themselves and abroad that Algerian democracy is here to stay, for such is the people's will! Just a scant three years later, however, the army calls off the legislative elections in the middle of the process to prevent the likely victory of the FIS (Islamic Salvation Front); the entry of this party into parliament as a major player is seen as potentially harmful to the future of public liberties … and to the bureaucratic–military elite that has, until then, led Algeria. The *coup*, the banning of the FIS and of its newspapers, the opening of internment camps in the Sahara, spark a civil war that puts off indefinitely the return to democracy. Why are democratic transitions so fragile?

Rabat, 1990: a book published in Paris and authored by Gilles Perrault, *Notre ami le roi*, disturbs the serenity of the Sherifian sovereign, King Hassan II, Commander of the Faithful.[1] The chronicle of a dictatorship, and based on information circulating clandestinely within Morocco, the book draws an unflattering portrait of the monarch: corruption, electoral fraud, vendettas, torture and disappearances are revealed to the French and international public. A vigorous international campaign follows with Danielle Mitterrand (the then French president's spouse) and Amnesty International as its main driving forces. In order to save his public image, the King decides first to release the most famous political prisoners: Serfaty, the Tazmamart prisoners, the Oufkir family, and the Bourequat brothers. Gradually, he also releases most of the other prisoners of conscience and multiplies constitutional reforms without the ever-dissatisfied opposition ceasing to press for more freedom.

Under this dictatorship, so much decried since Perrault's book, there nevertheless are opposition parties, which capture the majority of seats at the elections. Opposition newspapers, trade unions and human rights organizations are also able to criticize the state. All these people monitor and denounce violations of freedom. How can we explain such a capacity to speak out under a dictatorship?

Some thirty years earlier, in the 1950s, there was but one counterweight in the face of royal absolutism: the Istiqlal party, the hero of the struggle for independence, and the sole opposition party. Through a skilful mixture of compliant administrations and pitting the Istiqlal's left wing against its right wing, Crown Prince Moulay Hassan (the future King Hassan II) succeeded in provoking a split within the nationalist party. This split paralysed the opposition and would politically discredit it for years to come. The political vacuum thus created made it possible for the king to reign with an iron fist over his kingdom and to coerce his subjects into absolute obedience … for a while.

Tunisia, Algeria, Morocco: these three contrasting scenarios of political evolution in the second half of the twentieth century have one thing in common. In all three cases, alliances between the government and civil actors were formed at the expense of freedom. In Tunisia and Algeria, those alliances have been fatal for the development of two necessary counterweights to the temptation of authoritarianism and return to tyranny: strong civil institutions and the rule of law. In Algeria, more particularly, they have been used to legitimize the return of the military to the political arena, though, as we shall see, civil society has not lost everything. In Morocco, on the other hand, the civil actors have definitely been able to survive these dangerous friendships. After a long period of suppression, civil liberties have returned and, even in the absence of formally democratic mechanisms, civil institutions have been steadily growing.

This book aims to provide an account of the evolution of power relations prior to and following these dangerous alliances in order to understand how such friendships facilitate the closing off of the Maghreb's public forums or agoras. We will also see how this closing-off ensures a minimum of plausibility for the show democracy produced by Tunisian public discourses, and in Algeria made it possible to disguise a military *coup* as an enterprise for the rescue of democracy. There is something in it for the international media as well: initially hungry for the sensational, they feed on official discourses to develop a product that sells well. During this time, out of public view behind the smokescreen built up by propaganda, tyranny re-emerges and grows stronger.

However, the freedom virus has only been weakened, not destroyed, by the dangerous alliance. As time goes by, the 'medicine' loses its effect, and the social body develops new forms of resistance; new unarmed prophets (the phrase is Machiavelli's; the concept was brilliantly embodied by Sakharov, Solzhenitsyn, Walesa and others in the 1980s), backed by international support, little by little undermine the image of these democracylike dictatorships in the international public forum.

Meanwhile, within the countries themselves, a new fertile soil favourable for the growth of freedom may have formed. Of course, the authoritarian regimes have reasserted their power in both Tunisia and

Algeria in the name of democracy. Of course, the public discourses that the dangerous state/society alliances have given rise to have the perverse short-term effect of masking the reality of tyranny. However, when one reads the major newspapers, it becomes clear that these dictatorships, as they try to legitimize themselves by claiming that their aim is democratization, have unwittingly helped to foster a truly democratic civic culture. Alas, this culture legitimizes one front only; what will happen when the cracks become too visible? Have the new dictatorships already provided a justification for their potential gravediggers?

From alliances to conflicts and from openness to closedness, the concept of dangerous friendships will help guide us through Maghreb's narrow labyrinth of democratization processes, their failures as well as their successes. The public arena, the media, the flow of information, propaganda, culture: my discussion will focus on the political society as a whole, not solely on the state. As the argument unfolds, the illusory nature of the princely saying 'I am the state' will become more obvious: Tunisia is not Ben Ali; Algeria is not the military; and Morocco is not the king. Therefore, the enigma posed by the fragility of the democratic balance will be stated in terms of power relations and processes, rather than by reference solely to the personality of the prince or the ideal standards of law and political philosophy (of which the prince is, in fact, not the sole repository).

In passing, I will dissect a number of preconceptions on the inevitability of tyranny in Arab countries (or, for that matter, in Muslim countries, the Maghreb, or 'underdeveloped' countries generally): history, religion, culture, underdevelopment, the international geopolitical context do not represent insurmountable barriers to the development of freedom. On the contrary, all these factors have on occasion supported a favourable evolution.

Note

1   Gilles Perrault, *Notre ami le roi*, Gallimard, Paris (1990).

PART
I

THE PUBLIC ARENA IN THE MAGREB
Convergences and Divergences

'Setting the Stage'

Freedom, dignity and peace, a dream to which ancient Greece gave a name: democracy. But the words evoke also the anguish of a universal drama: why is it, throughout human history, that tyranny, exploitation and war are the rule? Why are freedom, dignity and peace the exceptions? Under different scenarios, from one century to another, it is the same drama: the confiscation and reconquering of freedom of speech. The location of the drama in which we are actors or witnesses is the public forum, the Athenian agora, or the Maghreb's *djemaa*.

A first scenario was depicted by Plato, the father of Western and Arab philosophy. Plato compared the public forum to a dark cave on the walls of which are projected reflections of reality. The show's actors and witnesses are condemned to contemplate nothing but shadows of the real, which is constantly denied them. This scenario has been staged in the Tunisian public forum, padlocked for ten years by a police regime built on censorship, terror and corruption, preventing any form of free expression. The first three chapters of this book will explain how the old demons of domination and submission have succeeded in silencing the Tunisian people.

A second scenario is based on the Greek legend of Oedipus, as brilliantly reconstituted by Freud, the father of psychoanalysis. Oedipus is the mythical representation of those who, out of a desire to emancipate themselves from childhood bonds, set out to undermine the Father's dominant position. After the downfall of the latter, his lone children take refuge in the protective arms of their mother, as Oedipus did with his mother, Jocasta. Oedipus was Greek; it was Algerians who, in 1992, after having rid themselves of the totalitarian government of the National Liberation Front (FLN), the single party, took fright in the face of their new-found freedom and invited the army to save the country from chaos. Chapter 4, then, gives an account of the evolution of Algerian civil society, the downfall of the Father, the temporary triumph of Oedipus the king, the return of the children of Jocasta to the brawny arms of their mother, the army, and the new emancipation of the Algerian Oedipus that perhaps is taking place.

Moroccans too have gone through the trials and tribulations produced by dangerous alliances, but according to a scenario that is, yet again, different. This is already an old story, which alternates between periods of intense civil activity and strongarm rule, between freedom and tyranny. This story is reminiscent of the legendary Sisyphus, the Greek hero condemned eternally to roll a heavy rock up a hill. He always stops halfway to rest, and hence, the rock rolls down again to the bottom of the slope and he must start work all over again. It has been the destiny of Moroccan civil society to be like Sisyphus, whose endless efforts to counteract the pull of authoritarian temptation do not prevent the rock of freedom from returning to the bottom of the slope. As we shall see in Chapter 5, Morocco's story is that of the slow and arduous achievement of liberties until the day when civil activity pauses; Moroccan Sisyphus then ceases to be vigilant and reconciles with the government in an unnatural alliance. Yielding under the weight of the monarchy's authoritarian will may lead to a catastrophic setback for civil and political rights. No, Morocco is not yet a democracy.

1

TUNISIA
THE DOMINATION OF PLATO'S CAVE

The study of Tunisian history may prove disconcerting for the researcher seeking to fathom the fragility of transitions to democracy and the reasons for their failure. This is a history that challenges the theories generally employed to explain the problems of democratic transition found in Yugoslavia, Russia, Poland. It is noteworthy that during its short life span, Tunisia's transition to democracy was confronted with no nationalistic tension, as was the case in the former Yugoslavia. No economic crisis occurred to compromise the feasibility of the democratic project, as in Russia. Neither did Tunisia's transition to democracy suffer from anything like what Korbonski called 'excessive pluralism' in post-communist Poland.[1] Tunisia's transition to democracy simply did not take place – save in the promises of the official discourse and in the hopes for democracy that civil society had unreservedly pinned on its saviour, the new president, Zin Al-Abidin Ben Ali.

The political blockade was complete. Just like those people in Plato's cave who were unable to see anything but shadows of reality, the Tunisian people have had an experience limited to no more than shadows of freedom. Consequently, the transformation of an authoritarian state into a totalitarian dictatorship went almost completely unnoticed by the public, both in Tunisia and abroad. This is why it is necessary to start by bringing to light those little-known facts that will make more comprehensible the analyses presented in this book. Based on reports of international organizations such as Amnesty International, the International Federation for Human Rights, Reporters Sans Frontières (RSF), Article 19, the International Commission of Jurists, but also drawing on private archives and eyewitness accounts of events, I will shed some light on the mechanisms of domination of a police state which have been systematically reinforced since the coming to power of Ben Ali.

The Tunisian Transition to Democracy Did Not Take Place

In fact, the locking up of the Tunisian public forum started at the time of the fall of prime minister Mohamed M'Zali, in 1986, while Ben Ali, who had recently been called back from Poland, was Interior Minister. The human rights situation deteriorated quickly during the interregnum of prime minister Rachid Sfar. Opposition leaders, such as Khemaïs Chamari and Najib Chebbi of the left-wing tendency and Rachid Ghannouchi of the Islamist tendency, were thrown in prison. By early 1987, the situation was ripe for a crackdown on the opposition and a wave of arrests among Islamist militants began, which led to the first big political trial. Torture and executions soon followed.

At this time, tension was running high in the streets and on campuses. On the night of 7 November, Ben Ali – by now prime minister – summoned to the Interior Ministry seven doctors who, without even examining President Bourguiba, declared him unfit to rule the country. As provided for in the Constitution, Ben Ali replaced the deposed president. His next move was to issue a statement promising to re-establish order and undertake democratic reforms.

These promises were soon broken, and instead diametrically opposed policies were pursued. It is true that the position of public prosecutor and the state security court were abolished, but the long-awaited general amnesty gave back to the amnestied neither their civic rights nor their lost jobs. Amendments to the Constitution, far from laying the foundations for democratic institutions, further reinforced the power of the president *vis-à-vis* parliament and the government. In particular, the president no longer has to resign if he loses the confidence of parliament. As for the government, it became a passive tool in the hands of the president, answerable only to him. The new laws upheld the prohibition of any form of criticism of the government and confirmed the powers of the Interior Ministry over political parties and the media. The so-called constitutional reforms provided the smokescreen needed to further consolidate presidential authority while producing the illusion of democratic transition. The Tunisian political system kept the various branches of government in an almost total merger: as the head of state has at his disposal all the resources of the administration which he can freely use to mete out reward and punishment, and the executive is not subject to any form of control by parliament or the judiciary, which are in fact institutionally sub-ordinated to it. Without a countervailing force within the state apparatus, without a separation of powers, as Montesquieu observed, tyranny will only flourish.

A prevailing view of power that confuses the state with political leadership, a machine for police repression that is ready for action, a judicial system that is subordinated to the executive, legal and informal rules that prevent rotation in office: such are the resources that President Ben Ali has exploited to the full, as we shall see in the following sections. His aim is for the emasculation and marginalization of all civil actors and the reconfiguration of the public scene around a central figure, the president, presented as the source of all benevolence and the generous donor to all those in distress.

'I am the State'

A first tool for the reinforcement of tyranny is inherent in the political culture and in the history of independent Tunisia. It consists in a patriarchal view of power, predicated on the notion of the supreme interest of the nation and consensus around its human embodiment. The patriarchal moral order identifies state authority with the charisma of the man at the helm, the only person able to 'grant' opposition parties, free media, cultural organizations, trade unions to civil society. Following Stalin, who used to call himself 'father of all people', Ben Ali has become a father figure, at the same time threatening and benevolent: threatening for those who have mis-givings about his enlightened rule, benevolent for all the unfortunate ones who will eventually turn to him whenever they are faced with difficulties in dealing with government officials. Such, at least, is the presidential image conveyed by the media and commonly taken up in private conversations.

One of my interviewees, who evidently adheres to this patriarchal paradigm, gave me the following account:

> The President said: '*I* saved you from the gallows. *I* gave you permission to have a newspaper and a union. *I* am ready to give you representation in the Economic and Social Council and in all the other advisory councils, but … *I* ask you to stop … After that, if …, *I* will give you your party.' [emphases added]

Is not the expression 'I gave' this or that, in my interviewee's statements, suggestive of the pervasiveness of the image of the president's benevolent authority which ultimately substitutes itself for the figure of the Father in a society that has not yet reached 'full maturity'?

In fact, the patriarchal benevolence of the president extends to a sphere that is apparently neutral and outside the domain of political competition, namely humanitarian emergencies. One day, a butcher was murdered in the Kasbah. A young man in his twenties was convicted and sentenced to death for the crime. As a result, his mother was left in utter poverty without any source of income. Charitable organizations did not dare provide any assistance to the poor woman. Neither did the local chapter of the Tunisian League for Human Rights. At last, it was people of the ruling party who found her a job in a hotel.

This general lack of solidarity towards the bereaved mother of a convict is remarkable in a Maghreb society. But in Tunis, at that time, it can be explained. The ruling party or the government perhaps can help the families of prisoners, even those of political prisoners, but ordinary citizens who dare do so run the risk of having to answer to the police: helping the poor without permission, is it a mere act of charity? Isn't competing in this way with the patriarchal regime a kind of political gesture? In any case, the police are there and may check. As we shall see later, only the government can decide if it is right to help the families of prisoners, whether political or not.

Understandably, such a political culture has proved useful for Ben Ali's strategy. More particularly, it inspired the leaders of the human rights movement to embrace a strategy of caution, consisting in quietly trying to reform the structure of the state from the inside, rather than openly and publicly criticising the president's policies. This is why some of my interviewees who are close to government circles sometimes tell me, 'I have close relations with the president. I would like this conversation to remain confidential to protect this relationship which enables me to serve my country.'

Thus, the patriarchal view of power weakens a first countervailing force against the authoritarian temptation: the democratic idea of popular sovereignty in the moral order on which state authority is founded. However, moral authority by itself is not enough. It is also necessary to be able to tame recalcitrant elements. This is a matter no longer of just symbol, but of organization, and what enters the picture here is the police machine, on which the benevolent Father of all Tunisians has the monopoly.

A Police State

The USSR was a party-state and the head of state was an apparatchik. In socialist Algeria, the system of military surveillance of the population could only function under the command of a high-ranking officer. In Tunisia, by contrast, it is the police force that constitutes the main instrument of control of all government bodies: ministries, the ruling party and the judiciary.

The ultimate rank in a police officer's career

The personality of President Ben Ali goes hand in hand with his style of government. The president is a career police officer. After a few months of training at the Saint-Cyr military academy in France, then at the Senior Intelligence School at Fort Holabird in the United States, he headed the Military Intelligence Services from 1967 to 1978. During the general strike that took place during that period, his troops shot dead 200 people according to some sources, 94 according to the authorities, and left hundreds injured.[2] As a reward for this victory over the UGTT (Tunisian General Union of Labour), in 1979 he was appointed Director-General of National Security. In January 1980, an attack on Gafsa by an unidentified insurgent group took place. Bourguiba held Ben Ali responsible and removed him from office. On M'Zali's suggestion, Ben Ali was then appointed ambassador to Communist Poland. Called back after the Bread Riots of January 1984, he was reinstated in his former position. He became Minister of the Interior in 1986, three months before the removal of M'Zali, then prime minister in Autumn 1987. His experience prepared him to make full use of the police force in order to bring to their knees the not-so-docile and to scare into inaction those who might be tempted to follow in their footsteps.

The President 'sees all and hears all'

One lunchtime in Tunis, I was walking with my colleague Hamid (fictitious name) when suddenly a man approached my companion and yelled in Arabic, 'Police! Your papers! What are you doing with this foreigner? I know what you were talking about.' Hamid turned pale with fear.

Fortunately, it was just a joke. The man, the son of an acquaintance of my companion, was very proud of himself because the trick he had played had worked. Hamid's reaction and the very idea of the joke testify to the climate of terror that reigns and show that police surveillance is so common that everybody is terrified by it.

The Sûreté Nationale and the National Guard, the former in the cities and the latter in rural areas, watch closely the activities of everyone and, when necessary, step in to restore order. In doing so, they rely on the support of local police stations. However, that is not enough to keep the opposition in check. So the interior ministry has created two civilian squads, made up of 'volunteer' and supposedly benevolent citizens: the Neighbourhood Watch Groups who spy on people in residential areas, and the Citizen-spy Brigades, who monitor their colleagues' activities at the workplace; the ruling Constitutional Democratic Rally party (RCD) and the Tunisian External Communication Agency (ATCE, the equivalent of a ministry of propaganda) are also engaged in activities of infiltration and surveillance. All these agencies serve to gauge fluctuations in enthusiasm for the patriarchal benevolence of the regime. The performance of every member of the surveillance structure is evaluated based on his or her ability to sniff out unenthusiastic and recalcitrant elements. The multiplication of intelligence agencies, often with overlapping missions, is reminiscent of Iraq, Syria and states usually defined as totalitarian: Nazi Germany, the USSR and China.

Let us take, for example, the propaganda scheme called Tajfif Al-yanabii (Nip the Evil in the Bud). It was uncovered by journalists and brought to light in a number of Arabic newspapers.[3] The scheme aims at preventing the Islamist Al-Nahdha movement from channelling all forms of opposition. The scheme's strategy, which was to be shrouded in utter secrecy, consisted in infiltrating civil institutions and destabilizing the Islamic movement from within, through the spreading of lies and rumours, enticement (promises of material rewards, employment and promotions), intelligence gathering and exchange of information with the interior ministry. The opposition parties and organizations associated with them were the target of the propaganda plan. The objective was to persuade them that the Islamist opposition was the enemy not just of the regime but of society as a whole.

The heavy institutionalized surveillance produced a directly observable effect which no foreign reporter who visits Tunis can fail to notice; a crippling fear which is bound to discourage the slightest initiative on the part of civil society. Hamid was not the only one who was haunted by police terror. Sonia (fictitious name) invited me to her house for breakfast. The radio was on at full volume. To my amazement, she explained to me that everyone was being watched. Upon my insistence, she emphatically repeated, 'Everyone!' She was convinced that the telephone, when the receiver was in the cradle, was used as a bugging device. So, with the radio at full volume, she believed herself to be relatively safe.

During the meal, she received a phone call. When she asked the identity of the caller, 'a man with a smooth voice' called her by her first name. He asked her how things were going at work (notice the veiled threat), and how she felt about the election results (won by President Ben Ali by the usual margin). She hung up and explained to me that before, during some political trial, someone had tried to scare her in the same way.

Before I left her, she suggested that we agree on what to say to the police in case we were taken for questioning. I reassured her that I was protected by virtue of my status as foreign researcher and that no one could force me to reveal even the identity of my interviewees. But still, in order to reassure her I had to destroy the notes of the interview and hide my notebook under my coat. In the evening, she decided to spend the night at her parents' house, in another district.

Intimidation can take many forms other than anonymous telephone threats. My interviewees had to endure retaliatory measures such as car thefts, break-ins and ransackings or criminal fires, and at times power and telephone cuts, interrogations at the interior ministry, 'friendly advice', and visits to their homes. In short, the repertoire of intimidation measures which I have documented, though little known by the general public, accords with the reports of Amnesty International since 1991.

Targeting of opponents and their families

Like Mohamed Moada, the party leader, Khemaïs Chamari was a prominent figure in the Socialist Democrats' Movement (MDS). He is a former member of the Tunisian parliament, and he and his wife Alya are well-known human rights defenders. Both took part in an international campaign for the release of Moada. After they declared that Moada's arrest was politically motivated, the Chamaris suffered constant police harassment. In late October 1995, they were denied permission to travel to Malta to attend an international conference on human rights and had their passports confiscated. When Khemaïs Chamari wrote to France requesting a piece of evidence that could clear Moada, the letter was intercepted and he was thrown in jail (see page 21). He was stripped of his parliamentary immunity and charged with divulging investigative secrets in the Moada case.

Police surveillance and harassment are not enough, however. Many civil actors are targeted through their private lives, reputation, career and family. The most infamous ploy consists in spreading rumours about the morals of political activists which the press propagates, and of which the scandal sheet *Al-Hadeth* (Announcements), makes a speciality. These rumours can be devastating for the reputation of opposition figures in a Muslim society.

Other dissidents have seen their career achievements targeted. Moncef Marzuki was one: for having attempted to stand as a candidate in the presidential elections, he was punished with the abolition of the Department of Community Medicine he had established at the University of Sousse. Similarly, Mustafa Ben Jaafar had wanted to create a political party close to Marzuki: the Democratic Forum for Freedom and Labour. A diplomat and head of a hospital department, he was transferred to a maternity department: 'At the time, not even a labourer could be transferred without clearance from a joint employer/employee board!' former prime minister Mohamed M'Zali commented when interviewed in Paris in 1996.

Political exiles, of course, are out of reach. Instead, their families are targeted. M'Zali was apparently the first victim of this new instrument of political terror:

> As soon as I reached my destination abroad, I learnt that my other children too had been arrested and tortured, and that my wife [a former minister and feminist militant] was under house arrest. Their passports had been confiscated. Two of my sons were dismissed from their jobs and could not subsequently find employment. There have also been dismissals among members of my wife's family. One of my relatives had his coffee shop licence, his only source of subsistence, taken away from him. Others have been arrested and tortured. Before Ben Ali led the police forces, there had never been such generalized campaigns of terror against the families of exiles.

Women had never been implicated before Ben Ali. The wives of the exiles of Al-Nahdha and of other exiled opposition members have suffered enormously as a result of police terror.[4] One of them, who is currently seeking political asylum abroad, described to me the horrors of what they went through after the escape of their husbands:

> Neighbours and relatives are forbidden to provide us with any assistance. Members of the militia search the rubbish bins of prisoners' wives. If they find the leftovers of a good meal, with meat, the woman is taken away for interrogation as to the source of it.
> I had even had my identity card and family record book taken away

from me. So I could neither work any more nor legally leave the country. We were like outcasts, living on the fringes of society.

Whenever my husband telephoned me from abroad, I was automatically summoned by the head of the intelligence services. I had to give them a detailed account of what had been said. And if I happened to forget anything, it would be pointed out to me: 'Such and such ... why hide it?'

Forced divorce is used to break the spirit of political opponents, not only by destroying their careers and mercilessly breaking up their families, but also hurting their honour (in the strong, Mediterranean sense of the term): their wives face humiliation by the police, threats of sexual assault and prison – even their daughters are not spared – unless they agree to ask for divorce.

Torture

The generalized practice of torture in police stations, prisons and the interior ministry is too well documented to necessitate any lengthy treatment here.[5] The exact number of torture victims will probably never be known, but according to the least pessimistic estimates, those of Amnesty International for example, they are in the thousands. Those who survive the ordeal will have to endure the effects of the resulting physical and psychological damage all their lives. Torture completes the edifice of terror erected by President Ben Ali.[6]

A Legal System in Captivity

In order to maintain its iron grip on the whole society, what is in effect a praetorian state is not content to increase police resources and engage in a campaign of terror. It must also prevent the legal system from righting the wrongs caused by abuses of power and from bringing to justice those responsible. In order for fear to paralyse society effectively, there should be no way of escape through the justice system, this being the second possible countervailing force against the tendency towards authoritarianism in a state of law. Thus the regime uses the police machine and patriarchal authority to neutralize the country's lawyers, judges and due process.

Due process

On the surface, Tunisia has a model legal system which should be the envy of its Moroccan and Algerian neighbours. The penal code, as amended following the 1987 coup, limits to four days the period for which arrestees can be held in police custody without charge. This period can only be extended under exceptional circumstances and via a monitoring mechanism which, theoretically, must make any abuse by the police impossible. Any officer violating this law can incur very serious penalties. He may even lose his job and all his civil rights, which may further delay the trial.

In practice, however, the police can keep a prisoner in custody for as long as they want: through the falsification of police records which has become common practice. The period between the moment the person is brought into custody and his or her first appearance before a judge can be very long, and during this time prisoners are tortured without being able to consult a doctor or a lawyer, or to inform their families. Once confessions are extorted, a long period of time in custody may be needed for the marks of torture to disappear.

Hundreds of Tunisian prisoners of conscience have informed the courts that their self-incriminating statements have been obtained by means of coercion and torture. Their efforts have been wasted: no doctor would dare certify in writing the existence of physical evidence of torture, nor would judges have the courage to order the investigation of defenders' complaints.

Lawyers

Lawyers who requested the opening of investigations into allegations of torture saw their offices broken into and ransacked, were subjected to interrogations and faced threats of legal prosecution for 'dissemination of false information'. Many were denied access to their clients and trial files.

Some lawyers had serious trouble with the courts after they represented defendants in political trials. Two well-known examples which were at the centre of international campaigns are that of Nadia Nasraoui, who has been charged before the court again and again, and that of Najib Hosni, thrown in jail and tortured after he acted in the defence of Moncef Marzuki, the human rights activist who committed the imprudence of trying to run for president in the 1994 election. At the end of 1996, after several years in detention and a strong international campaign for his release, Hosni was granted a presidential conditional pardon – and was subject to police/judicial harassment from then on. In early 2001, after becoming an overt dissident, he was thrown back in jail.

Judges

Tunisian law provides many guarantees of the defendant's right of defence, but these guarantees cannot be respected so long as the judiciary is structurally linked to the executive. The main problem is that the Supreme Council of Magistracy is chaired by the head of state. Of course, this structure exists in other countries too, but the position of the head of state in the latter cases is only symbolic. In Tunisia, on the contrary, the head of state has full authority to decide on the nomination, promotion, transfer, retirement and dismissal of judicial officers. At the start of every legal year, the magistrates express their support to him and promise to work 'under the guidance of his enlightened leadership'.[7]

Consequently, with only a few exceptions, magistrates never dare display any sign of independence. In December 1994, the Geneva-based International Commission of Jurists organized a seminar in Tunis to discuss several issues, notably the independence of the judiciary. In the final report, young Tunisian magistrates criticized the interference of the executive in the work of the judiciary and made a number of recommendations on how to address the problem. A few days later, they were summoned to the Ministry of Justice one by one and forced to sign a new text.

Under such conditions, generally judges prefer to turn a blind eye to patently falsified police reports and refuse to investigate complaints about torture in custody. Their decisions cannot go against the police establishment and the patriarchal order, as was manifested in some typical political trials.[8] One such trial involved Bechir Essid, the ex-president of the Arab Lawyers' Association and leader of an (unauthorized) opposition movement with some affinity with the Libyan regime. He fell victim to a series of mishaps for no other crime than that he spoke about the private life of Ben Ali during a trip to Libya. His remarks were tape-recorded and brought back from Libya (notice how far the Tunisian security services can go in spying on the citizens!). Not long after Hosni's return, he employed a new secretary in his office. The latter turned to be an intelligence agent, who denounced Hosni for attempted sabotage and illegal nighttime fly-posting of leaflets on the walls of the building housing the law courts. He was arrested on 14 September 1989, one year after the denunciation, and was sentenced to three years' imprisonment. Following an appeal from the Tunisian Bar Association and the Arab Lawyers' Association, he was pardoned by the president eight months before the expiry of his term.

A Western diplomat (source: private interview, 1996) told me how one day, when he went to see the Minister of Justice pleading for one of his compatriots, the minister reassured him by informing him, in advance, of the exact sentence that would be passed and the presidential pardon which would follow. This was a clear indication of the relationship of dependency that exists between the administrative and judicial authorities.

Another typical political trial was that of the leading human rights figure Moncef Marzuki. In 1994, while the legal proceedings which were taken against him were under way, he was also brought before the disciplinary board of his university, where he was censured for having travelled abroad without authorization (in theory this is prohibited, but professors used to do so at the time without being penalized).

Marzuki was convicted on the strength of a photocopy of an article that bore neither the name of the newspaper nor that of the journalist who wrote it, only his or her initials. Marzuki denied having made the said statements or having met anybody corresponding to the initials. This 'article' must have been a put-up job. For Marzuki had just come back from a visit to Morocco and Spain, and a Tangier-based newspaper had just been seized at the request of the Tunisian embassy. Surely it would have been easy to find an actual interview to corroborate the accusation that he left the country without authorization? Conclusion: anything can be proved against anyone. Moncef Marzuki was deprived of his passport for several years; not before summer 2000 could he travel abroad, and his first trip overseas cost him his university position.[9]

Al-Nahdha, the Islamist Movement, was a victim of the same kind of unfair trial based on trumped-up charges. After the Bab Souika arson case in February 1991, the rope that allegedly had been used to tie up the building's guards before they were burned alive was produced at a press conference: 'the rope was unscathed', Amnesty International reported, 'without any marks of burns'.[10] The trial, which was covered by Tunisian newspapers, which then unleashed their rage at the terrorists, took place in the absence of the defence lawyers who withdrew from the court in protest against what they saw as a wrongful prosecution. In spring 1991, at a press conference attended by Tunisian and international journalists, the authorities announced that they had uncovered an Al-Nahdha plot to shoot down the president's plane with a Stinger missile, kidnap foreign diplomats, and overthrow the government. The leaders of the movement were brought to trial and convicted on the basis of a single prosecution affidavit. Nevertheless, for the Tunisian press and public the sentences that resulted from the two trials are enough to give credence to the official thesis that Al-Nahdha is a terrorist movement, backed by Algerian Islamists whose aim is to import subversion and violence. In this context, one has reason to wonder how a political police force as well organized as that of Tunisia was unable to gather any evidence that could stand up in a court of law.

In Tunisia, with its heavy surveillance machine and countless spies, it is astonishing that the authorities still find it necessary to convict people on the basis of manufactured evidence, confessions and prosecution affidavits obtained by coercion. But no one dares bring this fact out: neither lawyers who are terrified by the prospect of defending dissidents, nor judges liable to dismissal and subject to the directions of the executive; a judicial system so subordinated to the executive makes state actors untouchable and exacerbates the vulnerability of civil actors to abuses of power. This subordination also has the advantage of giving President Ben Ali the opportunity, whenever he thinks fit, to order the release of prisoners, something which he does readily and regularly, after the prisoners have served most of their terms. Under such a legal system, salvation can come only from presidential clemency, on which ultimately all depends.

It could still be objected that if the Tunisian regime were so tyrannical, Tunisians still have the possibility to change things by removing their leaders from office, since they have political parties and elections. Unfortunately, since 7 November 1987, the possibility of an electoral change has proved impossible, given the way political parties and elections are organized.

Alternation in Office Impossible

The law of 3 May 1988 'organizing political parties' is itself a pure product of the patriarchal view. It confirms the role of the government as manager of all civil institutions and parties, whose creation can be authorized only by the Minister of the Interior. The law provides that leaders of authorized parties must not have been 'deprived of their civic rights'. This provision excludes *de facto* most civil actors who confronted the ruling elite before the 1987 coup, who benefited from the 'general' amnesty but remain excluded from the public scene by virtue of the law.

The law also provides that a party can be authorized only if its principles, activities and platform are sufficiently distinct from those of others. It is up to the Minister of the Interior, in accordance with patriarchal logic and before the electorate has its say, to decide on the pertinence and morality of opposition parties. In this context, three 'big' opposition parties have been authorized: the Popular Unity Party (PUP), the MDS, and the communist party Al-Tajdid (the Revival). There is also the small Unionist Democratic Union (UDU), whose leader was in fact a plant by the ruling party, the Constitutional Democratic Rally (RCD). Four parties were still unauthorized when the first 'democratic' elections took place in 1989: the Democratic Forum for Liberties and Labour (FDLT), the Tunisian Workers' Communist Party (PCOT), the Popular Unity Movement (MUP) and Al-Nahdha. They nevertheless had the chance to form 'independent lists'.

For all parties, authorized and unauthorized, these elections were to be a first test of their real capacity to contend for power. From the outset, the result was negative with regards to the post of President. A series of belatedly issued electoral decrees prevented the candidates from standing for the presidency. First, their applications were rejected on the grounds that the decrees had not yet been issued. Then the applications were dropped again on the pretext that they were submitted after the deadline set by the law. The only candidate who managed to make it through this space–time legal thicket was President Ben Ali, who was back in office with 99.27 per cent of the votes cast.

The election campaign proceeded fairly smoothly. Some fraud was reported which was small in scale and could not possibly have had any serious impact on the results. On the day of the election, however, things suddenly turned sour. The monitors of the independent lists were driven out of the polling stations. Consequently, the poll proceeded without them being able to check the identity of voters or to monitor the vote count.

'Out in the streets, vote counters paid cash for the opposition ballot papers that were brought to them. Five dinars per ballot paper and an entry ticket to the victory celebration party, planned for the evening in the coastside hotels,' Ahmed Manaï observes.[11] The following day, according to official figures, the 'independent list' emerged as the only opposition force, with 22 per cent of the votes, against the ruling RCD which got nearly 70 per cent of the votes. Not a single deputy from the opposition could sit in the parliament; the first test of the Tunisian transition to democracy was negative.

Five years later the second test took place. This time, the election decree was issued in time but another obstacle stood in the way of the two presidential candidates, Moncef Marzuki and Abderrahmane Hani.[12] The electoral law stipulates that, in order to indicate seriousness, every candidate must obtain the endorsement of thirty members of parliament or municipal bodies before he or she can participate in the contest. But the parliament that had emerged from the 1989 elections included no deputies from the opposition. It came as no surprise that no deputy of the ruling party supported the applications of Marzuki and Hani, and 99 per cent of the electorate again voted for Ben Ali, the sole candidate.

The outcome of the parliamentary election was the same: no opposition party managed to have a single deputy elected. In its patriarchal magnanimity, however, the government had already provided itself, through its electoral law, with the possibility of redressing the imbalance in representation. So the president designated nineteen candidates from the opposition as members of the first pluralistic parliament in Tunisian history.

Immediately, the nineteen MPs, coming from the MDS, the PUP, the UDU and Al-Tajdid, reached an agreement to avoid any confrontation with the MPs of the ruling party (which should have been their very role if this were really a pluralistic system). Being the representatives of the opposition in a patriarchal political order, they took it upon themselves 'to seek to close the gap between the different viewpoints, minimize divergences and focus on the points of agreement', while at the same time rejecting 'a minority / majority pattern divorced from the real problems of the country'. The basis of their statements, issued soon after their nomination, is not contentious, but consensual: the '7 November Declaration' made by the President'.[13]

Even though appointed and without any real power, Tunisian political actors may be tempted to take themselves seriously, or at least somewhat to modify the informal rules of the game to their advantage. On 9 October 1995, the executive committee of the MDS issued an open letter accompanied by a press release, expressing to the president its growing concern over the increasing restrictions imposed on public freedoms. The following day, no newspaper had published the statement or the letter, but Mohamed Moada, the MDS leader, was arrested. He spent more than a year in prison.

The 1999 general election reproduced the same features. Thanks to the passive submission of the mainstream civil institutions,[14] President Ben Ali was re-elected with 99.4 per cent of the votes, according to the interior ministry. His party was given 80 per cent of the seats in parliament. Opposition parties therefore, appointed and not elected, having from the very beginning proclaimed their allegiance to the regime to which they owe everything, punished if they try to play their role, have been in no better a position than the satellite parties of some totalitarian states: Syria, Iraq, communist East Germany. Such satellite parties are used to lend the parliament an appearance of democratic legitimacy and conceal the fact that no alternation is really possible.

A patriarchal moral order, police state, the dependence of the legal system, the impossibility of rotation in power: these resources have been used to the full by the regime in order to reinforce tyranny. Such an enterprise, however, does not exist in a vacuum. We still have to explain the reason why nobody, or almost nobody, at that time seemed conscious of the fact that the totalitarian strategy of a state without any separation of powers was about to destroy civil society. Such passivity, such submissiveness, cannot be explained away just as the strategy of the president. The instruments of domination existed even before Ben Ali. Under Bourguiba, there was no separation of powers either. Yet there was more room for expression. What happened after Ben Ali came to power?

Notes

1. Andrzej Korbonski (1996) 'How much is enough? Excessive pluralism as the cause of Poland's socio-economic crisis', *International Political Science Review*, Vol. XVII, No. 3, July 1996, pp. 297–306.
2. Khaled Ben M'barek (1996) '*Tunisie: 10 ans de torture: 1987–1997'*, *Droits de l'homme sans frontières* (*Tunisia: 10 years of torture. 1987–1997*, Human Rights without borders), Centre d'information et de documentation sur la torture en Tunisie, Besançon, France, p. 8.
3. For example *Al-Chaab*, the official journal of the UGTT, was one of the newspapers that brought to light the campaign, in mid-July 1990.
4. Since 1992, Amnesty International has reported a steady stream of cases of harassment, arrest and torture of women. Among those targeted were women activists, but most were simply relatives of activists. The Comité de soutien aux victimes de la répression en Tunisie (Committee in Support of Victims of Repression in Tunisia) issued a report, prefaced by Dr Hélène Jaffé (president of AVRE in Paris and a board member of the International Council for the Rehabilitation of the Victims of Torture [IRCT] in Copenhagen), and listing, with photographs, names and dates, sixty-eight cases of Tunisian women tortured by the police for political motives (*Témoignages sur les femmes réprimées en Tunisie*. [Testimony on oppressed women in Tunisia], Paris: 1996).
5. A huge stock of horror stories can be gathered from the archives of the United Nations Human Rights Committee, the European Parliament, the US Depart-

ment of External Affairs, the International Federation for Human Rights, Amnesty International, Article 19, Reporters Sans Frontières, Human Rights Watch, and the Lawyers' Committee for Human Rights.

6. The high level of intelligence activities, blackmail and torture, plus the targeting of careers and families, implies a major input of financial and human resources. Actual figures belong to the realm of state secrecy but, according to well-informed observers, they are considerable. For instance, former Secretary of Defence Ahmed Ben Nour claims that the budget of the Interior Ministry tripled from 1985 to 1996, rising from US$140 million to 493 million (private interview in 1996). According to *La Voix de l'audace* (*Voice of Courage*), No. 2, October–November 1996, the presidential budget grew sevenfold in the same period, from US$3 million to 20 million. As for the police corps, it quadrupled during the months following Ben Ali's *coup*, rising from twenty thousand to eighty thousand men, according to Ignacio Ramonet, 'Main de fer en Tunisie' ('Iron Fist in Tunisia'), *Le Monde diplomatique*, July 1996. Dissident circles in Paris report that the police forces included 130,000 men at the end of the twentieth century.

7. The symbiotic relationship between the judiciary and the executive is portrayed and documented in Ben M'barek (1996), p. 17.

8. Since 1991, Amnesty International's publications have been reporting on the executive interference in the judiciary.

9. In the summer of 2001, after a vigorous international campaign by a network of Tunisian dissidents, Marzuki moved to France from where, as an exile, he continued his campaign for justice in Tunisia.

10. Amnesty International (1992) *Tunisia: Heavy Sentences after Unfair Trials*, MDE 30/23/92.

11. Ahmed Manaï (1995) *Le Supplice tunisien* (The Tunisian Torture), Paris: La Découverte, p. 27.

12. Both Marzuki and Hani were quickly thrown in jail. In line with the government's concern to cultivate its image, they were charged not with serious but only common law offences.

13. See the statements issued by Mohamed Moada (MDS), Nasr Ben Amor (Al-Tajdid), and Khemaïs Chamari (MDS) as published by *Réalités* (The Real), No. 442, 1–7 April 1994, pp. 6–11.

14. The UGTT, the MDS, the PUP and the UDU all played a passive role.

2

TUNISIA
THE SUBMISSION TO PLATO'S CAVE

Transitions to democracy unfold in climates of great uncertainty.[1] On the one hand, the rules of political competition become all the more ambiguous as they keep changing. On the other hand, old political recipes are no longer suitable for the new situation. Moreover, the political actors find it difficult to assess the objectives and strategies of their allies and rivals. Therefore, they have to ensure their survival without being able to predict the consequences of their decisions … or indecision.

During this stage, which proceeds more or less in the dark, the actors' perceptions and the strategies of alliance or conflict they develop will none the less be decisive for the evolution of power struggles and, possibly, for the whole outcome of the transition: for whether it is to be the re-establishment of a pluralistic political society or the reinforcement of monolithic power.

The first scenario corresponds to the democratic transitions that took place in Chile, Hungary, Germany, Poland, Czechoslovakia and South Africa. These successful transitions towards democracy were all initiated, as in Tunisia, following a long history of confrontation between civil actors and authoritarian regimes. From Chile to South Africa, confrontations could not come to an end, and the process of democratization could not be set in motion, until the contending actors succeeded in reaching an agreement on the conditions of coexistence that were acceptable to all. In Tunisia, too, the pact concluded between President Ben Ali and the civil actors led to some sort of social peace … but a peace that was gradually used by the former to destabilize, then to marginalize or destroy the latter, before even democratic reforms took place.

Some might be tempted to argue that there is little chance of success for a democratic transition that is initiated from above following a *coup*, but the *coup* that had taken place in Tunisia came after a long struggle for more freedom. A vibrant pluralistic civil society had existed before Ben Ali came to power. By promising this civil society the democracy it clamorously demanded, the president set himself up as a champion of pluralism. But while everyone in the public forum was singing his praises, a drama was unfolding behind the scenes: that of the destruction of civil society. On the walls of a public forum that from then on was turned into Plato's cave, we were to see nothing but the moving shadows of the social actors of old. This is the true story of the Tunisian democratic transition, as it has never been told before.

Tunisian Civil Society before its Collapse

The first form of civil organization emerged long before independence; it was in 1924 that the Tunisian General Union of Labour (UGTT) organized the first general strike and that the first political trial took place. Subsequently, the labour movement grew more and more influential as time went by. What distinguishes Tunisian history, though, is that, after independence, trade unionism was the only force capable of counterbalancing state power.

Not until the late 1970s did a second network of civil institutions emerge, following divisions within the sole political party, the Neo-Destour. One faction took it upon itself to work towards the establishment of the rule of law and the democratization of the party. One of those involved was Ahmed Mestiri. Already in 1968 he had resigned from the Neo-Destour amid controversy over the forced collectivization of agricultural land. He rejoined the Party eighteen months later, and in 1973 he led the party congress to adopt a reform motion stipulating that the members of the party's political bureau would henceforth be elected. Bourguiba rejected this decision and organized another congress. Mestiri was again expelled, and along with him the other members of his group, the Socialist Democrats' Group (GDS).

In 1977, the Tunisian League for Human Rights (LTDH) was registered as an authorized organization. This group was close to the GDS, and it was speculated that this move was intended to dilute the GDS's influence. The LTDH also included representatives from the Communist Party, the Popular Unity Party and, no doubt to twist Bourguiba's arm, from the Neo-Destour as well. Constituted in the manner of a political lobby group following a split in the ruling party, the LTDH was founded by people who were then banned from forming political parties. (As a result of this particular structure, which has characterized it from its inception, each subsequent congress of the LTDH was supposed to be preceded by negotiations between the parties about the composition of the next executive committee. Up until 1985, things followed this pattern, and the partisan aspect was never completely eliminated).

Government minister Hassib Ben Ammar, a member of the GDS, set up the newspaper *Al-Rai* (Opinion), while Mestiri founded the Socialist Democrats' Movement (MDS) and the newspaper *Al-Moustaqbal* (The Future). Around the same period, the Tunisian Journalists' Association, hitherto just a social club, was transformed into a professional organization under the leadership of several professors of the Institute of Press and Information Sciences.

Concurrent with the growth of trade unionism and a modernistic civil left, a third tendency emerged at the heart of civil society: the Islamist movement, based principally at the university, and made up of a group of intellectual students who were discontented with the secularization of society imposed by Bourguiba. According to them, this policy excluded religion from social and political life under the pretext that Islam was against progress and modernity. It was precisely that which provoked their reaction. However, apart from their stand against the secularism of the regime and the civil left, at the beginning they had little in the way of a political programme.

'From the beginning, we had to endure persecution from the Marxist left on campus,' says one of them, now a political refugee in Paris. 'They used to point the finger at us and assault us, accusing us of being the accomplices of the government in the repression to which they were being subjected. As they had the upper hand among opposition groups, they used to deny us the right to speak and disrupt our meetings, accusing us of propagating "the opium of the people", and dragging us into fights.

'However, their analysis was wrong. No one had encouraged us to combat the left. The simple truth was that we were not yet so important as to be persecuted. Very quickly, though, our movement gained momentum, first on campuses. From our relatives, our influence then spread throughout the whole society. And yet, even then, we were still afraid of being identified, and continued to hide.'

Over the years the Islamists became politicized as a result of the confrontations with the civil left and the government, confrontations that were stimulated by the events taking place on the international stage (the 1973 oil embargo, then the Iranian Revolution and Libyan threats to Bourguiba's power).

A sense of solidarity quickly developed between the labour movement, the left-wing constellation born from the splitting of the Neo-Destour, and the Islamists, alongside a more assertive attitude towards the government. 'We did not want to be the mouthpiece of some party,' Hassib Ben Ammar told me, 'and we opened our columns to all – even to Rachid Ghannouchi [an Islamist] and Mohamed Harmel [a communist], whose views we did not share. We did so in the name of freedom of expression. I even published an editorial defending the fundamentalists.' Likewise, the weekly *Réalités* organized a round table that brought together Islamist and leftist students and a minister. 'So, we got the idea,' Ben Ammar told me, 'to issue a call for respect of public liberties and to organize a national conference to which would be invited foreign observers, such as human rights organizations. In April 1977, the call was spread. After that, I embarked on a tour to a number of countries in order to enlist support for our group. On 9 June 1977, even though it was not authorized, the conference took place at the air terminal.'

In the same spirit of solidarity, in 1978, from their stronghold at the university, the Islamists brought support to the general strike called by the UGTT. However, on 26 June 1978, at the height of the confrontation between the UGTT and the government, the general strike was checkmated by the police forces led by Ben Ali. The GDS then made an appeal for the release of detainees and an end to the state of emergency, and got up a petition collecting hundreds of signatures. The government backed down and the UGTT regained its freedom of action. The newly born newspapers, for their part, were subjected to legal harassment but that did not matter: the people in the street jostled to buy them and lawyers competed to defend them in the courts.

The confrontation brought visibility and credibility to the various groups. It also generated violence, around the trade unionists first, then the Islamists. But it is important to make clear its true nature, if only to re-establish the facts, which have been distorted by the propaganda of the praetorian state. Fights between students, demonstrations, clashes with the police, acid-throwing and other acts of crowd violence – all these indeed took place. But, the then prime minister Mohamed M'Zali comments, 'Each time it spilled over into the streets, the police used to intervene. There was no terrorism as such. It may be the job of the Tunisian External Communication Agency (ATCE) to claim the opposite, but it is not mine. If Bourguiba was afraid of the Islamist project, it was because it seemed to him a threat to his achievements: secularism, women's emancipation. He feared that his efforts might go to waste.' It was for this reason that Bourguiba would not authorize the Islamists to form a party, M'Zali believes, and not because of terrorism.

Diversity of institutions, political pluralism, displays of solidarity, confrontational relationships with the government: these are the hallmarks of a true civil society, which emerged under Bourguiba. Its ceaseless struggle for freedom continued until the milestone date of 7 November 1987.

The Fatal Alliance

After ten years of tumultuous and precarious life, continually exposed to police and judicial harassment, by 1987 the young Tunisian civil society was well aware of the hard facts of pluralism and open struggle against the ruling class. In such circumstances, what happens if the civil actors suddenly find themselves faced with the opportunity to carry on the process of democratization – which so far has not gone beyond an awakening of civil society – with the authorities' support this time, and no longer against them? What happens if, after the collapse of an authoritarian regime, a pact between the rising elite and state actors results in the restoration of the authority of the state? The question becomes more pressing if the state takes charge of the development of the network of civil institutions before the latter have acquired the organizational resources necessary for political independence. In the Tunisian case, the answer to these questions would come with Ben Ali's coup, on 7 November 1987, under the banner of human rights and democracy. One year later, all civil and state actors had signed the *National Pact*, a document recognizing Ben Ali as the nation's outstanding saviour and leader.

The position of the UGTT
The main force in civil society, the UGTT, was already in a weak position when Ben Ali came to power. In 1985, the trade union's leaders had been thrown in jail and its offices had been taken over by the police. The government appointed a new, subservient executive committee. Then, at the instigation of Ben Ali, who by then had become Interior Minister, the government nominated that part of the committee assigned to conduct genuine elections for the UGTT's top jobs. The result was a sham convention at which less than 50 per cent of the struc-

tures were renewed. From the outset, the UGTT was technically offside. Understandably, therefore, its adherence to the National Pact was not much of an event.

The seduction of the civil left

As for the cluster of left-wing civil institutions (parties, newspapers, the human rights movement), they were facing in Ben Ali an actor who had already shown how dangerous he was. What he then offered them, each one separately, was the opportunity to collaborate with him as government officials or, at least, by publicly expressing support for him.

Thus, after ten years of repression, the actors of the civil left saw themselves offered the opportunity to take their revenge on Bourguiba, finally to assume power and, so they thought, to actualize their blueprint for society under the as-yet-vague title of democracy. Ben Ali derived a double benefit from this alliance: not only a legitimizing doctrine but also arguments against the Islamists, seen by the left as dangerous enemies of modernity. At the same time, he got the left to agree to put its democratic aspirations on hold. 'It's true,' he admitted to every new ally in a tone of confidence, 'there still are problems concerning liberties. Give me time to get rid of those old rusty nails of the party. That would give me greater leeway.' And as a gesture of goodwill, Ben Ali then offered the person he was speaking to a position within the state apparatus. By accepting it, the latter allowed himself or herself to be gagged.

The new ally of the left-wingers did not give any guarantee to those who adhered to the National Pact, but they nevertheless preferred the protection of the praetorian state to the advent of religious totalitarianism, which they saw as inevitable if the Islamists were one day to come to power. As a feminist activist once put it:

> Amnesty International and Western public opinion are wrong in defending the fundamentalists when they are subjected to torture or arbitrary detention. The fundamentalists are the enemies of human rights. When they assume power, there will be neither democracy nor human rights anymore, and it is women who will bear the brunt. Unlike you in the West, here we are directly exposed to this threat. No rights for the enemies of human rights! Arrests, assassination and torture? Is there any other solution?

In this way, the civil left rejected a solution that could have made possible the peaceful settlement of ideological disputes through open debate in the public forum. To use the words of Clausewitz, it instead chose the 'continuation of politics by other means': war. The problem was that by condoning torture and repression, these people politicized the concept of human rights and thereby destroyed the notion of its universality.

This reaction of the civil left, in the face of what it perceived as a serious threat, was also counterproductive: it facilitated both the introduction and reinforcement of authoritarian political practices and the secret character of the government. This would backfire on it.

The position of the Islamists

The 'it's them or us' attitude of the civil left towards the Islamist Al-Nahdha organization facilitated the final elimination of the latter from the public forum by the praetorian regime. In fact, since the time of political openness during the seventies, the Islamists had been no more than tolerated. They were permitted to travel, hold meetings and issue publications, but their party remained unauthorized. Then, a short time before the coup, in March 1987, fourteen members of the leadership (including Jabali, Bennani, Larayedh and Beldi) went into hiding, Muru went into exile, and the remaining leaders were thrown into jail. Some of them, now political refugees in Europe, gave me the following account of how they themselves were induced into signing the National Pact:

> From our prison, we tried to assess the situation; Ben Ali would never tolerate us, and sooner or later there would be a confrontation. But at that time, he employed delaying tactics, asking us not to rush things and promising to solve our problem as soon as he could. In the meantime, in our absence he promulgated the National Pact, had the law on political parties passed, and reorganized the Neo-Destour [which was renamed Constitutional Democratic Rally, hereafter RCD]. At the same time, Ben Ali negotiated with us through mediators who used to contact us in prison.
>
> First, he asked us for a gesture of goodwill.This he got on 17 April 1988, when we declared in *Al-Sabah* newspaper that Al-Nahdha supported 'the change' and was ready to cooperate. In addition to that, Ben Ali asked us to sign the National Pact, to commit ourselves not to politicize mosques, and to give him time. We agreed.

The conditions under which the National Pact was concluded put civil society in so weak a position that it is no exaggeration to describe it as a little more than an open mandate handed to a president who set himself as the sole key to salvation, but promised nothing specific. Ben Ali thus found himself in a strong position: both being in control of a police machine ready to impose his will and legitimizing himself by democratic objectives that society had been seeking for ten years, he had just peacefully neutralized all civil opposition. The event was fatal for the future of democracy.

Once they signed the National Pact, the UGTT and the civil left were naturally going to fall into the trap of passive collaboration. Still, if need be, to obtain this collaboration, there was terror and corruption. Moreover, thanks to the various networks of intelligence at its disposal, the regime can also infiltrate nondocile institutions, get its agents nominated into high leadership positions, and create internal crises. After all have been neutralized, no dissident voice can speak out without risk. Therefore, the only remaining survival strategy following the fatal alliance was to get into the government's good books. 'In the event of a problem, one could count neither on trade unions, nor on lawyers, nor on the parties, nor on the media. Even the Tunisian League for Human Rights was unable to intervene; to ask it for assistance could make things even worse,' one of my interviewees who worked for one of these institutions said to me. 'All we could do was to just wait and hope for the goodwill of the president.'

The isolation of the different civil actors was further compounded by the demoralized legal system that the patriarchal regime had brought about which Ben Ali did nothing but reinforce. The penal code prohibits any 'threats to state security'. The law on political parties prohibits 'disturbance of public order'. The press code prohibits criticism of the government, even when well founded. The law on associations prohibits unauthorized political parties. The law on public meetings prohibits meetings that have not received prior authorization. The new law on association of 1992 prohibits groups from engaging in any activities other than those that justified their creation. The logic of this emasculated legal situation can be stated in a few words: anything not pre-authorized is prohibited. Since 1993, any call for criticism or protest, whatever the methods, has in practice been actually outlawed, before even the isolated protesters could seek allies. This is the conclusion that two very influential civil actors, the Islamist movement Al-Nahdha and the Tunisian League for Human Rights have drawn from their own unfortunate experiences.

The Destruction of Al-Nahdha

The Islamists believed they would be able to resist Ben Ali, and in the pre-collapse context, their confrontation strategy against the regime could have succeeded. But the old bonds of civil solidarity were broken: 'We thought that the unions and the parties would support us, but they lined up behind the government,' comments the Al-Nahdha leader Saïd Ferjani. 'We thought that the Algerian democracy would provide us with international backing, but the 1992 coup and the dissolution of the Islamic Salvation Front deprived us of this support. Thus, we found ourselves completely isolated. We had misjudged the potential support that we would be getting. Our popularity was not enough. It would have been better if we had done like the other Tunisian political forces: been patient and waited for the right time.'

The story of Al-Nahdha is edifying in that it illustrates the risks surrounding the attempt by an actor to maintain a margin of freedom of action in a praetorian state. In 1987, while their leaders were in prison, Al-Nahdha militants took to the streets demanding the legal authorization of their party.[2]

When Al-Nahdha reluctantly adhered to the National Pact in 1988, Ben Ali started releasing grassroots activists 'drop by drop'. Each release was followed by massive demonstrations of joy which were joined by thousands of people. These were undoubtedly spontaneous reactions of the supporters, since their leaders, still in prison, could not easily transmit instructions. The demonstrations went on while secret agents watched and compiled lists of names.

On 8 June 1988, Al-Nahdha officially applied for registration. According to the law, the Interior Minister had four months to reject the application. One day short of four months later (and a few weeks before the general amnesty), the answer came, and it was negative; Al-Nahdha leaders had judicial records! A second application, lodged before the 1989 elections, produced no better results. The leaders, concerned not to scare the government into panic, then decided to run as 'independents', but only in five districts out of twenty-three. Soon, however, they found themselves overwhelmed by the enthusiasm of their followers: each region insisted on having its own list, which was drawn up in no time and with much ease. Huge support rallies in favour of the 'independent lists' took place all around the country.

On the day of the ballot, some Al-Nahdha sympathizers within the administration smuggled to the movement's leaders semi-official results of the 'independent lists'. According to the leadership (private interview in Paris in 1997), they got 92 per cent in Tunis, 80 per cent in Ben Arroz, 85 per cent in the Sahel (Bourguiba's district), and approximately 65 per cent in the interior districts. Again according to Al-Nahdha, the governors had transmitted the exact results on the basis of official vote count reports. It was at the Interior Ministry that the election results were tampered with.

This was an opportunity for Ben Ali to learn the real strength of the movement. Moreover, it provided him with region-based lists of Al-Nahdha members and sympathizers, drawn from three sources: the participants in rallies, the ballot centres (during the vote, RCD supporters deliberately acted in ways that reflected their preference, so that those who did not could easily be identified as non-supporters of the regime), and the regional delegations that had not been excluded from the vote count. And so it was not long before retaliatory measures, including dismissals and all kinds of administrative harassment (confiscation of passports, public accusations, and so on), were taken against Al-Nahdha sympathizers and activists.

A night raid was planned for December 1990 to arrest the whole leadership. But information about it was leaked, and so, to ward off the blow and bolster its public image, the Islamist leadership decided to make public the names of the members of the regional offices at a press conference to be held at the office of the party's newspaper, *Al-Fajr* (Dawn). By means of such a move, the leaders hoped to increase the people's knowledge of their programme and organization. The press conference did not take place; and in a raid on Larayedh's house, the police arrested him and laid their hands on an extended list of the leadership (sixty members instead of fourteen) in addition to the regional lists. The office of *Al-Fajr* was closed down by the police. A wave of arrests began while the Tunisian press looked the other way, even though Al-Nahdha kept sending them information on events.

Around this time, those who could among Al-Nahdha's leaders fled the country and sought asylum elsewhere. Those who remained called on their followers to organize peaceful demonstrations. But the situation was explosive, and demonstrators used stones, Molotov cocktails, and sticks.

In 1991 came the fabricated story of Al-Nahdha's plot to kill the president. 'Frankly, we did not have the political power to support you', an opposition leader confessed. 'We were afraid, and the balance of power was not in your favour.' As for the opposition newspapers, which had recently disappeared, they would be unable to benefit from the funds freed by the President for starting up again unless they backed the regime against Al-Nahdha. None but international observers were there to protest against the unfair trials that followed. Since then, Al-Nahdha has not appeared in the Tunisian public arena.

The Undermining of the Tunisian League for Human Rights

When Ben Ali came to power in 1987, the Tunisian League for Human Rights (LTDH) had just emerged from a first ideological and conceptual crisis, sparked off in 1985 around two issues: the presence of a Tunisian Jew, Serges Adda, on its Executive Committee, and the potential role of the organization in the promotion of equality between the sexes. This crisis took place at a time when the Islamists were calling into question the Code of Personal Status which, they argued, Bourguiba had imposed upon society. So, the government did not intervene in the dispute around this double problem, which became the subject of public debates, and topped the list on the agenda of the League's congress: against Serges Adda and against the equality between the sexes, whereas Arab nationalists and Islamists voiced their opposition to a notion of human rights that they rejected as a Western concept, alien to the Arab and Muslim mentality. The dispute was resolved, not without all the accompanying commotion imaginable, by means of a compromise text: the Tunisian Human Rights Charter, with its reference to 'the positive side of the Arab-Muslim mentality', was submitted to a national council (not a general meeting) and was adopted by twenty-five votes against twenty-four (the latter were the votes of the Islamists and Arab nationalists), following several successive drafts submitted to the executive committee.

Serges Adda kept his position on the executive committee and a Women's Affairs Committee was set up. In future, every applicant for membership of the League was to be required, at least in theory, to sign the Tunisian Human Rights Charter and prove his or her commitment to the organization's objectives in an interview with a senior member (these procedures, however, were not rigorously applied in practice, because of the lack of time to meet all applicants).

On the issue of the equality of the sexes, the League called for the law to be changed to acknowledge the absolute right of Muslim women to choose their spouses. Until then, the government still had not expressed any position on this question, considering that the Code of Personal Status was part of Bourguiba's heritage, which should not be touched. The Mufti of the Republic expressed his opposition to the code; some MPs declared to the press that women should 'stay at home'. The debate went on while there were rumours to the effect that a bill legalizing bigamy had been submitted to the prime minister. In March 1988, a few months after the coup, amid great excitement and fanfare around the burgeoning ideas of democracy and equality for women, Ben Ali stated his support for the women's cause. Until then, women's groups active in the League had not been authorized, as the issue of women was the monopoly of the ruling party. However, after the elections had revealed the extent of the fundamentalist resurgence, two women's groups were authorized in August 1989. The same developments also led to women's demands being incorporated into the strategy that emerged from the National Pact, which was unanimously endorsed. Ben Ali was going to become very popular with women, and the League was going to continue to exercise, for a very short period of time, a good deal of influence.

The departure of the president of the League, Mohamed Charfi, who was appointed a minister one month after its 1989 congress, contributed in the long run to the destabilization of the organization. Taken by surprise, the League replaced him with Moncef Marzuki. The latter would prove unable to build consensus over his leadership; now that the honeymoon between the government and the Islamists was over, Marzuki's declarations in their defence disturbed many people.

The debate around this core issue had not yet been settled when the Gulf War occurred, triggering yet another confrontation between the League and the Arab nationalist movement. While the general population expressed its support for the Iraqi president, Saddam Hussein, the LTDH denounced the invasion of Kuwait, and expressed its condemnation of Iraqi dictatorship, but it also warned the West against the temptation of trying to cash in on the conflict. A campaign soon ensued, led by the government and the newspapers, accusing the League's leaders of being the hirelings of foreign powers.

The Arab nationalists, for their part, described the Gulf War as a war of the West against the Arab world. It is noteworthy how again the universal character of human rights was undermined and the concept was made into a tool for selective use by governments in furtherance of their various strategies. A movement then emerged in favour of an Arab or Islamic declaration of human rights. Seven members of the LTDH executive committee publicly expressed their disagreement with the other seven, criticizing them for having 'sold out' to the West. Attacks on Marzuki and his group came from within the League, from Arab nationalists calling for their resignation, and from outside, from a number of organizations, among them the Young Lawyers as well as some political parties, which expressed their disapproval of Marzuki. Some League branches voiced their disagreement with the position of the executive committee. Within the latter, there were even discussions about dissolving the organization. Tension was running very high and meetings were no longer held for fear that they might lead to more agitation.

As if these problems were not enough to destabilize the League, its relationship with the government began to deteriorate. On 13 June 1991, it issued a statement denouncing human rights violations regardless of the perpetrator. Ben Ali invited Marzuki, along with the local president of Amnesty International and Hassib Ben Ammar for discussions. This appeasement attempt did not lead to any agreement, but the League decided to keep quiet and wait for the report of the commission of investigation, promised during the meeting, and for the trials of the torturers. In December 1991, the executive committee renewed its condemnation of torture and deaths. This statement was much stronger in tone than its previous one. For the first time, mention was made of the gap between the discourse of President Ben Ali and reality. The crisis broke out two days later: Marzuki was attacked in the Tunisian papers and reacted clumsily – by defending himself in foreign papers. (But what else could he have done?)

The response of the government came in the form of a special law requiring 'voluntary organizations' to open up their doors to all (which could only facilitate infiltration by intelligence agents), and banning party leaders from holding positions on their executive bodies (to prevent politicization). So the League was threatened with losing its autonomy if it yielded to the law and threatened with dissolution if it resisted it.

There was hardly any reaction on the part of civil society: to defend the League was tantamount to committing the heinous sin of criticizing the government. Only international NGOs could negotiate on behalf of the League for the provisional lifting of the suspension. A compromise was struck: the League would comply with the clause prohibiting plurality of offices. In return, the government would waive the provision opening membership to all comers. Technically, the League would remain delinquent and could be dissolved at any time. Henceforth, it would depend for its very existence on the good will of the president.

Yet during the preparations for the next congress, it became evident that the commitments entered into by the government would not be honoured: more than half of the six thousand applications for membership came from the ruling RCD. The tacit alliance between the MDS and the government contributed to that, since it was the MDS that sponsored the RCD applications; one thousand applications from the

RCD, that is, 25 per cent, were accepted; out of 300 congress delegates, 50 to 70 were going to be from the RCD. From being the party with the smallest representation in the League, the RCD jumped to the top in terms of influence. This infiltration and internal dissent precipitated the fall of Marzuki at the congress.

The relations established between the regime and Tunisian civil society following the fatal alliance thus led to the 'satellization' of civil institutions and their being drained of all substance. The only exceptions were Al-Nahdha, which was knocked out, and the League, which the government spared to avoid embarrassment, given Tunisia's international commitments in relation to human rights and the League's international credibility. Being gagged and isolated inside the country, however, the League had no audience except international institutions. Thus, the major countervailing force against the temptation to authoritarianism – a network of civil institutions capable of undertaking joint protest and challenging the government in ideological debates in the domestic public forum – had disappeared. All that was left was to drive home the last bolt in the totalitarian edifice that had been erected.

Notes

1. This phenomenon of uncertainty was thoroughly analysed in the comparative analysis of democratic transitions edited by Guillermo O'Donnell, Philippe C. Schmitter and Laurence Whitehead, *Transition from Authoritarian Rule: Prospects for Democracy* (Johns Hopkins University Press, Baltimore, 4 vols, 1991). Democratic transitions may succeed or fail. In either case, the outcome of the process can be foreseen neither by the political actors nor by sociologists. Can political sociology improve its capability to predict the future? In order to do so, the history of democratic transitions can serve as a quasi-experimental laboratory and the unintentional-effect phenomenon can serve as an explanatory paradigm.
2. See, for instance, Michel Deuré's article 'Nouvelle manifestation des islamistes en plein centre de Tunis', *Le Monde*, 18 July 1987, p. 5.

3

TUNISIA

LOCKING UP PLATO'S CAVE

Montesquieu's classical theory of the separation of powers proposed three countervailing forces to offset the authoritarian temptation within the state: the executive, the legislature, and the judiciary. Each one of the state branches, if autonomous, can prevent or redress the abuses of the other two.

In modern times, this theory can be complemented by a fourth countervailing force. Whether it is a democracy or a tyranny, the state does not exist in a vacuum. Oppression by the rulers is also rendered possible by the submission of the ruled, and it is generally believed that it is the media (including their sources) who, by relaying the discourses of both sides, contribute to either building up a consensus of opinion or undermining it. Thus regulatory mechanisms or, at least, mechanisms of mutual influence between rulers and ruled can be established.

From this neo-liberal perspective, freedom of information and expression represent essential resources for this alleged fourth power – the media: without press freedom, without pluralistic expression of opinion, the state can easily monopolize public debate. Therefore, the locking up of a public forum, Tunisian or otherwise, requires a tightened state grip on national and international media, as well as on the isolated witnesses who might still be tempted to speak to journalists. Thus the flow of information is stemmed. On the walls of the cave, men don't perceive anything anymore except pale and indecipherable reflections of reality.

In Tunisia, until 1997 this information gag was imposed through the state Secretariat for Information, in charge of the Tunisian media, as well as through the Tunisian External Communication Agency (ATCE), which deals with the foreign media. Competition between officials is fierce and errors are unforgiven. Each one is trying to outdo the others

38

in their efforts to muzzle the media and protect the image of Tunisia and President Ben Ali. At the helm of this structure, the personal adviser of the president, Abdelwahab Abdellah, known in Tunis media circles as 'Goebbels', has been serving as *de facto* Minister of Propaganda.[1]

The locking up of the media could not have occurred were it not for the catastrophic political blunder that Tunisia's civil actors committed when they unconditionally rallied behind the president. The civil actors having voluntarily surrendered, newspapers found themselves isolated in the face of a regime that confronted them with a dilemma: bow and scrape or disappear. With a few exceptions, the media did not fight back. On the contrary, after the National Pact, they were quick to join the public forum's well-orchestrated concert.

The Disadvantaged Media

This lack of combativeness from the media finds its explanation not just in their isolation. It is also reinforced by the scarcity of resources that the print media have at their disposal to ensure their survival and growth in a context of underdevelopment. This accounts for the ease with which the regime was able to reduce the print media to a state of total patriarchal dependence and make of them mere tools for its domination; rather than just an alliance, in fact a symbiotic relationship between the regime and the press was established. The few ways of influencing things that certain papers have managed since to develop did not enhance their power of initiative in any significant way, and so have not extricated them from their role of satellite to totalitarian power. This was how the Tunisian print media ensured their survival. Freedom of the press in effect succumbed to the blows it suffered as a result of the fatal alliance between civil actors and the police regime.

The scant resources of the Tunisian print media

A survey conducted in Tunis during the early days of the rule of Ben-Ali revealed that 70 per cent of journalists have achieved the educational level of a master's degree or higher. Some 85.8 per cent have permanent posts, but their working conditions are poor: only 29 per cent earn more than DT400 (US$539 at 2003 values) per month, and 80 per cent have neither computer nor typewriter. Career development is hardly conceivable under such poor working conditions; 39 per cent of journalists have a second job and 35.8 per cent have already changed newspaper.[2] At the Institute of Journalism and Information Sciences, further signs of lack of motivation among journalists were detected: lack of initiative in journalistic production, failure at times to check information prior to publication, investigations undertaken without proper planning, and a search for sensationalism. According to the journalists interviewed, the general demotivation is exacerbated by another factor: the pressure resulting from the bosses' hunt for immediate profitability, and the quantitative norms of production, which drive the journalist towards carelessness.[3]

Corporate culture too seems to discourage initiative. 'The newspaper's manager is either appointed by the government, or well thought of by the government. His contributors and journalists have just a few responsibilities, especially the latter, who seldom get the opportunity to discuss the future of their company and its broad directions.' So, with authoritarianism at the micro level of the company, combined with the more generalized authoritarianism at the macro level of the political system, self-censorship and the ritualistic reproduction of official slogans become the norm. Here, the line of demarcation between civil society and the state has been completely blurred (Chouikha, 1993 – see note 3).

The objective conditions of the publication of newspapers (equipment and distribution) also leave much to be desired. In fact, the majority of Tunisian newspapers have no equipment. They must contract out typesetting, do the editing on-site, then again contract out the printing. To the high costs engendered by this subcontracting is to be added the problem of paper shortages. When there is a shortage of paper at the printing plant, the newspapers must look for it elsewhere, buy some and come back for the printing.

The publisher of a daily paper who under such conditions manages to produce an interesting issue, without delay or undue costs at the printing house, is still not guaranteed success, all his efforts notwithstanding. Another obstacle stands in his way: there is no distribution company. Therefore, he must rely on news vendors only. In Tunis, there is a kind of newspaper brokers' network. In the interior of the country, newspapers are mailed by post or via a courier company, which is itself having difficulties. The result: a good issue is unlikely to reach all newsstands in time. According to the publishers I met, the problems of distribution constitute one of the major factors behind the sales problems. On top of these logistical problems there are political problems; under the scourge of police terror, the suppliers (printing, distribution and advertising) may decide to ignore a blacklisted newspaper for fear of reprisal.

As in Morocco and Algeria, the Tunisian print media, already weakened by organizational deficiencies and deserted by civil society, must face the authoritarian policies of the state on their own. On their own? What about their readers? Don't they support the press by buying newspaper every morning? Very few ...

The readership

Radio is the source of information for Tunisians. Television is the second. Print media lag far behind. In a 1992 survey that included 1,000 Tunisians distributed across eight major cities of the country, Al-Amouri revealed that daily newspapers are generally read or just leafed through once or twice a week.[4]

Topping the list, according to the reading habits of the people surveyed, was a daily Arabic-language popular newspaper, *Al-Chourouq* (The Dawn, read by 73 per cent of respondents), praised by its readers for its condensed political analyses and second-page news briefs, sports coverage and gossip column, the quality of its graphics and its entertaining and sensational style. Second was *Al-Sabah* (The Morning, 59 per cent), an Arabic-language daily newspaper that combines the entertaining style of the popular press and the more austere mode of the establishment press. Third most popular (42 per cent) was the French-language government-controlled daily newspaper *La Presse de Tunisie*. The respondents regarded it as the most objective and credible general-interest newspaper, less superficial than the other French-language dailies.[5] It is also worth noting the statistically honourable performance of the Al-Sabah group's French-language daily *Le Temps* (The Times, 25 per cent). Apart from these major newspapers, dozens of other ephemeral and low-circulation newspapers are read on occasion, mainly by people in the capital.

Let us suppose that, by some miracle, one of the four big dailies suddenly showed some independence by openly challenging the policies of the president and got away with it. In order to survive financially the loss of subsidies, advertising and subscriptions that its audacity would engender, it would need at the very least to double its sales figures (according to publishers' estimates). The objective would be achievable, providing the content was diversified and the design was improved. The 1991 Gulf War did demonstrate that the public buys more when a newspaper meets readers' expectations. And what the public expects from a newspaper (still according to Al-Amouri's research), is that it should take risks, develop its own ideas and analyses, not relying solely on official sources, and that it should reflect expertise on all subjects and support the views held by the public.

Assessed against such unrealistic expectations, the image of the Tunisian press is on the whole poor: Al-Amouri's respondents saw them as open to manipulation by the government, concealing what ought to be exposed, distorting reality, and often indulging in plagiarism. Even though the public claims to be aware of the material and political constraints that block information, it believes that newspapers could show more courage and competence. In short, Tunisian newspapers are boring and lacking in credibility.

Logically, in order to double their readership, the print media would have to 'double' their quality. But with what resources? With which professional journalists? What computers? What printers? With what government or civil support to fall back on in the event of censorship? The level of market acceptance as well as of other resources will remain low. And this structural deficiency, in a context of social anomie and under a regime without separation of powers, places the media in a state of absolute dependence *vis-à-vis* patriarchal benevolence. Consequently, the risk to a newspaper of getting into the government's bad books would be suicidal and so, very understandably, no newspaper has ever reached this point and survived.

How the Tunisian Media were Neutralized

A press law that makes it difficult for newspapers to be set up, to expand or to speak out, combined with generalized censorship, locks them in a relationship of dependence on a patriarchal regime that holds the power to give them life or take it away from them. In Tunisia the formal rules of control have been defined by the Press Code (1975) in the following way.

The formal rules of press control
In theory, people can start newspapers by submitting a notice to the Interior Minister. Upon receiving it, the minister issues a receipt acknowledging having been notified. However, the issuing of this receipt may take a very long time, or even may never happen. Thus, the minister has virtually full control over the process of choosing the individuals and groups who will be allowed to create newspapers.

The law prohibits any form of partisan or commercial monopoly in newspaper ownership (article 15). Moreover, newspapers can be funded neither with portfolio funds nor with foreign investment (article 19). These regulations encourage the multiplication of short-lived, low-circulation newspapers, in the face of the big pro-government newspapers that dominate the market, and inhibit the emergence of an influential private or partisan press.

It is prohibited to disseminate any information liable to disturb 'public order' (article 73, as amended in 1988) and to criticize ('defame') the authorities, even where the criticisms are based on proven allegations (article 75). And it is up to the Interior Minister to decide what constitutes 'defamation' or a 'threat to public order'. The minister may even proceed with the seizure of a newspaper without legal recourse.

The Press Code also provides for legal deposit of each issue of a newspaper before publication. And as the government very often informally appoints a censor at the printing plant, censorship and seizure become all the easier.[6]

Over the years the newspapers (especially *Al-Chourouq, Al-Sabah, Le Temps, Al-Saada* [Happiness] and *Réalités*) developed the practice of leaving blank spaces to draw their readers' attention to censored articles. One day in 1991, copies of *Les Annonces* newspaper were seized for having blank spaces. Since then, newspapers have become very reluctant to use this method of exposing censorship.

The practice of censorship

Directives to newspaper editors are straightforward and come from several sources, sometimes simultaneously. Most often, a minister calls to order the publication of a disclaimer or the sacking of the journalist, or to order the newspaper not to interview this or that person any more. Newspaper editors are also accustomed to friendly advice of the type 'You have exaggerated … You should not have …', and to threats of the type 'By writing that, you show that you are unreliable,' as well as seizures at the newsstands or the printing house. In any case, there is bargaining on articles in question: 'Listen, if we remove page 37, page 13 has also to be removed …' or 'We did not want to say that …' or 'We will ring up again.' Most often, the caller won't give up until a page is torn away or a word scratched out.

What happens when a Tunisian newspaper resists the pressures? After the Gulf War, the editor-in-chief of a big national daily was laid off on the order of the authorities because he failed to support the government's initial position on the war. He has since been demoted to a simple journalist. This is a common practice. *Le Maghreb* gave commercial and political conditions as the reason for its closing down, after it had denounced the domination of the media by the government and refused to fire three of its journalists. The director, Omar S'habou, then signed an article entitled 'Rising Values and Falling Values.' Three ministers filed a criminal libel suit against him, and he was sentenced to prison on charges of disseminating 'false news'.

During Bourguiba's time, the journalists of *Tunis Afrique Presse* (TAP), in which the government holds the majority of shares, had formed numerous pockets of resistance. Under Ben Ali, however, they have been restricted to the role of mere public servants. 'Our reports and investigations are truncated accounts which convey only that part of reality that the bosses and the government would be pleased with,' one TAP representative told me. 'No one can try to improve things; nobody keeps his position long enough to do it. Stranded between fear and our principles, we may be tempted to commit fatal mistakes. Resign? Yes, but without compensation.'

Before overt dissidence appeared in December 1998, most of the Tunisian newspapers took the side of President Ben Ali. They did so not just because they had no choice, but also hoping to derive some benefits from their submissiveness. The president did not disappoint them.

Patriarchal dependence: an exchange relationship

When it re-emerged in 1991 and 1992, after a short period of eclipse, the private press expected new trials. However, the 'change' was non-violent, which gave reason for optimism. 'So, we joined the battle for change,' explains the editor of a small newspaper.

In the opinion of some, however, the private press is not completely isolated. 'We now have an arbitrator who is being encouraging and understanding: Ben Ali,' another journalist maintains. 'Today we can, if necessary, ask for justice; we have appealed to him each time we had a serious problem. I have even met with him, I was able to clarify our position and speak to him about the importance of our newspaper.' The fatherly arbitration of President Ben Ali obviously presupposes that one is already well thought of by the regime.

This monopoly of arbitration is seen by some as an advantage: 'Today, there is a president who is in control, whereas under Bourguiba the last ten years were tragic; it was a total mess.' And, actually, the president does act like an arbitrator … between his right arm, the Ministry of the Interior, which punishes, and his left arm, the TAP, whose functions include the distribution of public advertising (from ministries and government-run companies) among the different newspapers.

Ben Ali also administers a financial assistance scheme, with no precise rules (on the price of paper, distribution, equipment etcetera), which increases newspapers' dependence on his patriarchal benevolence.

For the government-controlled *Presse de Tunisie*, at times, advertising represented up to 80 per cent of income. *Al-Sabah*, when it was still well thought of, used to publish four pages of advertising out of its sixteen pages, perhaps the equivalent of 40–50 per cent of its income. Advertising revenues do not exceed 20–25 per cent of income (three pages out of forty) for the popular daily *Al-Chourouq* and the low-circulation papers, such as *Réalités*. Were advertising cuts that were inflicted on *Al-Sabah*, *Al-Chourouq* and *Réalités* used as pressure tactics? Some publishers dared to admit it's true: 'When advertising decreases, we react by complaining to the authorities and negotiating with them to make sure the fluctuations are only temporary.' How about private advertising? 'Private advertisers are sensitive to the state's conduct; when they notice that government advertising allocated to us has dropped, there is every chance that, out of fear, they follow suit. The private advertising/public advertising ratio is 15/85. We have also tried subscription campaigns, but the readership is not very faithful and the results are disappointing.'

In this exchange relationship between the press and the state, both receive benefits; the state secures the collaboration of a subservient press in return for providing it with advertising revenue and news from the TAP. The press lives off public subsidies in return for a passive collaboration with the higher authority that holds the power of reward and punishment.

Such is the story of the housing project initiated by the Tunisian Journalists' Association (AJT) for the benefit of its members, in collaboration with SPROLS, a housing development firm. Under this project, named *Al-Ghazala*, construction of 190 housing units was started. Eventually, the AJT was to be the owner of the project.

After it had earned the backing of the presidency with regards to zoning, *Al-Ghazala* project gave rise to tensions. The sale price of a housing unit jumped initially from 28,000 to 40,000 Tunisian *dinar* per unit, which represented an increase in payments from 220 to 350 dinars per month, over a period of fifteen to twenty years. On the other hand, because the law prohibits Social Funds from asking salaried employees to pay more than 40 per cent of their salary in housing costs, such an increase in costs deprived between 60 and 80 per cent of journalist members of the AJT (those whose families do not earn two salaries) of the opportunity to benefit from this project.

This was a critical moment for the AJT, which feared the eruption of an internal conflict. In an attempt to gain the approval of the government, it started by showing its opposition to the position taken by the French press with regards to a money-laundering affair involving Moncef, the president's brother. Then it publicly declared its support for Ben Ali as a candidate in the 1994 presidential elections. 'I went for it,' one AJT representative explained to me. 'For a while this gesture rid us of many problems that resulted from our former positions, and it did not cost us anything.' Indeed, the AJT was far more confrontational under Bourguiba.

Survival Strategies

The press has adapted to the stifling patriarchal benevolence of President Ben Ali. Editors now know only too well how to avoid taboo subjects, how to approach sensitive issues without provoking the wrath of the state, and how to negotiate with the authorities a carefully sanitized public agenda.

The no-news zones

The absolute limit not to be transgressed is clear: the press should not disturb, either at home or abroad. 'Often,' an editor frankly admits, 'we do not use the information available for fear of reprisal. We keep information that is too sensitive for our own analyses and we refer to it only allusively.'

The taboos have to do first of all with the foundations of the president's discourse of legitimacy, that is, the institutions and the process of democratization; the press must agree with the official evaluation of the dangers allegedly lying in wait for democracy and approve of the oppressive methods used by the government. 'We are for the economic, social and democratic solutions, rather than the oppressive methods,' an editor acknowledges. 'Before, we dared to speak about political trials. That is why our present situation (sales, paper ...) is so bad. So, we don't speak about it any more.'

Likewise, the laws and government institutions that control the press are no longer questioned. Exceptionally, at an international conference on 'freedom of information in the Maghreb' held in April 1991 in Tunis, foreign journalists and academics openly discussed the evolution of the press in Tunisia and the laws that govern it. The event took place at a time when all the important private newspapers had just closed down as they could no longer cope with the legal and administrative harassment. Someone raised a question: 'Wouldn't the press be freer without a Press Code?' A Tunisian jurist sharply retorted that the code was vital for the freedom of information, and the audience fell silent.

Another area that is forbidden to the press includes anything that could suggest that the Tunisian public forum is not unanimous. One example is the viewpoints of opposition parties. When they are in favour of President Ben Ali, as was the case in the aftermath of the 1994 elections, the press may report. The press did not, however, publish the public letter of the opposition leader regarding human rights violations, in autumn 1995. Neither did it squander a drop of ink on his arrest. As for the banned political parties, the Islamist Al-Nahdha and the Tunisian Communist Labour Party (PCOT), they were completely ignored, as if they had never existed. The communiqués of the Tunisian League for Human Rights (LTDH) suffered the same fate.

A fourth zone forbidden to the press comprises all that may lead to external hostility or controversy: Tunisia must go on looking peaceful and friendly to all. As soon as a foreign diplomat intervenes, directives to the press immediately follow. When Qadhafi threatened Tunisia with reprisals against Tunisian workers in Libya, a report on the economic situation in Libya was not published. When, during the Gulf War, a certain journalist lashed out at the attitude of the French media, his newspaper was advised to reduce its Arab nationalist ardour. When the 1992 coup took place in Algeria, the Tunisian press, on the whole, hardly commented on the event, in contrast with the Algerian press. In all three cases, the Tunisian authorities invoked diplomatic reasons for interfering with the press.

The Happy Agenda

The main newspaper headlines are devoted to President Ben Ali's activities. The press regularly reproduces the patriarchal conception of government and feeds the Manichaean view of political opponents (they are all Islamists, all terrorists) into public opinion. Its representation of an apparent social unanimity serves to conceal the fact that nothing but official news can be released. Consequently, instead of the conflictual public debates typical of a pluralist political forum, the Tunisian press provides nothing for the Tunisian public forum but ornamental rhetoric and empty slogans, such as the 'change' and, still emptier, its hyperbole of the 'acceleration of the change'.[7] Applause for President Ben Ali, founder and saviour of the nascent 'Tunisian democracy', must inaugurate any public speech.

Nevertheless, large newspapers do try to make use of a tiny margin of flexibility still available where they may perhaps get away with it. One newspaper has managed to survive within this area of ambiguity by attaching importance only to official news that relates to social problems, development and elections. As for the other news, the daily agenda of the president for example, or a cabinet meeting that has decided nothing of importance, nothing is published, except on inside pages and in the form of short items. Following pressures, mainly by telephone, and after long negotiations with the editor, the government seems to have accepted this policy. To support its position, the newspaper resorted to the argument that the best images lose their power as a result of frequent repetition. It added that the newspaper would not sell unless it contained news of interest to its readers, and argued that a marketing strategy of relative indifference is not a sign of lack of political enthusiasm, especially when the newspaper regularly publishes the gossip that is spread against the opposition. The overt pressure ended, but the amount of advertising allocated to this newspaper decreased; a warning not to go farther?

Another director told me that unsigned articles are published in his newspaper without his authorization. He has protested, but in vain; other newspapers have suffered the same kind of intrusion. What can he do, aside from keeping his position for as long as he can?

Still, there is room for initiative, and even for controversy, when a newspaper wants to distinguish itself from its competitors. Such was the case with the polemic around the entertainment show, *Noujoum* (The Stars), which opposed the government-controlled daily *La Presse de Tunisie* to the popular newspapers *Al-Chourouq* and *Al-Hadeth* (The Event). At first, the latter stirred up public opinion against the show which was considered an affront to public morality. In a front-page article titled 'Let the Stars Shine', *La Presse de Tunisie* dubbed them fundamentalists. Notable here is the denunciation of rival newspapers by a term – 'fundamentalist' – which was given its political connotation by the official discourse. Thus the controversy ends with a subtle expression of reverence for the government. While sales increase …

Be it by sensationalism that sells or by a dilettantish and literary image that increases its credibility, occasionally a newspaper manages to compensate for the dullness of its political neutrality by finding something else to attract the reader. Sometimes, allegories or metaphors provide a convenient way to launch disguised criticisms. Thus, in a diary column published in *La Presse de Tunisie*, one may read fictitious dialogues between the journalist and his son of the following form: 'Father, tell me a story' – and the father tells his son a story with a very official moral. 'But father, at school I was told …' – 'Definitely not so, my son …'

What makes the journalist need to lecture an invented son in a fictitious dialogue? Is he being cautious not to clash with the powers that be? Maybe; but be that as it may, the message did get across … through his son's words … even if it means that only a few readers will be able to decipher the hidden message. For the uninitiated readers, this article is no more than a simple example of good literary quality in the press of a happy country.

Relations with the Foreign Press

But the foreign press, one might object, why would they accept being silenced? Are not foreign journalists protected by their embassies? Protected they are, but they are also prevented by the Tunisian authorities from having access to news sources and from disseminating disturbing news.

A prohibited territory

Prohibition and expulsion measures against the foreign media, and seizures of foreign newspapers at the border, have become common practice since the winter of 1994. In turn, the dailies *Le Monde, Le Monde diplomatique, Jeune Afrique Économie, Libération, Agence France-Presse, Le Courrier International, Info-Matin, Terre sauvage, Le Canard enchaîné* and the daily *La Croix* have been prevented from informing the Tunisian public. The English *Guardian* and *Financial Times*, as well as the BBC (London), underwent censorship, as did the Moroccan *Les Nouvelles du Nord, L'Opinion* and *Al-Alam*. The Kuwaiti news agency KUNA was shut down in 1994, its telephone line and electricity cut off. The matter was resolved between governments; the correspondent was expelled.

Sometimes the reasons for the expulsion of journalists are concealed. On one occasion, the Agence France-Presse (AFP) refused to publish a correction which had been requested by the Tunisian authorities but which in conformity with the professional code of ethics – no slander, no insults, no false information – had not been written. Not daring formally to expel the AFP correspondent, one week later they played on him this nasty little trick: a young girl fell to the ground in front of him screaming with pain, and as he rushed to her assistance, the girl started shouting 'rape'. A complaint was filed with the police. Following the intervention of the French embassy, the correspondent was allowed to leave Tunisia, but the charges were retained against him until his substitute was appointed.

Tunisians working for the foreign press

To work for the foreign press is not a right for the Tunisian journalist. It is, rather, a privilege to be requested from the authorities.[8] Sometimes, accreditation does not come. The journalist who works in a state of illegality has no security whatsoever. An arrangement can be negotiated between the agency's management and the authorities, but it is a matter of toleration that can be reversed at any time. When accreditation is granted, the journalist remains a suspect citizen, to be watched because he has dangerous connections (from the perspective of the locking-up policy), and to be subjected to obscure rules that render his situation precarious.

At the time of the 1994 election campaign, journalist Kamel Labidi was working for TAP. But it was for the French daily *La Croix* that he interviewed Moncef Marzuki, the president's rival. Labidi had already been doubly recognized: he had obtained the accreditation of the Tunisian External Communication Agency (ATCE) (card no. 033 delivered in December 1993) as well as the professional card of the Ministry of Culture and Information (card no. 038 delivered in December 1992 and renewed in 1994). Following his interview with Marzuki, he was dismissed from TAP; his director had not authorized him to work for *La Croix*. After his dismissal, Labidi could find no Tunisian employer who dared give him a job. Other administrative obstacles followed, preventing him from exercising his profession.

One year after his dismissal from TAP, Labidi wanted to go to Yemen for a conference on the independence of Arab media. The day before his departure, he received his passport, renewed for five years. That night, however, plain-clothes policemen came to take it away from him: there was a mistake in the passport. They promised to give it back to him at the airport, once the mistake was corrected. Thus he was prevented from leaving, at the last minute, when it was too late for interventions. The official explanation given to the daily *La Croix* was that the authorities were unaware that a new passport was issued then withdrawn: 'Kamel's passport had expired.'[9]

Working conditions of foreign journalists

Foreign newspapers may be banned or their Tunisian correspondents may be prevented from working, but there are nevertheless top-level representatives at the Tunis-based offices of foreign newspapers, and special correspondents still come to make reports. However, the surveillance, the intimidation and the directives to which they are subjected are based on a strategy of blocking out international information.

It all begins at the border, when the foreign journalist declares his status and the police officer disappears with the passport for several minutes, without uttering a word. Then comes the not-always-covert police surveillance throughout the journalist's stay. The story told by *Le Courrier de Genève* is but one example among many: 'As we left the Chamaris' house, the police officers rushed to take photos of us. The following day, a document from Pax Christi on the issue, which we left on the table in our Hammamet hotel room, mysteriously disappeared.'[10]

Barry Newman, the special correspondent of the *Wall Street Journal*, had in the past worked in Singapore, Malaysia and Eastern Europe. He was already used to the difficulties encountered by foreign correspondents working in a dictatorship. As his first mission in Tunisia was also to be his last, he thought he could do an honest job without fearing reprisals. But he had underestimated the climate of surveillance and terror he was going to meet with:

On my arrival, I asked the state Secretary for Information to assign me an interpreter, for I wished to talk with ordinary people in their own language. Someone was immediately sent to me. My interpreter started by giving me a long speech about the merits of his government. That did not bother me much; my experience in Asia and Eastern Europe had accustomed me to this sort of apologist. After having together prepared a work plan for my visit, we left each other.

The following day, my interpreter did not show up. I seized the opportunity to have a free walk around Tunis. In the evening, on my return to the hotel, I thought of avoiding the official channel that had left me in the lurch. So, I asked the receptionist if one of his acquaintances, a student or a young person wanting to earn some money, could work for me as an interpreter and guide the next day. Sure, he promised, I know someone. Hardly five minutes had passed when the telephone rang; it was my interpreter of the day before!

The following day, we went together for a walk through the countryside. Strangely, the interpreter seemed very reluctant to stop the car and let me talk with the people. Finally, we stopped to eat. At one point, the restaurant owner whispered in my ear asking if my companion were an official. Upon my affirmative answer, he disappeared, not to come back again. The remainder of the day was wasted between the vague and useless translations of my interpreter and the speechifying of the local worthies we met.

On the fourth day, I discharged my interpreter. Still in search of new information, I approached the British embassy: outright refusal to see me. At the American embassy, I could meet neither the ambassador nor the political adviser. As an ultimate concession, the Americans arranged for a meeting with the Counsellor for Public Affairs. The latter insisted that we had to meet incognito and outside the embassy. During the interview, he remained unwilling to open up, embarrassed, and kept parroting the Tunisian official discourse.

As for foreign journalists residing in Tunisia, their working conditions are no better than those of their Tunisian colleagues; they have to resign themselves to the fact that they cannot reflect anything but shadows of Tunisian reality, or else leave. How is this so? Often the minister calls: 'Why this false news?' But it also happens that the journalist is invited for a cup of tea by a state representative, and pressured not to publish this or to publish that. The general strategy seems to consist in using foreign journalists as accessories to the state information apparatus. If the correspondent shows resistance, he becomes undesirable; he gets framed and is forced to leave, without doing too much damage to the image of the regime, so it is hoped.

Banning International Human Rights Monitoring

At the beginning of the twenty-first century, only three states in the world continue to ban international human rights monitoring delegations from their territories: China, Burma and Tunisia. These are, then, the world's most closed dictatorships, well hidden from foreign observers.

Patrick Beaudoin, attorney-at-law in Paris and president of the International Federation for Human Rights, had not been to Tunisia for three years. In the meantime, alarming news reached him through some Tunisian lawyers and League activists. So he decided to check with the authorities and set a first date for his departure: end of 1995. He was persuaded to wait until the report of the League was published. Then a second date of departure was also deferred: relations between the League and the government were tense, while internal conflicts were dividing the League, and the timing was deemed inappropriate. Beaudoin set a third date: early summer 1996, and wrote a formal request to the Tunisian embassy asking for an appointment with the authorities. When he received no reply, he called by telephone: the ambassador was 'not around'. So he sent a fax. An answer came back: 'Delay your trip; the time is inappropriate.' As he was about to leave, at the airport, Tunis-Air handed him a fax from the Tunisian ambassador asking him not to leave before an appointment was arranged for him 'with the relevant authorities'. Beaudoin telephoned the ambassador to inform him that he was not going to delay his trip for a third time because of such evasive promises and left for Tunis, accompanied by the president of the Senegalese League for Human Rights. At Tunis-Carthage airport, they were turned back. The official pretext: Beaudoin had insulted the authorities on his arrival.

With Reporters Sans Frontières (RSF), it was the same attitude. 'The ATCE made it explicit that we would be turned back at the frontier, and that the decision about this ban was final,' said Robert Ménard. 'With the ATCE, messages have the advantage of being clear, but they are never written: no traces are to be left.' The delegations of Amnesty International also don't go to Tunisia any more: they are no longer granted visas, and their publications are no longer allowed into Tunisia. Understandably, a further attempt by Robert Ménard and Patrick Beaudoin to visit Tunisia, during the summer of 2000, ended with their arrival at Tunis-Carthage Airport, where they were denied entrance to the country. Other nongovernmental organizations (NGOs) are no more welcome.

The same is true of any book that criticizes the regime. Arriving on one flight in December 1994, one couple – the man bearded and the woman wearing the veil – were the only passengers intercepted by Tunisian customs. The customs officer who searched their bags carefully leafed through the books the couple brought with them. 'Intellectuals close to government circles', whose anonymity the AFP correspondent protected, had the following comment to make about the incident: 'A terrorist is even more dangerous with a book than with a rifle.' The correspondent linked the incident with another event: the international book fair in Tunis: 55,542 books were coming in from twenty-two countries, and the management of this event required the checking of each one of those books by the censors. Customs officers also act as censors: books entering Tunisia may get confiscated, just as the French version of this book of mine, *Le silence tunisien* (1998), has been.

Conclusion

This was how the Tunisian Plato's cave was locked up, following the fatal alliance of the National Pact; the public can no longer express itself, information circulates publicly no more. The silencing of civil society, which was more or less voluntary in the beginning, but was later forced, made it possible for the official actors to monopolize public speech. Consequently, the other bolts, applied to the legal system, the parliament and political parties were further reinforced. This allows the constant reproduction, on the walls of the cave, of an unreal spectacle: that of a unanimous consensus about the Tunisian 'responsible democracy'. President Ben Ali has become the sole director of a play where only one role is allowed: to applaud.

Hence the illusion of happy Tunisia, so different from its neighbours Algeria and Morocco. In that more real world over there, disagreement and the expression thereof are possible.

Notes

1. The State Secretariat for Information was formally abolished in 1997 in answer to international pressures for more freedom of expression. At the same time, Ben Ali blamed the media for their lack of initiative. The 'culprits' gave their mea culpas and the game went on unchanged. Censorship was even imposed on academic circles, with all conference papers subjected to legal deposit and organizers having to inform the authorities about programmes and participants.
2. Centre africain de perfectionnement des journalistes et communicateurs (1990), 'Enquête sur les besoins des Journalistes tunisiens en matière de formation permanente'. Unpublished research paper: Tunis.
3. See Larbi Chouikha's unpublished enquiries into Tunisian journalism (1990, 1993 and 1994).
4 . These data are taken from Tahar Al-Amouri (1992). *Les Tunisiens et les médias*. Vol. 1: *Étude quantitative* and Vol. 2, *Étude qualitative*, Tunis: Al-Amouri Institute.
5. These readership data have possibly been biased by the respondents' fear of denunciation, given the prevailing political climate at that time. None the less, they disclose a very interesting feature: respondents prefer the regime press's better graphic quality and estimate its enquiries to be better documented than those of the private press.
6. Can the requirement for legal deposit before publication be escaped by clandestine newsletters and photocopiers? President Ben Ali could foresee everything. This is how Lazhar Marco, a young Tunisian engineer, was put in charge of drawing up a registration system. As stated by *Maghreb Confidentiel* (No. 282, 6 June 1996), this makes it possible to identify the photocopier's owner on all circulating documents.
7. *Jeune Afrique* (No. 1882, 29 January to 4 February).
8. Until the late 1990s, such authorizations were delivered by ATCE.
9. 'Kamel Labidi récupérera son passeport', *La Croix*, 13 January 1996. p. 9.
10. Roger de Diesbach, 'Le Goût amer du loukoum sous le soleil', *Le Courrier de Genève*, 4 July 1996.

4

ALGERIA
THE CHILDREN OF JOCASTA

Liberal democracy presupposes a forum for debate in which contending views on issues of general concern are discussed and political
actors peacefully struggle to gain or retain power. Consequently, any
process of democratization implies the development of a civil society
which gradually escapes the tutelage of the state apparatus to acquire
the capacity to express itself freely through the media, parliament, the
courts, or any other public platform. This process is constantly fragile
and reversible, as was illustrated by the Tunisian example.

Algerian civil society, too, is in its infancy. Its birth accompanied the
decline of a totalitarian state and its downfall in the 1980s. Starting from
1992, while Algerian civil society was still developing, it had to
undergo the traumatic effects of a dangerous alliance between civil and
military actors. This alliance was meant to eliminate outstanding
political actors from the public platform. It has also led to the placing of
civil society in a very dangerous situation: that of hostage, caught in the
crossfire between the army and those who were then brutally excluded
from the political game.

The development of Algerian civil society, now cut off from its major
mobilizing force, was seriously compromised after the dangerous
alliance. It was resumed, however, slowly and dangerously, in the form
of dissidence and 'moderate' (in the sense of authorized) opposition
against a background of civil war. In consequence the hegemonic
ambitions of the military were somewhat curbed. The slow development of opposition is the primary characteristic that distinguishes
Algeria from the other scenarios of political evolution in the Maghreb.

The story of Algerian democracy is also striking for the prominent
role the press has played in it. Throughout the different phases of its
development, the Algerian press has served as a gauge of the state of

Algerian liberties; whether through its more or less polemical tone, through its ability to criticize government actors, and even through its more or less great dependence on the system for its survival. The Islamists would not have come so near to winning the 1991 elections had not the Algerian press got the messages of the Islamic Salvation Front (FIS) across. Likewise, the easy victory of Liamine Zeroual in the 1995 presidential elections was only possible because most of the opposition no longer had access to the press. Such is the importance of freedom of information and expression in the edifice of democracy: rotation of political power presupposes an opposition that is able to get its messages across to voters, and without information that circulates effectively in the public arena there can be no serious debate.

The Birth of Civil Society

The social vacuum that preceded the birth of Algerian civil society is a natural concomitant of the decadence of totalitarian states, as in the cases of Nasser's Egypt and the People's Democratic Republic of Yemen. During this period of social vacuum, the totalitarian state continues to maintain a monopoly on political power and occupy the public platform to the exclusion of all others. According to sociologists who have studied democratic transitions, this monopoly could not have been achieved without 'the total destruction of the resilience of society and individuals in the face of the central authority'.[1]

Hence the absolute ban on dissent, the imposition of censorship (official or unofficial), the compulsory supervision of all public functions by the single party or an equivalent control apparatus (such as the Libyan Revolutionary Committees), the contempt for the rule of law – as well as police and legal terror. Consequently, the idea of an organized society no longer in symbiosis with the state but, rather, disengaged and politically differentiated from it, is inconceivable. Long before Tunisia under Ben Ali, socialist Algeria did not tolerate any independent civil institutions; nothing could exist outside the structure of the National Liberation Front (FLN) and its mass organizations. Civil society therefore remained deprived of autonomous structures of expression and action until the decline and fall of the totalitarian state.

Throughout this period of latency, the Algerian press was not a significant factor in the liberalization measures which those in power undertook to reassert their legitimacy, because it belonged to the state. The latter controlled the press through the game of transfers, appoint-

ments, sanctions, arbitrary cuts in circulation and obstruction of distribution; serious problems might hit the newspaper that went beyond the
limits of the narrow margin of freedom allowed by the regime. In
particular, criticism of the authorities, the opening of newspaper
columns to dissidents, and disclosure of so-called 'strategic' secrets
were punishable by such sanctions as dismissal or expulsion (for
foreign correspondents).

In this phase of the decadence of totalitarianism, it often happens
that the press adopts a critical and polemic tone. Such a critical tone
should not, however, give the wrong impression: it is in line with
government or presidential directives. This official criticism is directed
at some pseudo-enemies of the 'Arab Nation' (Zionism, neocolonial-
ism, a 'Western plot' ...) or at the leaders who have recently been
shoved aside. Often it is nothing but an echo of the debates of the ruling
elite. It invariably provides the press with the opportunity to assert its
loyalty to the 'People', to the 'brother President', or to the 'Revolution'.
This illusory freedom of expression does not, however, replace the
clichés and cheerleading tone that continue to dominate the discursive
practices of the press. Polemics and criticism are little more than rhetorical devices designed to safeguard the credibility of a mobilization
press[2] that has always served as an instrument of state propaganda.

How the FLN state was put to death by its own leaders

What makes the leaders of dictatorships decide to give up absolute
power, start democratic reforms, and run the risk of political competition? There is a very natural reason: populations subjected to dictatorship always end up multiplying the signs of dissatisfaction and
rebelling. There are situations that spark popular anger: a military
defeat, for example. And when anger thunders, it may be more prudent
for leaders to make concessions through democratizing, rather than
maintain the dictatorship. Such was the case in Argentina, when it lost
the Falkland Islands to Britain. The political shock to public opinion
was such that at the same time as they laid down their arms, the military
had to return the keys of the City to the civilians.

In Algeria, it was the extent of economic failure that created the
favourable context for reforms. In the early eighties, tension reached
explosive proportions not just among the population, but also within
government circles. Starting in 1987, in a bid to initiate the social
dynamics that could get the country out of the crisis, the regime
brought down a good part of the socialist edifice that had monopolized
the public platform, henceforth permitting an independent league for

the defence of human rights, FLN-free organizations, transformation of public companies into shareholder corporations responsible for their own management, and the dismantling of the large socialist agricultural structures into small self-managed co-operatives. 'Because of the reforms,' former finance minister Ghazi Hidouci told me, 'the ruling elite were afraid that they might lose control. As for us [the reformers], our course was already mapped out: after the "technical" reforms, it was necessary to revise the Constitution, and in particular the unbending rule of public ownership of land and industrial enterprises.'

During the summer of 1988, President Chadli Benjadid's collaborators warned him, 'The FLN is preparing a congress against you.' Torn between the reformers and supporters of the status quo, the president gave a clumsy speech revealing the dissension until then hidden within the confines of the ruling elite. This speech, which was widely circulated by the press, was going to spark popular anger. Contrary to a strong rumour that circulated in Algiers, Chadli Benjadid and his team probably did not start the October riots. Why? Actually, for a long time the president had been convinced of the need for democratic reforms. But in the view of his rivals within the FLN, such reforms could only give rise to uncontrollable protests. The riots provided Benjadid with a perfect opportunity to carry out his plan: a scapegoat was needed. It was the FLN, the sole party, that was served up for media and public consumption.

In this way, popular riots and democratic reforms followed each other like question and answer. In fact, the popular riots, fuelled by the harshness of everyday life during a time of economic crisis, were spontaneous and did not revolve around any specific political demands. Since decision-making about reforms was confined to the president's entourage, they provided him with the opportunity to eliminate his rivals within the FLN.

The 'Big Bang'

When a totalitarian state collapses, two routes open up for the political evolution of the country: either the state is able more or less to control the pace and forms in which civil society emerges, or it loses much of its authority. The first route was that taken by post-Nasser Egypt, for example. The restrictions imposed by Sadat on the 'transition to democracy' did contain to a great extent the pace of emergence of political parties and the press; not until 1977 did opposition parties obtain the right to publish their newspapers. The Egyptian press, subsequently restricted in its freedom of expression, could play only a minor role in the 'democratic transition'.

Post-socialist Algeria first followed the second course. The erosion of state authority was already visible before the democratic reforms: a popular fever for overseas migration, absenteeism from work, the black market, and especially public rumours about the corruption of government officials were all signs of the population's demobilization and disillusionment. October 1988 saw the public rupture of the consensus between rulers and ruled. As a result of this rupture a new sign of the decline of state authority appeared: the incapacity of the police to intervene over breaches of the law: theft and misconduct went unpunished. Even road regulations became useless as motorists grew contemptuous of the traffic police.[3] This temporary erosion of state authority did not, however, produce a parallel development of a civil force. When the erosion of the totalitarian regime takes place, the immense clamour about freedom that comes out of the emerging civil society can only disguise the vulnerability of the civil actors. When civil society is destroyed, the fall of totalitarianism has often brought with it violence and chaos: in Algeria as in Russia, Yugoslavia or Albania.

It is important to remember that before the 1988 riots, Algerian society had been kept for more than two centuries in a state of subjugation: first by colonial rule, then, since the 1954 revolution, by the totalitarian FLN regime. A society in so poor a condition could not re-emerge, after the riots of October 1988, other than in the form of an explosion of social forces (organizations, political parties, newspapers ...), most of which were without any significant weight in political developments.[4] In fact, the local elections of June 1990 would expose the extreme fragmentation of the so-called 'democratic' opposition.

The emergence and rapid growth of an influential – even if vulnerable – press was another consequence of the temporary collapse of state authority.[5] The Algerian press emerged in a fragmented form: newspapers mushroomed; the profession split as a result of a serious division that took place in the Journalists', Writers' and Interpreters' Union, formerly an instrument of monopolistic control in the hands of the FLN; moreover, the creation, during this restless period, of the Algerian Journalists' Movement marked a new era of open contention without precedent in the history of the profession. Not long after its creation, however, rival journalists' organizations emerged, adding to the movement's divisions and slowing its momentum. Meanwhile, away from the goings-on behind the various manifestoes, the demands for freedom and assertions of the right to speak filled the headlines.

The favourable power relationship created by the collapse of state authority temporarily enabled the Algerian press to secure a substantial margin of freedom, despite its dependent relationship *vis-à-vis* the president. Between the 1988 riots and the 1992 *coup*, the Algerian press was able to exploit to the full the leadership crisis and to address to successive governments endless demands for freedom of expression and democracy. At the same time, professional solidarity among journalists grew stronger. Any arrest of a journalist, any suspension of a newspaper, automatically made the headlines, while the journalists signed petitions in support of their colleagues and took to the streets demanding greater press freedom. Little by little, private media companies wove a network of alliances with both state and civil actors: army officials who financed newspapers, opposition parties, and the two human rights leagues.

A close examination of the Algerian case, however, shows how artificial such a nascent freedom show can be. The new newspapers were born under the patronage of the president, who provided them with office space, equipment and distribution facilities, in addition to granting three years' wages to journalists willing to leave the public sector to contribute to the emergence of an independent press. In such a context, the Algerian press was able without any difficulty to climb on the bandwagon of pluralism and political contest, criticizing and informing on topics that were previously taboo.

However, the image of a press that dares to inform and express itself on everything does not stand up to analysis. The capability to inform? Not yet; as soon as it comes to those in power or the debates at the top, information flows no more. The power to express itself? Not really; the obvious difficulty, at first, to criticize a president who is actually in favour of pluralism but who monopolizes power, then the all-out press campaign across the whole spectrum against its guardian just as he was losing his authority, following the 1990 municipal elections, look more like the old unanimity around the single party.

After the 1988 riots, the vigorous press campaign against the authorities was used to support the steady stream of references to democracy in all the newspapers. However, the domination of democratic themes did not reflect a press power, but rather the fact that the idea was in vogue throughout society. The press, just like other actors, capitalized on the vogue for democracy to consolidate its power of influence by setting itself up as the defender of these new values. And especially, it took advantage of the collapse of state authority to go hammer and tongs at anything that moved at the top. To drift with the tide was thus the only strategy of influence it was able to develop prior to the 1992 *coup*. For what had just occurred was a momentous awakening of civil society, animated by three major forces: the Islamic movement, the agricultural movement, and the cluster of so-called 'democratic' secular political parties and organizations.

The FIS, a rallying and mobilizing force

Within living memory, Algeria had known nothing but a distant and dominating elite. The Islamist FIS, with its network of charitable organizations and clandestine trade, was the first institution to address the daily problems of the population and to bring together peasants, workers and the educated elite. Basically, it was a composite movement, combining within its ranks a mass basis (including the many unemployed and school drop-out youths), and an intellectual elite (imams, professors, journalists, civil servants and military staff), which provided the party with a solid structure throughout the country.[6]

Even though the FIS contained within it several conflicting political tendencies, the ideas of freedom of expression, an independent justice system, a liberal economy and decent public debate made significant inroads within it until 1992. This led Ghazi Hidouci (Finance and Economy Minister under the Hamrouche government) to say that, at that time, the Islamists were the only ones who truly sincerely played the democratic game.[7]

The high level of organization and mobilizing potential of the FIS were manifested through the party's thousands of charitable organizations, the *Trabendo* trade (or black market, which alone survived the 1992 *coup*), the communication network woven by its newspapers and mosques, and, starting from the June 1990 municipal elections, the communes which voted the FIS into office. The demonstrations it organized drew huge crowds, which could only impress the state and voters.

The FIS's organizing capacity gave it formidable efficiency. During his speech at the Kouba mosque on 15 June 1990, Ali Bel Hadj did not at all hide his disappointment with the election results: the FIS's narrow majority (54 per cent) of votes astonished him. The lesson of the municipal elections was clear: in order for the electoral exercise to do justice to the party, it was necessary for FIS officials to monitor the progress of the whole process from inception to completion.

This is what they did at the next elections, and this is an occasion to correct distorted historical accounts: perhaps there were some irregularities here and there, but they were never proved before the Constitutional Court. Overall, the 1991 legislative elections results were undoubtedly the most reliable in the history of Algeria. Here is the reason why.

In each one of the thousands of polling stations around the country, the followers of the FIS were present from the very first hour of the ballot, to see to it that things happened as they should. All day long, they were present in sufficient numbers to check the identity of each voter. Once voting closed, not only did they attend the count at each polling station, but they even mobilized themselves to follow the boxes and the count at every stage, from the polling station to the district, from the prefecture to the Interior Ministry. Thus, at no time did state officials have any opportunity to falsify the results. The FIS exercised control of the election process peacefully, by sheer force of numbers.

By contrast, the presidential elections in late 1995 took place while the FIS was banned (see pp. 65–6). The elections were strictly controlled by the military 'mafia', not by representatives of the candidates; the opponents of President Zeroual did not have sufficient personnel to do so. After the elections, Mahfoud Nahnah, leader of the Movement for the Islamic Society (HAMAS), talked about 'several ballot boxes being hijacked like aeroplanes' and other irregularities, and promised to initiate procedures before the Constitutional Council. Later, however, Nahnah received two ministerial portfolios for his party, and no mention of the said frauds was made again. No one among HAMAS's followers has been able to answer my enquiry about the fate of Nahnah's complaint. It will probably never be known how many votes HAMAS had actually obtained.

Thus did the renewed military rule pass the electoral test. The 1995 election scenario was reproduced faithfully in subsequent elections, in spite of demonstrations by the parties against electoral fraud, and even in spite of the resignation of six presidential candidates prior to the 1998 election, which Abdel-Aziz Bouteflika thus won in their absence.

Farmers: from the private sphere to parliament

In fact, the emergence of Algerian civil society started before the milestone of October 1988. First, there was the dissidence (Berberist, Islamist, and the human rights movement) that shook the last decade of socialist Algeria.[8] In addition, the emergence of Algerian civil society was stimulated by some state actors, particularly certain officials at the presidency. Among them were Hidouci, then adviser to the president, the future prime minister Hamrouche and Secretary General Mohammedi, who drafted the laws reforming the socialist agricultural system and establishing freedom of association.

Since 1985, these state actors had been aware that in a closed system it is difficult to develop the critical attitude necessary to get a country out of crisis. So they created a low-profile think-tank with a structure mirroring the government hierarchy, and commissioned it to make a thorough review of state policies and activities. It was this group, which became known as 'the reformers', that was at the origin of laws ordering the dismantling of socialist agricultural collectives, implementing capital-share within companies, and allowing the establishment of organizations free from FLN control.

What was initially envisaged by the reformers was the dismantling of the agricultural collectives into small production co-operatives. The impact of the reforms was far-reaching. The reformers' group, isolated within the government, suddenly won many allies.

The reform was particularly popular with farmers: 90 per cent of reallocations were done without judicial arbitration. Later, anticipating problems in connection with sales and in their relationship with the government, the farmers founded their local farming organizations, thus taking advantage of the newly conferred right to set up associations. Also, thanks to enterprise reforms, these local organizations were able to gain a foothold in the management of banks and agribusiness companies (for the manufacture of seeds etcetera). Organized in this way, the peasants were the first civil actors able to operate outside the controls of the Party–State and to negotiate with it on their demands.

The first manifestation of this capacity was the peasants' successful bid to obtain the creation of the Agricultural Bank. After that, they attacked the problem of the realignment of commercial services both upstream and downstream of agricultural production. The new constitution, ratified early in 1989, had abandoned the principle of state monopoly of landed property. In spring 1990, the farmers invaded parliament and engaged MPs in negotiations for ten days, at the end of which a new land law was passed authorizing farmers to become owners of the land they cultivated.[9] After the 1992 *coup*, the military elite tried in vain to regain control of the agricultural sector, which proved to be the only economic sector to remain resistant to the state's attempt to reassert its dominance until the massacres of 1997.

The secularists

The secularists were not a homogeneous social force, but rather a loose coalition embracing political parties born *ex nihilo*, newspapers, women's groups, and isolated but well-known figures such as Miloud Brahimi, founder president of the Algerian Human Rights League, and the writer Rachid Boujedra.[10] It also included a few more significant institutions that appeared more frequently on the public platform: the Front of Socialist Forces (FFS, a Berberist party), the Rally for Culture and Democracy (RCD, an FFS rival), and the former sole party in the country, the FLN.

The FFS, banned and underground until the reforms, was led by one of the historic leaders of the Algerian revolution: Hocine Aït-Ahmed. It has been characterized by an irregular political line, and by a capacity, first, to criticize the regime, then, when the civil war broke out, to call for an end to violence, rather than by any specific ideological orientation. The FFS boycotted the first free elections – the municipal elections – wrongly thinking that they were only going to bring back the FLN.

The RCD was formed following a split within the Berber cultural movement. The 1991 legislative elections credited it with 3 per cent of the votes, and those of 1997 with 10 per cent; in Algeria, however, its audience was confined to Kabylia and a certain elite in the capital. It has shown little ability to compromise with adversaries.

As for the FLN, it suffers from two major handicaps in the eyes of the electorate: the attempts by the regime to regain control and its past as the single party.

In this leaderless, diffuse political formation, the desire to increase support is expressed by references to democracy. It is not always evident, however, that these diverse organizations accept all the consequences of this new value (in particular an unfavourable verdict from society). More particularly, the democratic groups proved unable to gather their forces before the 1991 legislative elections, nor even to state the terms of the new social contract they proposed. After the elections, their only strategy (with the exception of the FFS) was to count on the military to protect the Republic against the Islamist threat. Without much of a support base, the secularist representatives were not going to have any legitimacy except that of intellectuals subjected to persecution from all sides. None of the secular political parties, not even the FLN, proved to be a credible competitor to the ruling elite.

The Oedipus Temptation

By the end of the first round of the legislative elections in December 1991, the Islamist FIS had secured the majority of seats. Already, President Chadli Benjadid had declared his intention to cohabit with an FIS parliament. The FFS organized a march in favour of freedom. Its leader, Hocine Aït-Ahmed, wanted to sound reassuring by promising that his party would stand against any fundamentalist drift. Thousands of Algerians joined the march in the streets of Algiers. On 29 December, speaking to the French-language radio station Chaîne 3, the leader of the RCD, Saïd Saadi, called for the cancellation of the second round of the elections. The following day, he added: by all means, including violence (*Libération*, 1 January 1992).

Saïd Saadi's stand was supported by most self-styled 'democratic' groups and newspapers, which called for the resignation of President Chadli Benjadid and the dissolution of the FLN-controlled parliament without taking into consideration the institutional vacuum that their demands entailed, since the secular political parties had just been defeated at the elections. Aware that in the short run they had no chance of winning popular support, the 'democratic' parties had to give up their craving for power temporarily, and invite the army to eliminate their main competitor, the FIS. The movement for the cancellation of the elections was soon joined by the General Union of Algerian Workers (UGTA), which was afraid that it might lose its followers to the Islamist trade union.

The attitude of the UGTA was predictable. Behind their union, the workers of the industrial sector were terrified by the economic reforms which made them responsible for the sector's profitability. Conscious of a threat to their privileges (job security, wages and subsidies), they had showed resistance from the very start, to the extent of triggering, in summer 1988, a movement of spontaneous strikes preceding the riots of the following autumn. For their part, the top executives owed their positions to a system of clientelism and were frightened by the prospect of being accountable to stockholders and of facing competition from unemployed professionals. Liberalization of the economy, therefore, was welcomed neither by industrial workers nor by executives. Neither were democratic reforms, as a result.

The opportunity to move against the reformers and the FIS was too good to miss; and, if we are to believe public rumours, the military may have had a hand in provoking it.[11] The military elite, which had been publicly threatened in FIS speeches, yielded easily to the 'pressures', which were magnified by the press of the RCD, the Socialist Vanguard Party (PAGS), the trade unions and the Algerian Human Rights League, which had just come together in the National Committee to Safeguard Algeria; the elections were cancelled early in 1992, and the president was forced by the military to resign. A state of emergency then began under the control of the military elite. The FIS was dissolved and its newspapers were banned. Its local councils were abolished and replaced by administrators appointed by the regime. Its elected municipal and national officials were banished to the Sahara. As repression increased, the weight of radical Islamists within the FIS increased. A logic of war emerged, alongside the electoral strategy that had failed.

As for the secular groups, strict controls were imposed on their public activities. Political meetings were practically prohibited, and phone tapping became common practice. Press freedom became impossible to exercise without the dangers of suspensions, trials, fines.

The risks were financial as well. In late 1992, the prime minister ordered all ministries and state enterprises to hand exclusive responsibility for media buying and placement to the National Editing and Publishing Agency (ANEP), and to limit advertising to 30 per cent of the surface of each newspaper. If the logic behind this move had been related to the profitability of the government's media-buying programme, the government would rather have ordered the ANEP to consider newspapers' circulation ratings by employing market indicators, such as the 'average frequency of exposures' or 'cost per thousand exposures.' But the fact is that another logic was at work: by adopting the 30 per cent standard, the state signalled that it was going to continue to be responsible for the development of the Algerian press, its quality and its mission.

Already made vulnerable by its dependence on a state playing the multiple roles of customer, supplier, regulator and police, the press was associated formally with the campaign of psychological warfare carried out against the Islamists by the ministerial decree of 7 June 1994. Jointly signed by the ministers of Information and the Interior, this decree instituted a communications unit with the exclusive function of drafting official statements on the crisis. An explanatory letter, addressed to newspaper editors but not published, prohibited them from publishing anything on the crisis except official information. The letter included recommendations about how the newspapers were to participate in the psychological war: on the agenda and terminology they should adopt, on self-censorship, and on the values they should highlight in order to reinforce in readers a 'collective reflex of self-defence'. The trap set for the secularists had just snapped shut. How could they have allowed themselves to be dragged into it?

The dilemma of the children of Jocasta
According to the advocates of the tough 'crack down' approach, the calculation was simple: 'either flu or AIDS'. The flu is the military regime;

AIDS is the FIS which was fatally advancing towards power. The democrats' dangerous alliance with the military had just struck a fatal blow to the democratic reforms; it had eliminated some civil actors from the public platform and had placed the others in a more or less paralysing dependence on the military regime.

In the great drama of the 1992 *coup*, which led to such bloodletting and mass suffering for the people of Algeria, two groups of forces were ranged against one another. On the one hand, President Chadli Benjadid and his team, as well as the FIS, who symbolized real innovation, but at the cost of fundamentally altering the Algerian political order with consequences that could not be foretold. On the other hand, the so-called democratic groups, the managers of industry and the army that was willing brutally to restore the former political order.

We may describe the Algerian drama since 1992 and explain the conduct of its actors, using the Oedipus legend and its lessons. Chadli Benjadid, the father of the democratic reforms, was rejected by the self-confessedly rebellious new elite: industry owners, 'democratic' groups and the ruling elite, who panicked at the thought of power slipping out of their hands, and who coalesced with the secularists against the danger that was threatening the Republic. Democracy? This cursed gift of the deposed Father was not going to produce anything, in their view, but history being thrown into reverse. Once the deposed father had been politically eliminated, his disgraced image was soon wiped from memory, and the generation of rebellious sons took refuge in the brawny arms of their protectress: the army. The result was a major cataclysm which shook the foundations of the nascent civil society, involved the destruction of its most dynamic component, the FIS, and heralded civil war. Like Oedipus, the Algerian people did not reign for long.

In fact the army, having used the secularists to discredit the Islamist adversary in the eyes of the public, would before long devour its dearest children by denouncing them as 'secular assimilationists', and rule on its own, having imposed a state of emergency, with no more press freedom, and sham pluralistic elections.

The independent justice system set up during the democratic transition was restructured by the anti-terrorist law of 1992 into a network of special courts, presided over by anonymous judges. Arrests were carried out without warrants by men in hoods. Raids, kidnappings and extrajudicial executions of unarmed civilians were reported as clashes between the army and 'terrorists'. Those who were not immediately executed were summoned for preliminary investigations which were systematically accompanied by torture, and sometimes by public confessions in front of television cameras. The denunciations and confessions thus obtained were used as evidence in chief, as in Tunisia, to pass the death sentence on thousands of suspects, often without the anonymous magistrates investigating allegations of torture.

We shall never know ...

Had it not been for the 1992 *coup*, the FIS would have occupied the majority of seats in the parliament. This possibility did not yet mean power, which was still basically held in Algeria by the president backed by the army. But a democratically elected FIS parliament could have allowed a continuation of the rapid development of civil society. Would this have been towards democracy or towards crowd fanaticism? Opinions on this subject diverge, in Algeria and elsewhere, but in light of the *coup* and the war, the question will remain unanswered. Nevertheless, beyond the extreme opinions expressed on the 'true' nature of the FIS, it is important to restore the facts: its statements were contradictory, and its definitive position on democracy and individual freedoms was never made clear.

Some Algerian women had their throats cut by unidentified men for not wearing the veil. At the same time, after the first round of the elections in 1991, according to the press, Mohamed Saïd declared that Algerians would have to prepare themselves for changes in their dress habits (this famous statement was sometimes wrongly attributed to Ali Bel Hadj, the imprisoned Sheikh).[12] According to another spokesman, Abbassi Madani, on the contrary, it was more appropriate to apply the basic Sunni Islamic rule in matters of dress – 'there is no compulsion in religion' – and to try to convince rather than coerce. Another leader, Hachani, gave public reassurances that 'the Islamic Salvation Front will not prevent women from going out and working' (*Algérie Actualité*, 2–8 January 1990). Rabah Kebir, to one of my questions about the role of women in the FIS, smiled and replied, 'You know, in the world, there always are men and women!' The FIS was actually deeply divided on the issue of women: the opponents of coeducation refused sport and work for women, while others reminded that Aïcha, the favoured wife of the Prophet Muhammad, used to race him and often beat him at this game.

Ali Bel Hadj declared that democracy was *kofr* (impious) and his supporters paraded in the streets echoing this charge. Madani, on the other hand, repeatedly stated that disagreement was normal during the time of the Prophet, and promised that both secularists and communists would have their place in an Islamic state. This did not prevent Bel Hadj from declaring that the communists were apostates and, for this reason, deserved death. It was therefore not without reason that the leaders of the PAGS should be terrified, like most of the secularists, by the growing audiences of Bel Hadj, and that they should seek the protection of the military.

If the FIS were one day to seize power through presidential elections – an unlikely proposition – it is impossible to predict with what majority it would do so, nor which tendency within its ranks would prevail, or how it would choose between its more moderate and non-Islamist allies and its radical grassroots. The role it would then be called on to play in the political evolution of Algeria is unforeseeable. But one thing is now certain: the FIS as an apparatus has been destroyed. Even though on several occasions it has condemned violence committed against civilians and foreigners, it is far from being in control of all the armed groups.

Since 1992, Algerian civil society has functioned not under a democratic regime but in a context of war. Nevertheless, civil actors have not been completely isolated, and nor has the future become completely hopeless.

The Unfinished Business of Remaking the Public Arena

Since the *coup*, the balance of power between the new regime and civil society has seemed to be based on a relationship of interdependence: civil society's so-called democrats called for the cancellation of the elections and the safeguarding of the Republic; they needed military rule not just to get rid of the Islamist threat, but also to preserve and improve their social and political status in the absence of democratic institutions. Whether spontaneous or orchestrated by the military, the support of the 'democrats' helped to legitimize the military takeover.

A first serious, though unsuccessful, attempt to form a new independent civil force took place in the arena of politics. In November 1994, the three major opposition parties, the FIS, the FFS and the FLN, met at Sant'Egidio (Rome) with other groups in order to work out together a peaceful strategy to end the crisis.

This was a purely civil initiative, and it aimed at reintegrating the FIS into the public arena: a sign of political maturity which nevertheless failed to convince the army that it could return power to civilians without running the risk of trials, judgements and loss of privileges and fortunes: the pact concluded in Rome made it explicit that human rights violations should not go unpunished. Moreover, the commitment of the FIS to civil peace was unconvincing; its internal divisions were too significant and its influence over the armed groups was too dubious. These were the reasons that apparently prevented those in control from adhering to the Rome strategy.

The signatories to the alliance, for their part, lacked the internal cohesion necessary to impose their strategy, even in the medium term. As for the FLN, it was divided between the advocates of a strategy of alignment with the regime and those who preferred to be on the opposition side. The weak link of the alliance since the May 1996 congress, it was going ultimately to opt for reconciliation with the regime. The FIS, on the other hand, still banned as it was, was unable to maintain harmonious communication between its representatives in exile, its leaders in prison and its officials who, remaining free in Algeria, kept in contact with the regime and with the HAMAS party. For his part the FFS leader, who had settled abroad for years, was not going to get away easily with having entered an alliance with the FIS.

The Sant'Egidio alliance did not survive the 1995 presidential elections and its awkward call for a boycott of them. In hindsight, this empty-chair strategy looks less like the result of a political miscalculation than a manifestation of the weakness of an alliance that failed to reach consensus on a candidate to represent it. Consequently, the electorate had no other reasonable choice but to pledge support to President Liamine Zeroual, who was the only remaining credible candidate. Since the victory of the latter, the Rome alliance has dropped out of the picture (even if its platform for the political resolution of the crisis may inspire future trials).

Meanwhile, the regime has been more than ever in need of support from civil society to protect its legitimacy. This was the case at the late 1995 presidential elections; Zeroual owes the pluralistic facade of those elections to a leadership until then insignificant: the RCD and the Islamist party HAMAS. The latter, in return, seized the opportunity to politically eliminate their rivals; the FIS, being banned was henceforth supplanted by HAMAS. At the same time, the dangerous alliance found itself expanded by the inclusion of a 'moderate' Islamist party, apparently in favour of democracy and willing to make compromises with the regime.

The dangerous alliance did not completely destroy Algerian civil society; part of this society continues to survive, as reflected in the capacity, limited as it is, that the newspapers and political parties have maintained to criticize the government. Moreover, since the alliance serves as a legitimizing device for the military in its policy of eradi- cating Islamism, the regime is obliged not only to tolerate the existence of the FFS, and to let its allies, the RCD and HAMAS, sometimes sharply criticize its policy, but also not to react too severely when the press defies censorship. Even though limited in practice, the freedoms of association and expression remain reference values which all civil actors feel at some point obliged to sacrifice for. In fact, the psycholog- ical war has been somewhat mitigated by the defiant freedom of expression which makes it possible for the press to disseminate, even if only sparingly and against government orders, some information that departs from the official discourse.

The Press and its Role in Political Developments

In order to understand the place occupied by the press in the Algerian transition, it is necessary to disregard a phenomenon which, though terrifying and spectacular, did not stop the development of civil society altogether: the war, and the terrorist threat to the press which came with it. In the abundant literature on the assassination of journalists and the climate of fear which developed within the profession, little attention has been paid to a phenomenon that is more significant in the long run: the press has become more professional. It has developed a remarkable sense of professional solidarity in the face of the threats aimed at it from all sides. It has established stronger international relations (useful in the event of censorship or a major crisis). Moreover, in only a few years after the 1988 riots, newspaper circulation rocketed and maintained a high level. The Algerian press may have lost some excellent journalists, including Islamists, who were assassinated or fled abroad. Perhaps it has too often agreed not to say everything and not to denounce. Still, this vulnerable social actor did achieve some progress since the riots. It survived the civil war (attacks and censorship) after the *coup*.

Its undeniable progress notwithstanding, the Algerian press seems the most vulnerable among the democratization actors; instead of serving as a catalyst in the power struggle within the political arena, more often than not all it could do was simply react to the changes spurred by the other actors. The factors explaining the vulnerability and passivity of the press deserve discussion, if only to do away with the cliché of underdevelopment as the determining factor. It is rather towards civil society that we must look in search of the reasons that dictate to this vulnerable press its alliances and its conflicts with the actors of democratization. It has been only by drawing advantage from the favourable decisions of other actors, and by avoiding alienating the actual rulers, that the press has been able to survive and grow. Too fragile, it never acts on its own.

The fatality of underdevelopment

Third Worldist intellectuals who haunt the corridors of universities often explain the vulnerability of the press in transitional societies and its dependence on the other actors in the transition to democracy by its financial weakness – a consequence of underdevelopment. Deprived of proper financial resources, in addition to being susceptible to judicial harassment (suspensions, arrests, trials etcetera), this press can hardly afford to engage in investigation and reportage, so much so that it becomes dependent on official information released by the government or opposition parties. This explanation presents economic development as a necessary and sufficient condition for press freedom. In the Algerian case in particular, the hypothesis is all the more attractive, because many papers are owned by co-operatives of journalists set up in 1989 thanks to the facilities (wages, buildings etcetera) granted by the Algerian government, and because there are no large press companies in Algeria.[13] Underdevelopment would, therefore, seem to constitute an insurmountable obstacle to press freedom.

This thesis is invalidated by empirical data: even though under-developed, Costa Rica has an independent and influential press. Similarly, underdevelopment in Lebanon was no hindrance to the Lebanese press attaining an international repute. On the other hand, economic prosperity is not necessarily accompanied by press freedom. Many Third World dictatorships have reached remarkable levels of economic growth without the press being able to distance itself from the government. In the Arab world, for example, William A. Rugh has observed that the Saudi press grew richer at the end of the 1970s without becoming less susceptible to the pressures of the state.[14] In the same vein Jac-Kyong Lee has noticed, in the case of the 'four dragons' of Asia (South Korea, Taiwan, Hong Kong and Singapore), that the prosperity of the country and press companies did not put an end to the absence of freedom of information and expression.[15] He explains this paradox by the state of civil society, considered as the main factor affecting the role of the press; without a strong civil society, he argues, there is every chance that individual liberties and 'democratic' principles will remain subject to the arbitrary will of the prince. The freedom of the press, in particular, will depend above all on the 'benevolence' of those in power.

Perhaps one might object that the growth experienced by the 'four dragons', Saudi Arabia and also Algeria did not succeed in eradicating illiteracy; hence the low capacity of the press to make a healthy profit from circulation. Thus, the economic variable would still be a determining factor for the press of the Third World; not displeasing those in power is a *sine qua non* for financial survival.

This argument, however, overlooks the fact that docility towards the authorities is not an exclusive phenomenon of dictatorships with high rates of illiteracy. Lars Willnat describes how in the communist German Democratic Republic (GDR) during the transition to democracy the press clung to the journalistic practices of the totalitarian period in defiance of the tide of liberalization and *glasnost*. Yet, the newspaper-readers of the GDR, Willnat notes, were regarded as among the most avid media consumers in Europe, with an average of 1.5 daily and 1.4 weekly newspapers read per inhabitant; the high rate of literacy, in this case, was not a sufficient condition for the emergence of an independent press.[16]

In short, the experiences of Saudi Arabia, of the four Asian dragons and GDR show that it is necessary to relativize the influence of economic prosperity and growth on the development of a non-governmental press; it is the perception the actors have of the situation that is determining for the direction taken by the process of transition. The economy can be a hindrance – by no means absolute – or a positive factor – by no means essential – in the 'transition to democracy'.

Can there be a free press without a pluralistic parliament?

The question is fundamental: the parliament, just like the press, is a platform for the control of the leaders by public opinion: those who represent it or those who shape it. The Algerian parliament occupies a marginal place in the agenda of the press, contrary to the old 'democracies' of Europe and America. On the topic of the management of public funds, for example, most often we come across bits and pieces of news, spread by public rumour, on the personal wealth of the leaders of socialist Algeria as well as reports of investigations and trials relating to old cases of corruption: General Ben Loucif had been sacked in 1986, but it was only in 1992 that the press learned that he was the subject of an investigation about misappropriation of public funds. What is significant in this event is that the press came to know about the investigation report through a 'leak' from the army, and not from a debate in parliament. If it takes six years to reopen the books, there is a problem: the control over the management of public funds does not have a preventive effect. The term 'taxpayer' is not even mentioned in public speeches. Political parties may well demonstrate in the streets against this show democracy but their elected representatives still attend the parliament's sessions.

The weakness of the theme of public expenditure in the agenda of a press which presents itself as witness and torch-bearer for democracy is a problem in itself: 'No taxation without representation' has been the slogan of democrats since the Boston Tea Party ... except in the Arab world. The problem, therefore, goes beyond the particular case of the Algerian press. Why is this issue absent from the parliamentary agenda? Logically, that is a consequence of the strategy of the executive which, without the countervailing factor of the threat of dismissal by parliament, exercises full control over the agenda through the policies and reforms it announces. It is easy to understand the reluctance and lack of imagination on the part of the executive in creating parliamentary and judicial mechanisms for the control of public expenditure, while the actual leadership, patriarchal in nature, continues to rely on clientilist networks as its foundation.[17] Thus, the absence of real opposition in parliament, even after the legislative elections of May 1997, has deprived the press of an alliance capable of reinforcing its influence in the transition process, which could not but impair the press's development.

Deprived of the backing of a multiparty parliament and the support of a strong 'democratic' opposition able to stand up to the government, the Algerian press has had no other choice but to seek the protection of the people in power or, at least, to avoid antagonizing them beyond certain limits; the executive and the military can punish newspapers that are too aggressive.

The press alone in the face of the executive

The 1992 anti-terrorist law suppressing freedoms and the unpublished 1994 decree imposing the publication only of official information on the crisis are, in principle, temporary measures. Regardless of these measures, however, henceforth the government has at its disposal three permanent supports to muzzle the press and keep it within certain limits:

The judicial

In 1990 the law put an end to the state monopoly of the press, while at the same time it curtailed freedom of information by prohibiting 'false information' and 'libel', breaches of national unity and state security, as well as criticism of Islam and the other revealed religions. This law was used to justify suspensions of newspapers and other administrative measures which increased in number after the *coup*.

Such a support is quite tricky for governments to use, though. In Yemen, for example, not only have the courts overturned administrative decisions, but the amount of time and the costs involved in legal proceedings often make the authorities back down. However, such a deterrent would not be fully effective in Algeria unless the judiciary were independent *vis-à-vis* the government, that is, unless the military mafia was no longer in control of the game.

Advertising
The government remains the main customer of the press. As already noted, in 1992 the prime minister called on the managers of ministries and public companies to do their media placement through an official agency, the ANEP. About 70 per cent of advertising comes from the public sector (*Al-Watan*, 30 January 1993, p. 1). Thus, the authorities have the ability – at least theoretically – to use media placement as a blackmail tool against newspapers that displease.

Logistical support
The state monopoly on newsprint and printing facilities represents another potential threat against newspapers that displease. Newsprint shortages (to impose arbitrary limits on circulation) and publication delays (blamed on technical problems) may be nothing but harassment measures.

The press and the military 'mafia'
Since independence, Algeria has become increasingly run by a military mafia, also called a 'clans network' by the French press. I prefer the name 'mafia', which now better describes informal power in Algeria than the idea of family links evoked by the term 'clan'. Here is why.

The term 'mafia' refers to a kind of organization characterized by personal clientist links of subordinates with one or a few 'godfathers' who spy on everyone, whose will has to be obeyed to the letter, and who forgive no failure. The godfathers are never personally known, except by a few. They represent an informal but real leadership hiding behind designated stooges. In return for their loyalty, the subordinates are protected and provided by their 'godfathers' with important material rewards. In cases of disobedience, the 'godfathers' mete out violent punishment, through their death squads for instance, in order to issue a warning as to what should never be done. In fact, the military groups who have informally ruled Algeria since even before independence have become increasingly closer to the 'mafia' type since the *coup* of 1992.

It is very important not to confound this military mafia with the Algerian army. As a matter of fact, the military apparatus has been subject to important cleansing by its 'godfathers', and as a result several military officers trying to save the honour of the army, some of them top-level staff, were transferred, forced to retire, arrested, tortured and in some cases assassinated for resisting the influence of this mafia. The most famous of these officers are the former president Mohamed Boudiaf, assassinated just before he launched his anti-corruption plan, and former prime minister Kasdi Merbah, assassinated as soon as he started secret negotiations with the FIS. President Liamine Zeroual resigned soon enough to escape this fatal end.[18]

There is a historical tradition in Algeria according to which state institutions are regulated not by the rotation of elites in power but rather by the sharing of power among all influential individuals. Even if clans and their leaders can dissolve over time, there remains a permanent feature: that of an occult influence network pervading all the institutional centres of power (the presidency, the army, the administration, trade and mainstream industries, the press).

Historically, the Algerian military has never tolerated being threatened or defied. On the whole, the Algerian press has perfectly complied with this informal rule of the political game. Sure, it has been able to criticize the president or the government harshly and get away with it, but it cannot challenge the military 'godfathers' of the country.

Actually this kind of taboo has become traditional in the Arab world. When newspapers attack the ruling elite (the Saudi royal family, the Alawi clan in Syria, the military in Algeria or Egypt), the response is immediate: suspensions or trials when criticism is mild, or outright closure when the newspaper breaches the threshold of tolerance of those in power. Thus the press is not in a position to break the last taboo, and the only information published involving those in power (including top-level debates on the broad orientations of the state) is likely to remain official information, purged by censorship and clichés.

In short, this is what we can learn from the Algerian experience: when newspapers can rely neither on a mature and differentiated civil society, nor on an opposition capable of overthrowing the government, nor on a legitimate parliament, nor on independent courts with the power to defend them against abuses of power, they have to adopt a low profile and observe caution in their dealings with the military elite, because in these circumstances this actor has the capability to crush them. Such is the precarious and vulnerable position of the press in transition circumstances.

When this vulnerability reaches a critical level, however, it may activate a survival reflex leading to a more serious attitude towards the mission of informing and to an attempt to regain some freedom. Perhaps this reflex explains why some Algerian newspapers have become increasingly willing to risk breaching the unpublished 1994 decree and to disseminate their own information on the crisis. In doing so, some have even made use of the international support which they have meanwhile acquired to defy openly the psychological war carried out by the authorities.

Thus Salima Ghazali, editor of the daily *La Nation*, wanted to publish a report, but feared seizure. Accompanied by the director of Reporters Sans Frontières (RSF), Robert Ménard, she submitted the report to *Le Monde diplomatique*. The agreement was that the report would be published at the same time in *La Nation* and *Le Monde diplomatique*, while RSF would post it on the internet. As expected, the issue of *La Nation* containing the report was seized in Algeria, but the report itself nevertheless did get circulated via *Le Monde diplomatique* (number 504, March 1996, pp. 17–20) and the internet. Since then, RSF have begun to publish regularly on the internet information about the problems facing press freedom in Algeria and to reproduce censored articles.[19] Sometimes, the international reach of the Algerian press gets extended, through non-governmental organizations such as RSF, to a significant number of European newspapers which then draw from it controversial issues. Such was the cartoon campaign which a score of French and Belgian newspapers took part in on 29 July 1996 as a demonstration of solidarity with the cartoonist of the Algiers-based daily *La Tribune*, who had been jailed for his political humour at the expense of the military.

Between Open Dissidence and 'Moderate' Opposition: Prospects for a Rebirth

The unnatural alliance between the secularists and the army could well have led to irreversible destruction of civil society and a return to totalitarianism. Only the erosion of state authority, memories of the brief democratic interlude, and the persistence of the newly created bonds of solidarity can explain the fact that Algerian civil society was not completely annihilated.

The shock of what happened was significant, particularly for the newly created opposition parties. Even though they lack the internal cohesion necessary effectively to oppose the regime's clampdown, those that remained in legal existence, or have since appeared, do try to distance themselves publicly from the regime, though with unequal vigour: some boycotted the national reconciliation conference organized by President Zeroual in September 1996 (the FFS, MDA and Ettahadi) or have refused the President's offer that they enter into a coalition government before the legislative elections (the FFS, MDA, RCD, Ettahadi).

Apart from these authorized political parties, one segment of civil society continues to grow, at a slower pace and on an infinitely reduced scale: that of the dissidence which has taken shape in the form of interpersonal networks rather than in the exploded and massive form of the civil institutions of the pre-1992 *coup* period. This dissidence is open, not underground as in the 1980s. Its emblematic figures (Aït-Ahmed, Ali-Yahia, Salima Ghazali, Louisa Hanoun and others) are well known. They travel, publish abroad, make public statements, maintain contact with political exiles, mobilize support from governments,[20] NGOs and large media, in spite of the legal and police harassment to which they are subjected at home.

One interesting component of this dissident information network is Hoggar, a publisher in Geneva, which in 1999 released *An Inquiry into the Algerian Massacres*, a detailed account of the Algerian civil war, running to over 1,400 pages of testimony, archives, charts, figures and analyses. By this means, an informal international civil network continues to expose the secret sides of the Algerian war, namely atrocities by the regime. Does it not by so doing help little by little to neutralize one weapon of war – information – and to discredit the military solution in the eyes of the public? Obviously, this is a role in which dissident information networks can make some difference in power relations; how much more time does the Algerian regime still have to solve the crisis?

Thanks to the civil war, which does in a way limit the military elite's hopes of regaining total control over the country, perhaps time will allow other actors – political parties? lawyers? trade unions? social movements? – to break free from dependence on the state and to openly support the dissident networks. Unfortunately, the long-lasting civil war has also contributed to rendering military rule necessary in the eyes of Western diplomats and of the international media less sensitive to war atrocities in Algeria. Will time eventually swing the balance in favour of Algerian dissidents or of the military 'mafia'? It is difficult to say, but both eventualities are possible. As the Moroccan example will show us, once the test of the dangerous alliances is passed, time may allow a steady development of civil society.

Notes

1. Bertrand Badie and Guy Hermet (1990) *Politique comparée*, Paris: PUF, p. 181.
2. The expression was coined by William A. Rugh (1979) *The Arab Press: News Media and the Political Process in the Arab World*, Syracuse: University of Syracuse Press, pp. 31–49.
3. Pierre Guillard (1994) *Ce fleuve qui nous sépare: Lettre à l'imam Ali Bel Hadj*, Paris: Loysel, p. 38.
4. Robert A. Dahl labels this form of society 'unstable polyarchy' (*Democracy and Its Critics*, New Haven and London: Yale University Press, 1989).
5. Private newspapers have reached a circulation of 100,000 in less than a decade of existence and could continue at this level while criticizing the government and surviving seizures and arrests.
6. Séverine Labat (1995) wrote the internal history of the FIS in *Les Islamistes algériens: Entre les urnes et le maquis*, Paris: Seuil.
7. Ghazi Hidouci (1995) *Algérie: La Libération inachevée*, Paris: La Découverte, pp. 239–61.
8. The plight of these actors of the Algerian democratic transition was described in my previous book, *L'Obsession unitaire et la Nation trompée: La fin de l'Algérie socialiste*, Ste-Foy: Laval University Press, 1993.
9. 'Bill 90-25 about land policy', *Journal officiel de la République algérienne*, No. 49, 18 November 1990.
10. Rachid Boujedra (1994) *FIS de la haine*, Paris: Gallimard.
11. In his *Mémoires du général Khaled Nezzar* (Algiers: Chibab), General Khaled Nezzar claims that such support had been planned by his services.
12. Brahim Taouti commented to me, in a personal communication dated 26 August 2001, that Saïd was then preaching against the Algerians' habit of spending more than they can afford in the context of underdevelopment. As published by the press, Saïd's sentence finally took on a very different meaning.
13. The famous newspapers of the Arab world are mainly based in the Middle East.
14. Rugh, *The Arab Press*, pp. 71–88.
15. Jac-Kyong Lee (1991) 'Press Freedom and National Development: Toward a Reconceptualization', *Gazette/International Journal for Mass Communication Studies*, Vol. 48, No. 3 (1991), pp. 149–63.
16. Lars Willnat, 'The German Press during the Political Transformation of East Germany'. *Gazette/International Journal for Mass Communications Studies*, Vol. 48, No. 3 (1991), pp. 193–208.
17. Prime minister Belaïd Abdessalam issued no further comment on this issue but admitting that there was nothing he could do.

18. This is not new information. For detailed accounts and analyses, see Youcef Bedjaoui, Abbas Aroua and Meziane Aït-Larbi, *An Inquiry into the Algerian Massacres* (Geneva: Hoggar, 1999) and, more precisely, the sections 'Reactions of the Algerian Army to the Massacres', pp. 471–509, and 'Multinationals in Algeria: The Political Economy of Brutality', pp. 985–92. Also see 'What is the GIA?', pp. 374–454, about the counter-guerrilla hypothesis. See more on the German Algeria Watch web site (http://www.algeria-watch.de, in French and German, operated by Salimah Mellah, about the clan war). Finally, I recommend sociologist Lahouari Addi's articles in *Le Monde diplomatique*: 'L'Armée algérienne confisque le pouvoir' (February 1998) and 'L'Armée algérienne se divise' (March 1999).

19. Salima Ghazali was invited, all expenses paid, to press conferences abroad organized in Stockholm and Göteborg by the local section of Reporters sans frontières in the early months of 1997 thanks to funding from Publicistklubben. Similarly with the June 2000 colloquium organized by Hosni Abidi from the University of Geneva in co-operation with the alternative publishing house, Hoggar. This gave rise to the Geneva Declaration, signed by prominent Algerian dissidents, which pleaded for an urgent reinstallation of democratic rule in Algeria.

20. An early and uncommonly significant support to the Algerian resistance came from the European Parliament, in December 1997, which gave Salima Ghazali the Human Rights Sakharov Prize.

5

MOROCCO

THE SLOW ASCENT OF SISYPHUS

The current Moroccan political system is the product of a power relationship that has evolved slowly but unsteadily in favour of civil society. The process started before independence. Unfortunately, it was halted by a sequence of dangerous alliances between the future King Hassan II and the factions of the nationalist party, Istiqlal (Independence), which eventually split up in 1959. Moroccan civil society was thus considerably weakened and a dictatorial regime took control of Morocco.

Civil society subsequently performed better than in Algeria. Starting from the 1970s, after being eclipsed for approximately a quarter of a century, public liberties progressively re-emerged in Morocco, with the creation of civil institutions such as the Moroccan Human Rights Organization (OMDH), the Kutla ('Block') electoral alliance and the revitalization of trade unionism (which itself dates back to the 1930s). What distinguishes the Moroccan model of civil society development, since then and beyond the dark years of dangerous alliances, is its stable character, with neither progress nor setback of the spectacular type.

To understand the why of such stability, I will examine an event where it manifested itself most strikingly during the 1990s: the Amaoui affair. The strategies adopted then by civil and state actors revealed a confrontation between protagonists with comparable political capabilities of contending speech in the public forum. Such a balance, as we shall see, is the product of a long history of development of political pluralism, an essential characteristic of both past and present Moroccan political life.

The Amaoui Affair

The Amaoui affair unfolded during March and April 1992, in the form of a formidable confrontation between the ruling elite and some of the most influential civil institutions. Amaoui was an opposition trade union leader. Since the early 1990s, he had been devoted to uniting and mobilizing the Moroccan left in a campaign for democratic reforms. He went everywhere, repeating that no social development was possible without a reduction in royal prerogatives, and that it was necessary to give more power to parliament and the government. In early 1992, he was charged with libel. His trial took place in April. Despite significant support both at home and internationally, the trade union leader was quickly convicted and thrown in prison.

Key issues surrounding the crisis

In the public debate that accompanied Amaoui's trial, the majority of the political actors (official and civil) exchanged contradictory viewpoints, and the general mobilization around the trial reached a level unparalleled in Moroccan history. The confrontation in this crisis was between two visions of political power: a patrimonial model based on a system of clientilism (in this model, the state actors protect and dominate civil actors) and a pluralistic model of state (comprising separation of powers and an autonomous civil society, following the liberal tradition in its purest, Enlightenment form). The patrimonial model implies, by definition, a strict dependence of society on the state apparatus and a rather peaceful public forum where everything seems to be all right. By contrast, the pluralistic model is predicated on competition for power and conflictual public debates.

More particularly, two fundamental principles of the Moroccan law were in conflict in this ideological confrontation: on the one hand, freedom of thought, as defined in the Covenant on Civil and Political Freedoms and ratified by the Moroccan parliament, and, on the other hand, royal supremacy over the law. According to the pluralistic view of government, freedom of thought must have the priority. It must even include the right to call in question royal supremacy. In contrast, the patrimonial view subordinates the first principle to the second; freedom of thought is protected and guaranteed by the principle of royal supremacy. Therefore, there should never be any conflict between the two; thanks to royal wisdom and magnanimity, and only thanks to the king, the kingdom can be ruled by progressive laws and policies. To put it simply, the pluralistic model pleads for more power for civil society, whereas the patrimonial model supports the status quo. In the Amaoui crisis, the strategies of the actors were divided between these two views.

The royal judicial strategy of camouflaging the political dimension of the conflict

King Hassan II had obvious reasons to fear Amaoui. How was he going to neutralize such an influential adversary? Could he be content, as before, just to throw him in prison or make him disappear? The vogue for freedom at that time made this solution politically risky, especially as the image of the king had already been tarnished by revelations of political repression and torture, and by hunger strikes, disappearances and deaths of prisoners. Could he corrupt him? If it was actually attempted, it proved insufficient to neutralize Amaoui. Therefore, only a resort to legal sanctions was left.

Amaoui was arrested following statements he made to the Spanish newspaper *El País* (on 11 March 1992) in which he denounced corruption and renewed his call for constitutional reforms to restrict royal prerogatives. In this interview, Amaoui called prominent government figures 'foreign consuls' deserving to be expelled from the country. The authorities seized this latest opportunity, which came just before the campaign for a referendum on constitutional reforms and general elections, and charged Amaoui with libel and isolated him in prison. He would not reappear in public until fifteen months later, after the election, a timing that is particularly relevant.

It was necessary to camouflage further the ideological dimension of the Amaoui affair and its significance for the political contest. The authorities invoked Article 400 of the Penal Code to send Amaoui to prison immediately after the trial, before he could appeal. This article normally applies to nonpolitical offences: for offences relating to the press it is provided by law that all recourses must have been exhausted before a citizen is imprisoned. By using Article 400, the Moroccan courts treated Amaoui as an ordinary, not a political prisoner. The speed with which it was possible, legally, to imprison a leader of the opposition, and therefore to reduce him to silence in the middle of the public debate on constitutional reform, was the result of a legal trick: the use of Article 400, which allows an ordinary trial for a nonpolitical offence (libel).

However, the calculation had underestimated the importance of Amaoui in the public sphere. First of all, he was very popular with a large informal network of sympathizers, among whom were peasants and unemployed people. Behind him, moreover, there was the powerful Democratic Confederation of Labour (CDT), itself related to a significant opposition party, the Socialist Union of Popular Forces (USFP). And the USFP had, among its newspapers, the big national

Arabic-language daily *Al-Ittihad Al-Ishtiraki* (Socialist Union). The CDT also had an old ally: the Istiqlal party, with its equally important dailies *Al-Alam* (The Flag) and *Opinion*,[1] and its trade union confederation, the General Union of Moroccan Workers (UGTM), with which the CDT had organized the general strike of December 1990. Consequently, Amaoui was not isolated during those dark days.

Al-Ittihad Al-Ishtiraki and *Al-Alam* spark the crisis

The two Arabic dailies *Al-Alam* and *Al-Ittihad Al-Ishtiraki* placed the Amaoui affair at the top of their agenda, with daily news, headlines and photographs. The front page of *Al-Ittihad Al-Ishtiraki* was full of articles on the crisis during the trial. It contained everything, from the statements of defence lawyers and Amaoui himself (16, 17, 18 and 19 April) to communiqués from civil institutions and political and legal analyses of the trial (3, 5, 7, 8, 10, 12 and 14 April). *Al-Alam* proved only a little less obsessed with the affair. It did publish news on a daily basis, but the items were shorter and not always in the front page, except towards the end of the trial (16, 17 and 18 April). It also became known for the polemical cartoons to which it devoted its last page.

Such an extensive coverage gave the two newspapers and their political parties several strategic advantages. They were able to show the public the internal cohesion of each party and its satellite organizations by publishing at length their statements and communiqués of solidarity. Moreover, the USFP and Istiqlal were able to prove the solidity of their alliance by each publishing the positions of the other and of its satellite organizations (1 to 8 April). The two parties were also able to publicize widely their argument that the real motives behind this unfair trial were to weaken the cohesion of the USFP and its trade union confederation, to put an end to their demands for constitutional reform, and to restrict freedom of thought. Specifically, the Istiqlal and the USFP loudly denounced the harassment of their newspapers when they continued to cover the trial in spite of official prohibition.[2] In so doing, they neutralized two traditional strategies of any dictatorship: ignoring the opposition's political motives, and hiding repression behind a legal façade. At the same time, Istiqlal and the USFP succeeded in moving into the public arena a conflict between the ruling elite and the opposition, while continuing to take the initiative in the controversy directed against that elite (*Al-Ittihad Al-Ishtiraki*, 2, 4, 8, 11, 13, 15 and 18 April).

This unanimous cohesion between two political parties otherwise in competition dominated the conflict and probably encouraged some weaker actors to take part in the debate.

Al-Bayan (PPS): a position of weakness behind reconciliatory neutrality

As a left-wing opposition party, the Party of Progress and Socialism (PPS) was fairly close to the USFP. However, it had become more and more isolated within Moroccan politics since the fall of communism. Moreover, its relationships with the French Socialist Party had deteriorated because of divergences on the issue of Western Sahara. Finally, during the Gulf War and just before the Amaoui affair, its stand in favour of the United Nations Security Council made it look anti-Arab in the eyes of the major political parties. The decrease in popularity that followed meant that the PPS had to try to maximize its chances of taking part in a future government. The position of the PPS, therefore, did not enable it to follow the aggressive line taken by the USFP in the Amaoui affair; on the contrary, it had to try to win royal understanding and sympathy. As a left-wing opposition party, however, if it were to avoid discrediting itself in the eyes of the public it could not escape the need to show some sympathy to Amaoui.

The position of the PPS in the crisis was, therefore, ambivalent (likewise it lent its support to the royal project of constitutional reform and backed the candidates of the ruling elite in the 1993 elections: its strategy of moderation was going to exist for quite some time). Having to take into consideration both the king and the opposition in its two daily newspapers (one in Arabic and the other in French, both called *Al-Bayan* – Communiqué), first it avoided placing the crisis at the top of its agenda. The news reports of the trial were kept short and were limited in number compared to coverage in the Istiqlal and USFP newspapers (only seven issues of *Al-Bayan* in the whole month of April dealt with the trial), and most of the time very factual. *Al-Bayan* did nevertheless publish some statements of solidarity issued by other groups. Overall, it covered the affair only minimally, in addition to publishing the few statements of solidarity made by the PPS (7, 8 and 19 April).

The Amaoui affair was never on the front page of *Al-Bayan* except on 8 April, the day the hearing began, when the PPS had just declared its official stand. *Al-Bayan*, organ of the PPS and bound by its discipline, did no more than publish official positions and display an attitude of neutrality and understanding towards all protagonists. Its expression of solidarity with the other left-wing parties was weak; it criticized both the state's policy of provocation (18 and 19 April) and Amaoui's conduct (8 April), as though the rule was never to blame only one side at a time and to try to calm things down. In fact, the discourse of *Al-Bayan* made it look like an objective actor – not a weak one – which, as an opposition paper, was still able to arbitrate public debates, to report on their merits and the faults in a balanced way, and to sacrifice party particularism for the sake of Morocco's best interests.

Le Matin cannot go with the tide

The French-language daily *Le Matin* belonged to a newspaper group owned by Moulay Ahmed Alaoui, a cousin of the king and a minister. Its editorial line was thus equivalent to an official position. *Le Matin* published nothing on the Amaoui affair, except for a few lines, on 16 April, to announce that the trial was still under way, and a few more lines two days later. Its silence on the crisis, in contrast with the vigorous campaign of the opposition, is very significant: neither the trial nor the opposition campaign were going to be covered. Nor was there any social or political analysis when, at the end of the trial, *Le Matin* announced laconically that the secretary-general of the CDT, Mr Amaoui, had been sentenced to two years in prison for insulting the government. This was the ultimate in acting unaware of the political dimension of a crisis that was creating big headlines in the major newspapers. Maybe *Le Matin's* editor-in-chief attached no importance to Amaoui, one could object. Except that this indifference suddenly appeared only at the beginning of the trial: in the past *Le Matin* had published against Amaoui a number of editorials described by Nadir Yata as 'inflammatory'.[3]

There is nothing mysterious about the sudden reversal of attitude on the part of a quasi-official newspaper when a conflict breaks out between the government and a famous dissident. For the editor of *Le Matin*, apparently the safest line was to ignore the debate rather than discuss the issues, and to let the court do the dirty work.

The four major newspapers I have just analysed represent the main forces in competition in the Moroccan political arena, namely the monarchy and the three major opposition parties.[4] Considering their respective positions in the crisis, we may safely draw the following conclusions on the outcome of the Amaoui affair.

The outcome of the clash

The opposition had little to lose in the crisis, except maybe the fact that henceforth the king may say, 'We are not that bad, after all. See what they were able to say against us.' Thus the king would score a good point, on the level of rhetoric, over the opposition's capacity to criticize the kingdom's authoritarianism.

In fact, it was the monarchy that was most at risk in the confrontation. Without pretending to be hoping for more than a weak argument against the opposition, it was to put to the test the cohesion of its clientilist network, its control over its press and state apparatus, as well as its capacity to censor and punish. When the crisis ended, the king had succeeded in preserving those resources essential to his authority: a judiciary less faithful to the law than to the ruling elite, Alaoui's press which takes no interest in an issue that has become heated, and the capacity to punish whoever defies royal authority.

On the other hand, the publicity surrounding the affair led Hassan II to realize that his image, abroad as well as in Morocco, was tied to a minimal observance of international conventions regarding human rights. His strategy of political terror (imprisonment, banning of newspapers) especially could be costly, to the extent of undermining his public image; henceforth, the opposition was ready to go this far (a political price that the king, clearly, did not wish to incur).

In terms of gains by the opposition, the Amaoui affair was an important event given the mobilization that it caused. Moroccan and foreign actors took the side of Amaoui in this political contest: political parties, trade unions, youth organizations, organizations of lawyers, of journalists, of writers. The three Moroccan human rights leagues also spoke out for Amaoui and freedom of expression. All these Moroccan civil institutions attended the trial, alongside foreign observers such as the Algerian Human Rights League and the International Association of Democratic Lawyers. The international press covered the event. Support came also from the European Parliament, from Amnesty International and from the Union of Arab Lawyers.

The image of the opposition emerged stronger, at the expense of that of the king. The opposition had increased legitimacy, for, henceforth, it could add to its historical legitimacy that of its fight for freedom; it had more credibility, as its internal cohesion had proved effective enough to protect its newspapers, reassert its power of mobilization, and resist legal harassment; and it had a leadership strengthened by its capacity to form effective alliances between the trade unions, the political parties, the press, lawyers and human rights organizations. The opposition had also gained in visibility, having occupied centre-stage on the political forum and monopolized attention for a number of weeks.

Such a context prevented the king from getting any support from the public during the Amaoui crisis. In addition, it became possible to inform and criticize; in the event of censorship or any other assault on freedom of expression, the press is eager to take up the ensuing controversy. As access to information is the cornerstone of democracy, so secrecy is essential for dictatorship. But hide-and-seek games are no longer easy in the face of a pluralistic society that has become conscious of its power of speech.

In short, the opposition's gains in legitimacy, credibility, leadership and visibility constituted a remarkable demonstration of independence on the part of civil society, particularly since the opposition's gains corresponded to parallel losses on the part of the government. However, the balance of power between civil and state actors revealed by the Amaoui affair was such that each side was able publicly to defy the other and exhibit its influence. The opposition was able to defend its viewpoint, and the king to reassert his authority; but none among the protagonists of the crisis was able to eliminate the other side politically. Such a scenario left little chance for the kind of radical shifts in power relations that characterized the history of Algeria after the 1988 riots and that of the Tunisia of Ben Ali, which generated periods of great uncertainty; the Amaoui crisis revealed a high level of stability in Morocco resulting from the balance between state and society. What conditions made possible such an evolution?

A Long Pluralistic Tradition

Moroccan political pluralism is an old and firmly established tradition. Its history began with the emergence of the nationalist movement in the 1930s, with the Morocco Action Committee (*Comité d'action pour le Maroc*), a rather select and conservative club led by important figures such as Allal Al-Fassi and Hassan Al-Ouazzani. It was the nationalist movement – rather than Sultan Mohamed V – which would start the struggle for independence from France, then restore the monarchy. From this time onwards, Moroccan civil society repeatedly proved its capacity to act independently from the authorities and to establish conflictual relations with the state actors.

The first signs of state/society differentiation

The first Moroccan political party, Istiqlal, was born in December 1943. In its founding document, the *Manifesto for Independence* (*Le manifeste pour l'indépendance*), it openly defied French colonial rule. It was, therefore, as a rival of the authority of a foreign state that Istiqlal was born. It would maintain the same attitude of opposition during the reign of Mohamed V, after independence was achieved in 1956 – the demand for democratic reforms having replaced, in its discourse, the project of national independence that had by then been achieved. Istiqlal was rapidly joined in this by the National Union of Moroccan Students (UNEM) which in 1956 already called into question the status of the royal army forces and appealed for democracy in Morocco. The capacity of civil institutions to challenge state authority was once again manifested during the crowning of King Hassan II in March 1961: neither the Moroccan Labour Union (UMT) nor the National Union of Popular Forces (UNFP) – a dissident wing of which would found the USFP – attended the enthronement ceremony.

At the time of the coronation, the leader of Istiqlal, Abderrahim Bouabid, stated in the following terms the democratic social contract that his party called for: 'a union of the parties outside the king's umbrella; the latter can only be the arbitrator, the righter of wrongs, he must reign but not rule', perfectly *à la* British.[5] The idea of democracy, therefore, appeared in Morocco as a right to be snatched from the state, and not as a gift from the king.

The struggle for freedom was accompanied by the rise of trade unionism. From 1952 until the end of the 1970s, strikes, demonstrations and riots regularly challenged the king's rule . It was during this period that the Moroccan League for the Defence of Human Rights (LMDDH) was created, under the umbrella of Istiqlal. Later, during the 1980s, following the rise of the human rights movement, the freedom of the press, torture, the conditions of detention and the status of the judiciary would become the central issues of the public agenda. The OMDH, in particular, became known for its regular public reports on the state of human rights in the country.

First models of civil organization

These recurring forms of civil society development and autonomy were facilitated by the rapid development of the notion of legitimacy, a mass social base and communication channels, but also, and more important, by emergence of what became Morocco's traditional configuration of party organizations.

The struggle for independence, then the Greater Morocco project (to include the Sahara, Mauritania and Algeria in the state) provided Istiqlal with the first of its resources: legitimacy. Istiqlal added to it promotion of the Greater Maghreb and even, under the influence of its left wing, Arab unity. Such ideological resources cannot but support the process of state/society differentiation; each time the opposition wanted to challenge the ruling elite, it was able to draw on a moral credibility that was difficult to contest. Along with political legitimacy also came the resource of a mass social base; by the time of independence in 1956, Istiqlal claimed 2 million members and the UMT 600,000. For recruitment, the dissemination of its message and mobilization, Istiqlal had set up around twenty schools; its newspaper, *Al-Alam*, had been operating since 1946. Its trade union, the UMT, itself had its own newspaper and schools. Omar Benjelloun, a famous post-independence trade unionist, was a member of the UMT.

A first riot took place in Casablanca in 1952, organized by Istiqlal and trade union members against the French protectorate. At the same time, two trade unions, the Moroccan Union of Trade, Industry and Handicrafts as well as the Moroccan Farmers Union, joined the Istiqlal party. It was, therefore, a long time ago, under French colonial rule, that civil society, trade unionism in particular, developed the practice of organizing its institutions around political parties. Later, following the split of Istiqlal in 1959, the new UNFP party reproduced the same structure: a constellation of institutions that it ran, which were soon joined by the UMT and the Moroccan Students Union (UME).

A long tradition of solidarity

After the few years of hesitation and mutual suspicion following the split, political life in Morocco got back on track, this time in the form of co-ordinated actions involving Istiqlal, the UNFP/USFP and other Moroccan and international civil institutions. Such bonds of solidarity facilitated public debate and provided a better framework for demonstrations and strikes.

During political trials, particularly, long before the Amaoui affair lawyers developed the practice of forming teams of ten or more for the defence of the accused. Since these trials tend to receive extensive media coverage, where lawyers can get a lot of exposure, involvement in them is much sought after. In the Amaoui trial, for example, a group of some eight hundred lawyers was put together for the defence.

Such joint actions over human rights often led to the mobilization of international support: Amnesty International since 1977, the European Parliament in 1985, and 1991 following the reports of its Human Rights Subcommittee, various European groupings, the US State Department, the United Nations' Human Rights Commission in Geneva. With such national and international mobilization for freedom, challenging arbitrary state actions became part of Moroccan political culture. Amnesty International's reports, in particular, were numerous and regular. During the thirtieth anniversary of the reign of Hassan II, Amnesty spoke of 'thirty years of systematic repression of the

Moroccan people'. International co-operation with Moroccan civil society grew as the years went by and even led to joint actions such as co-operation between the OMDH and Article 19 (a private organization based in London, dedicated to the defence of freedom of expression) in an assessment–research on the development of the press and information in Morocco, published in 1995.[6]

The fall and slow ascent of Sisyphus

Early in the reign of King Hassan II, Istiqlal had somehow or other to live with the principle of royal supremacy, while the king had to wrestle with the hegemonic ambitions of Istiqlal. In his attempt to neutralize his adversary, the king played the main role in a long story of corruption and police terror, a story to which the left-wing press in France has already given ample coverage. What is less known, however, though more instructive for our argument about the danger of state / society alliances, is that, even before his accession to the throne, King Hassan had succeed in raising tensions between the factions of Istiqlal through the alternation of monochrome cabinets, now left-wing, now right-wing, but all assigned to defend unpopular policies. This strategy, as has been so well described by Monjib, exacerbated the rivalries between the left and the right tendencies within the party.[7] That contributed to the destabilization of Istiqlal, then to its 1959 split. His adversary having thus been destroyed, the future King Hassan wasted no time in using the opportunity to re-establish and consolidate his connections with the traditional Moroccan elite, which was more experienced in the advantages of patrimonial authority than in democratic rule. The opposition would remain helpless for years.

Deprived of the support of an influential party, the press inevitably suffered a series of repressive measures. The *dahir* (decrees) of 1 June 1959, of 28 May 1960, of 13 November 1963 and of 10 April 1973 subjected the press to seizures by the Interior Minister in cases of libel against the authorities or violation of the kingdom's institutional, political or religious foundations, reduced the maximum period of detention prior to a court appearance to forty-eight hours, extended the limitations period to one year, made optional the proof of bad faith in libel cases, and forced newspapers to reveal their sources at the request of a tribunal.

Thus a series of dangerous alliances had made it possible for King Hassan II to lock up the Moroccan public forum and to reign supreme over his kingdom for several years, while abroad Morocco and its dreams of freedom were little by little forgotten. Starting from these dark years up until the Amaoui affair, only the organizational resources (party constellations, historical legitimacy, social bases) of civil society explain its survival, its slow and arduous resurgence between 1960 and the late eighties. Seriously weakened in 1959, opposition parties have nevertheless remained the focus of Moroccan political life and the centres around which revolved the satellite civil institutions: trade unions, newspapers, professional and intellectual associations, women's groups, human rights organizations, and other similar institutions. Understandably, such a model of civil organization prevents fragmentation of the social forces and enables society to withstand difficulties. Over the years, civil society quietly developed its resources, multiplied the number of parties and kept weaving the fabric of its international alliances, thereby managing to survive infiltration, corruption and police terror, then clamorously to resume its development during the last decade of the twentieth century.

In conclusion to this story of a stable development of civil society, which unfolded over a period of seventy years and has kept going on after the Amaoui affair, we must acknowledge that such a process requires time in order for the reflexes of autonomy to be acquired, for the organizational resources of civil society to be developed, and for viable mechanisms of collaboration between institutions to be established. One may even ask how long a civil society takes to reach a stable level of development. An American sociologist once ventured an estimate: ten years seemed to him a reasonable amount of time after which state authorities would no longer be able to arrest the development of a civil society.[8] The Moroccan case allows for a more valid evaluation of the time factor. Not only is the notion of a ten-year period mere speculation, but it is possible that no fixed time frame can be determined for the attainment of the stable phase of development. This is because the process is nourished not just by time, as in the case of living organisms, but also by historical experiences, that is, by trial and error – the actors involved cannot always evaluate with certainty the ultimate consequences of their strategies. The time necessary to rectify mistakes can be long … and new obstacles can crop up.

Such was, perhaps, the warning given to the Kutla parties by sociologist Rkia El-Mossadeq after they called on the king to intervene as arbitrator during the drafting of the new electoral law in 1997. 'The king answered the invitation, not by intervening before the parliament, but through secret dealings with the parties,' she wrote. The result was the establishment of an electoral reform commission, in which the Kutla parties were a minority, despite their having the majority in parliament.

Electoral reform has thus escaped parliamentary control and been left, for whatever purpose it may serve, to the discretion of royal authority. It was therefore not surprising, and in perfect conformity with constitutional provisions, that when the electoral law was passed on 2 April 1997, the parliament irrevocably lost all control over the conduct of elections, which was then left to the Interior Ministry. 'Without changing the other rules of the political game, it was, nevertheless, the possibility of rotation in power that was hampered by this latest alliance between the king and the *Kutla*,' the Moroccan sociologist complained.[9]

Rkia El-Mossadeq's remarks were first confirmed by the 1997 general elections. The Kutla managed to win the largest single share of seats: 102 of the 305 seats to be filled. But in spite of this clear swing in representation to the left, it was a loose right-wing coalition, the Wifak (Consensus), with 97 seats, and the centre-right united around the National Rally of Independents, with 100 seats, that once more held the majority in parliament. Obviously, the king remains the master of the game.

In considering the length of time necessary for the development of a stable civil society, it must also be remembered that the accumulation of organizational resources of each actor depends on exogenous factors that are difficult to predict: military, economic, political, cultural. Let us imagine for a moment what would have happened to the Maghreb had Nazi Germany won the Second World War; perhaps the French Vichy regime would have been in a position to annihilate the Moroccan nationalist movement. Let us imagine again that oil had been discovered in Morocco rather than in Algeria: Moroccan nationalism could have been as proud as Algeria's, perhaps it would have been in Morocco that a single party would have emerged, Istiqlal, and that all this oil wealth might have been wasted, while the Algerian neighbour was content with a modest agricultural development. And what if France had made of the Maghreb a French province and of its inhabitants full citizens, instead of fuelling nationalist anger by its contempt? And what if the revolution of 1789 had taken place in the Maghreb rather than in France?

The highly fanciful character of these questions should remind us that political systems are open to unforeseeable external influences. Therefore, the time required to reach a phase where the development of a civil society is irreversible and the social fabric indestructible, insofar as such a phase is inevitable, depends on the national particularities of each society concerned. Therefore, it is more reasonable to analyse each particular case while considering the recurrence of moves towards autonomy on the part of a civil society, than to try to determine a time limit, even distant, by the end of which a stable civil development would be reached.

A Moroccan Model for the Construction of a Civil Society

In the years that followed the 1992 Amaoui crisis, civil society resumed its conflictual relations with state actors. Its external alliances were renewed and consolidated.

Differentiation and state/society conflict

The confrontation between civil and state actors in the Amaoui affair was very intense. It was followed by other shows of force on the part of civil actors. Thus, during the Gulf War the same year, the opposition mobilized its forces in what was, according to some, the strongest expression of support for Iraq in the Arab world. The regime reacted prudently by withdrawing its troops from the Persian Gulf. At the same time, the OMDH continued to publish its yearly reports on Moroccan political prisoners and reiterate its demand for their release.

Civil society's potential for autonomy manifested itself even on the level of language. Highly contrasted discursive structures had, in fact, appeared in the four newspapers mentioned above in connection with the Amaoui affair: *Al-Ittihad Al-Ishtiraki*, *Al-Alam*, *Al-Bayan* (the left-wing opposition) and *Le Matin* (close to the power elite). These results were revealed by a content analysis of 850 articles on the development of freedoms, randomly picked from 1988 to 1993.

The differentiation of the discourses

The content analysis has shown that the opposition's agenda was different from that of the ruling elite, and that the polemical tone of the opposition newspapers was much stronger than that of *Le Matin*.

In terms of agenda, *Le Matin* gives more attention to government- and administration-related news (43 per cent of its articles) than the newspapers of the opposition (only 20 per cent). The latter, on the other hand, are the only ones to report emergency situations (strikes, riots, etcetera: 16 per cent of the articles), whereas the pro-government newspaper totally ignores these events. Likewise, events relating to human rights abuses make the headlines of opposition papers in 46 per cent of the cases, but this rate drops to 28 per cent in *Le Matin*.

Apolemical portrayal of actors such as the head of state, the state and international actors is less frequent in the opposition papers (7, 5 and 22 per cent of articles respectively) than in *Le Matin* (35, 26 and 40 per cent). By contrast, derogatory portrayals of international actors, of illegal physical and symbolic coercion, and of threats to human rights are much more frequent in the opposition's papers (51, 49, 43 and 80 per cent of articles respectively) than in the pro-government daily (29, 28, 12 and 45 per cent).

In short, the human rights theme is used to announce the good news concerning government officials in *Le Matin*, while it is used for political polemic, and in the headlines, in the newspapers of the opposition. It is noteworthy that no such contrast could be identified in the Tunisian press around the same period, at a time when the process of state/society differentiation had just been reversed and civil actors were undergoing rigid domestication by the police machine. In Morocco meanwhile, the network of civil actors was reinforcing its autonomy and its capacity for action.

The development of new alliances

Civil society came close to reaching another stage of its development, in 1979, with the establishment of the representation of the OMDH outside of a party umbrella. The idea of an institution that would be independent from both the state and the parties had come from a group of USFP officials. Paradoxically, the latter contributed to the setting-up of the first civil institution within which all Moroccan political parties, right-wing as well as left-wing, could be represented. With such an interparty umbrella, the OMDH quickly gained credibility, both nationally and internationally, thanks to its campaigns denouncing human rights violations, regardless of the political affiliation of the victim or of the persecutor. Later, however, the interparty character of this platform faded away and the OMDH was informally taken back under the USFP umbrella.

A more significant phase of civil development was reached during the 1993 election, when the main opposition parties joined forces in the Kutla electoral alliance. This alliance lasted well beyond the election; in fact, it was not until the opposition leader Mr Yussufi was appointed prime minister that the parties of the Kutla accepted ministerial portfolios in the cabinets formed by the king in line with electoral results. Such a cohesion saved the opposition from falling again into the trap of unconditional alliances with the king. Such was the lesson that the parties apparently drew from their defeat in 1959: coalitions against the king, and without participation in the government, are better than losing one's opposition status by joining a government in which the party would be bound to support the king while having no control over politics.

The parties continue to associate with other civil actors, particularly lawyers, during political trials. Lawyers grew used to forming voluntary defence teams in any political trial; that gave them a lot of publicity, since such events received extensive coverage in opposition newspapers, which devoted much space to the hearings, and were also publicized by international human rights organizations monitoring irregular trials. As a result, political trials have become very sought-after in Morocco. The political pressures on judges have become even more obvious.

The status of the press in party-based constellations

In this civil development model, the press is not 'free'. It is an official press whose management is linked to a party that protects it and whose political line it defends. But this does not make this press less of a support for a pluralistic opinion.

The mission of the partisan newspaper consists in promoting the programme of its party and supporting it against its competitors. During elections, it must also support the party's candidates and denounce electoral fraud. Generally, the newspaper undertakes the task of educating the public. As the editor of *Al-Alam* said in connection with the 1990 general strike, 'We explained to the public the reasons for this strike. We denounced government actions that provoked it. We protested against the arrests and the sentences that followed. In all that, we had the assistance of the party and the trade union.'

In addition to the protection the partisan newspapers enjoy in the event of a political crisis, these newspapers also need the logistical support of the party in normal circumstances. As editors and journalists put it, the context of illiteracy and underdevelopment does not allow newspapers to generate significant income from sales. As a result, they are in no position to pay for correspondents or telecommunications equipment. Therefore, they must rely on official sources, particularly those of the state and the party, for news and even for analyses. And as state sources are not used to having contacts with the press, they are likely to be reluctant to give information to an opposition newspaper – which can only reinforce the dependence of the newspaper *vis-à-vis* the party.

The party MPs too can supply information to the newspaper, by asking during a parliamentary session, in a reproachful tone, 'We have learned that …, but you had said to us that …'

Most important, however, is the fact that press readership is limited: all Morocco's newspapers together sell no more than 300,000 issues daily, and these mainly within the ranks of the parties (source: private archives). It is not surprising, under these conditions, that no independent newspaper has been able to survive long in Morocco. Even the periodicals *Kalima* (Word) and *Lamalif* (NO!), despite their circulation beyond the borders, had to cease publication.

The professionalization of journalism as a next step?

Traditionally, Moroccan journalists were recruited from among the parties' activists. Some of them, like Jamaai of *Opinion* and Ghallab of *Al-Alam*, took part in the struggle for independence. Others participated in the Arab nationalist movement in the Middle East or hold senior positions in the parties or the human rights movement. A number of them went through prison and torture.

The National Union of Moroccan Journalists (UNJM) was founded by Istiqlal in the sixties, just after the split, and it continued for a long time to be directed by representatives of that party. Since the eighties, however, young journalists without a previous political career have little by little swelled the ranks of the union. Since then, questions of a purely professional nature have begun to be discussed within the UNJM, in addition to the traditional political issues. The journalists of the Alaoui group also joined the UNJM.

At its 1993 annual conference, the UNJM was restructured into two chambers: that of journalists and that of bosses. Discussions with the information minister and the parties are about journalists' individual and collective rights: freedom of the press, professional status, collective conventions, a code of ethics, etcetera. And, of course, solidarity is sufficiently developed within the UNJM that its members count on it in the event of a confrontation with the government.

It is premature to speculate about the future of an independent professional press in Morocco, but a movement in this direction has indisputably started. This movement is nourished by an increasing awareness shown also by the journalists I interviewed, of the drawbacks of the profession: dependence on political parties, financial and technological deficiencies, low wages and poor working conditions in general, official censorship within the administration, the general atmosphere prevailing in the country, and in particular the absence of a democratic humanistic culture. The climate is therefore favourable for a new differentiation, not any more just of civil actors *vis-à-vis* the state, but also in the future, of unionized journalists *vis-à-vis* their bosses, the parties.

How far should the process of differentiation go? Until when should countervailing forces be multiplied to prevent any risk of despotism? The question is important: is it necessary to go so far as to cause the break-up of the state and the social forces? What is the equilibrium that should be maintained between autonomy and co-operation? For there must be one, otherwise social and political life would be impossible.

Facilitating Factors and Obstacles

In the particular case of Morocco, several stabilizing factors make the possibility of a social rupture less likely. One of these factors helping to minimize the risks of rupture is often hardly noticed, but none the less most interesting from the viewpoint of a developing civil society; this is a culture of compromise which manifests itself in exchanges of legitimizing resources among the political actors, in a minimum ideological common ground, and in an ability of the political actors to reach consensus, on a temporary basis, to avoid crises.

Exchanges of legitimizing resources

Maati Monjib (1992) has argued that in the mid-twentieth century the alliance of Sultan Mohamed V (the father of Hassan II) with Istiqlal in the struggle for independence helped to reinforce the authority of two institutions: monarchy and party. On the one hand, Istiqlal's aura was enhanced by getting closer to the source of authority both traditional (two centuries of Sherifian monarchy) and religious (the king considers the Prophet Muhammad to be one of his ancestors). On the other hand, the restoration of the monarchy had served as a symbol for the struggle for independence. The reconciliation of the sultan with Istiqlal, therefore, brightened his royal image with the aura of martyrdom and the patriotic redemption of exile. One of the effects of these symbolic transactions was that the long history of complicity of the sultan with the colonial power immediately disappeared from public discourse.

It thus becomes easy to understand that the opposition and the king, in Morocco, cannot do without each other: sacred symbols, such as History, Islam and the epic of Independence, form the basis of the legitimacy of the state. The magic of these symbols makes them unassailable in the collective consciousness, in a way that makes it politically perilous to defy openly one or other of the two institutions that founded independent Morocco. As a result, the opposition press has attacked the king only indirectly, through intermediate targets such as the Interior Minister (generally).

An incident that occurred during the summer of 1993 clearly illustrates this somewhat hypocritical obligation of courtesy that the protagonists of the Moroccan public forum owe one another, which serves as a factor of political stability. Jamaai, the editor-in-chief of *Opinion*, had been summoned by the Interior Minister after criticizing the government in an editorial. He replied through an open letter, published in his newspaper, in which he denounced the political pressures placed on the press, quoting the Prophet Muhammad and the Caliph (the Islamic term for 'king') Abu Bakr. Everyone in Morocco was well aware that it was to King Hassan II, and not to the minister, that the letter was actually addressed. By evoking the prestigious peers of the king, himself a religious leader, Jamaai was daringly suggesting to him that he should live up to his sacred duties.

Even expressed in a contentious mode, the comparison was too flattering for the king reasonably to take offence. In addition Jamaai had behind him, in the event of a problem, the same supports as Amaoui: opposition parties and their newspapers. After the Amaoui crisis, the king could not afford to carry the burden of a Jamaai affair. Nothing serious happened to Jamaai, neither trial nor car accident; the authorities endured in silence, and *Opinion* emerged even stronger. On the sacred ground of the symbols of the Moroccan 'nation', the mainstream political actors cannot destroy one another. This limitation on public debates has never been infringed in Morocco.

A minimal ideological common ground

In Morocco, the contradictions between the two views of power, the traditionalist clientilist model and the modern pluralistic model, are by no means absolute. There is a minimum of common values between these two antagonistic views, making it possible to produce stable modes of co-operation between state and civil actors. Such a common value was the objective of a Greater Morocco, which allowed a quasi-unanimous mobilization of the opposition behind the king on the policy over Sahara. Another such common value is the nationalistic conception of Islam (see Chapter 10) which enriches the legitimacy discourses of both King and opposition. Most important, however, is the non-partisan, universal and uncompromising vision of citizenship and human rights, which made Abdelkrim Ghallab (*Al-*

Alam, the Istiqlal) say the following in reply to one of my questions:

> The Istiqlal is a Muslims' party. We believe that Islam is neither extremism nor violence, but rather tolerance. We are also a democratic party. We oppose Islamist violence, but we also oppose the government when it prevents the Islamists from fully exercising their rights. We are against violence regardless of its source. The only solution lies in a true democracy not only in Morocco, but in the whole Muslim world from where it can spread. Violence has multiple causes, but the only real choice is between democracy and dictatorship.

It is therefore unlikely that a possible co-operation between the king and Istiqlal will serve, as in the case of Algeria, to eliminate from the public forum some of its actors.

A compromise consensus

Even aside from the minimum set of political values that they share, civil and state actors have on many occasions shown themselves capable of ending confrontation and working together, if only temporarily. As far as the opposition is concerned, participation in the legislative elections is a sign of such a capability (which was lacking in Algeria during the 1990 local elections, when the FFS abstained, and during the 1995 presidential elections, when the Rome alliance failed to reach consensus on a candidate). The capacity to lay down arms and join forces again manifested itself in the press campaigns against international actors, such as Danielle Mitterrand in July 1991, the European Parliament in January 1992, and the International Human Rights Federation the following February, which criticized the regime of King Hassan II. The capacity to co-operate was evident again during the October 1996 referendum campaign, when the opposition parties supported the constitutional reforms proposed by the king, and called on the population to vote for them.

As for the king, he has long learned how to soothe public anger by appeasement measures such as the suspension of political trials, the creation of the Advisory Council on Human Rights, the subsequent creation of a human rights ministry, and the periodic amnesties for political prisoners.

Such measures are taken in response to specific political demands. It is worth noting that the advisory council was created and a number of civilians were immediately appointed to it after a vigorous international campaign had tarnished the image of the regime on the issue of human rights. Famous political prisoners (Serfaty, the Tazmamart prisoners, the Oufkir family, the Bourequat brothers) were released after Perrault's book *Notre ami le Roi* (*Our Friend the King*) revealed to the international public their cruel fate and sparked controversy.

Obstruction factors

The culture of compromise is by no means the only factor promoting stability in Moroccan political evolution. Among the other factors of balance – or perhaps rather of obstruction, as they make civil development more difficult – are the royal regime's own resources: its network of clients, the economic power the law confers on the king, his prodigious fortune, his traditional and religious legitimacy, and the police machine. All these resources make of the king Morocco's dominant political figure. This has led experts, sociologists and journalists of the Moroccan forum, to argue that the corruption and terror that were made possible by the regime's resources continue to influence the balance of power. However, the advantages available to the king have enabled him only to slow down progress towards freedom; they would not prevent the development of a pluralistic civil society, had the king wanted such a development.

Obviously Morocco is not a democracy. Electoral fraud is serious enough to deprive the opposition of its electoral gains and prevent rotation of power. The judiciary is not independent of the executive, and royal supremacy over the law is still entrenched in the constitution. However, the accumulation of organizational resources (party constellations, communications channels etcetera) by civil society, along with its domestic and international alliances, have reinforced the capacity of the opposition to act independently and to confront state actors, whenever necessary. At the end of such an evolution, a reinforcement of despotism is unlikely, and the prospects for democratization, although remote, seem promising considering the dynamism of the civil institutions.

Such are the advantages of the Moroccan model of the development of civil society. Such are also its limitations: the liberties were developed without the democratic institutions that guarantee them, instead simply as a result of a power relationship that is favourable to the civil institutions. This is why, so far, they are just *collective* liberties (political parties, trade unions, organizations, newspapers). The isolated individual still does not have the citizenship status that would allow him or her to speak and act freely and openly (as enjoined by the Universal Declaration of Human Rights). He or she can always join the ranks of a party, but alone, the citizen has no existence in the public forum.

Ambiguity and the sluggishness of power games also remain dominant characteristics of Moroccan politics. Before King Hassan died, he apparently wished to comply with the recent election results as he co-opted Al-Youssoufi, the leader of the main opposition party, the USFP, to the position of prime minister. In other words, on the eve of succession, alternation in office was in the gift of the monarch rather than obtained through electoral mechanisms. And after his father's death, King Mohammed VI was applauded by Al-Youssoufi's government and all public figures as a 'good' king likely to promote human rights and democracy. Hassan II is dead! Long live Mohammed VI!

A good king and a good government do not, however, mean the advent of democracy, especially if counterweights to tyranny weaken, following a new alliance of the opposition and throne. In King Mohammed VI's reign, there are multiplying signs that freedom of speech is shrinking. First, the OMDH, after becoming famous for campaigning in support of political prisoners, has taken a quieter line since its founders, the erstwhile prime minister Al-Youssoufi and justice minister Azzimam, went on censoring and repressing just like previous governments. This is why, in May 2001, thirty-six activists were sentenced to jail after publicly naming those who had been responsible for torture and demanding that they be punished. This is also why the Moroccan justice minister did not co-operate with the French judge who wanted to hear witnesses to Ben Barka's assassination, which had taken place in France during the first years of King Hassan's reign. Protest demonstrations and foreign books are often banned and journalists are often censored.

In short, civic freedoms, however real they have proved over time, remain limited and fragile and the monarchy's ability to control the game should not be underestimated. In a socio-economic context in which the rural population, women and youth are becoming increasingly marginalized and forgotten, Sisyphus's mountain looks more and more like a volcano. Hence, some leader's government may one day be caught in the dangerous position of managing the next popular uprisings.

Still, one thing in Morocco is perhaps henceforth irreversible. The OMDH's rival, the Moroccan Human Rights Association (AMDH), and the Moroccan Union of Labour (UMT) have valiantly succeeded the USFP and the OMDH in the challengers' position, and the king remains liable for his political management. Before, there were things that the 'top boss' could secretly do 'at the back of the shop'. Today, human rights violations take place 'in the shop window'. This advantage is far from being insignificant, if we are to speculate on the long-term chances of the advent of democracy in Morocco.

Notes

1. See, for instance, in the issues of 10 and 17 April of *Al-Alam* and *Al-Ittihad Al-Ishtiraki*, the pictures portraying the political bureau of the USFP and Amaoui surrounded by his lawyers.
2. As illustrated in the issues of 1, 3, 5, 7, 13, 20, 21, 22, and 24 April of *Al-Ittihad Al-Ishtiraki* and *Al-Alam*'s editorial of 17 April: 'La logique du bâton n'arrêtera pas le cours de l'Histoire'.
3. Nadir Yata is chief editor of the French-language version of *Al-Bayan*. See more particularly his editorial of 4–5 April 1992.
4. The readership of these four newspapers at the time of the Amaoui affair can only be roughly estimated because their circulations were not made public until 1995. However, according to private archives I was able to consult, these four newspapers had the widest circulation of all those published in Morocco: *Al-Alam*'s was never below 25,000 copies, *Al-Ittihad Al-Ishtiraki* issued as many as 70,000 copies a day while *Le Matin* fluctuated between these two figures with an average circulation of 50,000 copies.
5. United Press wire news published by the French daily *Le Monde* on 8 March 1961, p. 6.
6. Abdelaziz, Bennani, Abdellah Eloualladi, Jamal Eddine Naji and Saïd Essoulami (1995) *Liberté de la presse et de l'information au Maroc. Limites et perspectives* (London and Rabat: Article 19 and OMDH).
7. Maati Monjib (1992) *La monarchie marocaine et la lutte pour le pouvoir* (Collection 'Histoire et perspectives méditerranéennes'), Paris: L'Harmattan.
8. Robert A. Dahl (1971) *Polyarchy/Participation and Opposition*, New Haven and London: Yale University Press.
9. Rkia El-Mossadeq (1995) *Consensus ou jeu du consensus?* Casablanca: Najah El Jadida, pp. 25–32, and (1997) 'La tactique du consensus dans le discours et la pratique des acteurs politiques marocains', research paper presented at the International Political Association's 1997 World Congress in Seoul.

6

CONCLUSION

THE PUBLIC POLITICAL ARENA IN THE MAGHREB

Are there any alternatives to the Moroccan model of civil society development? Did not the late King Hassan II himself express his preference for a democracy bestowed by the prince to one that comes through contention? For democratic reforms to have a lasting impact, is it enough, as some sociologists believe, that those in power be willing to assist the development of civil society?

But then why would they want to do such a thing? Why would they need to facilitate the growth of a rival political force? Since when have politicians been angels? If there is any clear lesson to be drawn from the evolution of the public forums in the Maghreb, it would be that only under social pressure do liberties develop. Just like the rock of Sisyphus, they roll back down as soon as the citizens stop caring for them or cease their efforts to secure them.

The Tunisian and Algerian examples illustrate that democratic reforms initiated from above, without a civil society that is capable of sustaining and supporting them, are scarecely viable. At most, if the circumstances are not too unfavourable (Algeria), the very short experience of freedom might keep society in a state of quasi-awakening and prevent the instinct for civil action from fading away totally. On the other hand, the history of pluralistic development in Morocco shows us that even without democratic institutions, demands for freedom may emanate from society.

Nevertheless, none of the Maghreb's political societies (in the sense of communities of state and civil actors) has presented the features of democracy. The hypothesis that civil society is a prerequisite for democratization does not mean that civil society constitutes a sufficient condition.

A dynamic civil society is nevertheless necessary, as is clearly shown by the Moroccan case, in order to produce a balance of power between civil and official actors such as to make high the political cost of authoritarianism. In such a case, rulers prefer to give away some power to the civil actors in order to preserve their authority. This more balanced power relationship will be reached only when civil society has mobilized enough organizational resources and sufficiently developed its bonds of solidarity to be able to challenge the rulers in public debates and threaten the legitimacy of those in power by disseminating the relevant information and publicly pointing at sensitive issues.

This is why the development of civil society has been described as a process of state/society differentiation, empirically manifested in the recurring capacity of the civil actors to exist without the government's assistance, to act without asking for authorization, to disregard prohibitions, to survive reprisals, to inform and speak out against the rulers.

Absolute differentiation, that is, continuous and all-out conflict between civil and state actors, is inconceivable without the risk of fatally undermining the political system. Political stability presupposes minimal interdependence, common objectives and a culture of compromise between rulers and ruled. It is in this sense that we may say that Morocco has stabilized the development of a pluralistic civil society, unlike the Algeria of the 1990s, where the process is still reversible, where the actors have not reached this level of minimum interdependence, and unlike the Tunisia of Ben Ali, where civil society has been destroyed as a result of being too vulnerable *vis-à-vis* those in power.

It is precisely because of the need for a reciprocal minimal dependence, whose ideal level is difficult for the competing actors to estimate, that the process of development of civil society is fragile and reversible, particularly following certain alliances between state and civil actors. These alliances become dangerous when the bond of trust that they create is established between weaker civil actors and a dominant state actor in order to eliminate an emergent competitor. They then constitute something totally different from the kind of covenants that lay down the rules for co-operation and peaceful settlement of conflicts between all contending actors; in this unbalanced power relationship, the weaker actors, thinking of the dominant actor as the only chance for salvation in a hostile world, can, as in Tunisia, go so far as unconditionally to give up all powers.

In such instances, then, the weaker actors are totally indebted for their political survival to the central actor and will not dare, during the initial honeymoon period that the latter enjoys, do anything that could provoke his anger. At this point, the future of the weaker actors appears to them to be related to that of the dominant actor, to the extent that, at least at the beginning, they will show no resistance to his attempts to transform his allies into satellites of his central power. The connection thus established in the form of an alliance quickly becomes organic; civil actors start acting like government bodies, while state actors assume the role of civil actors. Therefore, just as the development of civil society could be described as a process of differentiation (Morocco), conversely, its destruction can take the form of merging the actors into the sole role of serving the rulers (Tunisia).

When the weak actors finally become aware of the danger, it is perhaps already too late. They have been completely isolated from the external world, and the state leviathan will no longer let them escape without crushing them to death – political and social death at the very least and, if not, exile, torture, 'accidents', and even 'terrorist' attacks.

The future of the fragile process of democratization rests, in a necessary and sufficient manner, in the hands of the political actors (civil and state). It is their respective political capabilities and their alliance or conflict strategies, whose long-term outcomes are difficult to predict by the actors involved, that will determine the future of the process: consolidation or destruction of freedom. Therefore, even when sufficiently developed, civil society does not necessarily manage to impose the institutions of democracy (Morocco). Under what conditions can it achieve this goal? Or on the contrary fail to do so?

It would be too ambitious to infer, based on the sole case of the Maghreb's public forums, a complete and final explanation. Nevertheless, the three different scenarios of political evolution that are unfolding there suggest some keys to the enigma. First, they tend to confirm what sociology has observed in other processes of democratization.

First

The real distribution of the strategic resources between the civil and state actors – who is likely to be either too weak to overcome or too strong to be overcome – as well as their assessment of power relationships can suggest alliances that will be critical to the direction of the political change: towards more or towards less freedom.

Second

A feared threat to the legitimacy of those in power can also render uncertain the prospects for democratization. This threat may consist in an economic crisis, in a civil war, or simply in an obsessive and exaggerated assessment of the risks, as in the case of Tunisia. Be that as it may, such a threat can be sufficient to convince those in power of the urgent need to take back control of political life and to domesticate civil institutions one after the other.

The Maghreb's public forums also hold certain specific lessons, which not all transition experiences necessarily teach us. They include the following.

Third

Generally, the purpose of any alliance that occurs between the political actors (civil and state) is to bring about a change in the current power relationship. When the alliance takes the form of a pact in which the political actors (state and civil) agree on the conditions of coexistence and peaceful competition, the democratic transition is likely to succeed (Spain, Chile, Argentina). However, alliances that are established between those in power and weaker civil actors to counter the influence of a civil actor that is causing concern (Algeria and Tunisia) are far more fragile. In transition periods, it could be the possibility for peaceful alternation of political incumbents and the development of civil society that these alliances compromise. Hence the violence that they engender: state violence supported by the civil actors of the alliance (Algeria and Tunisia), or even civil violence provoked by the illegitimate stopping of the democratic transition (Algeria).

Fourth

A hasty coalition between state and civil actors, occurring before civil society is sufficiently developed to be able to negotiate its objectives with the rulers, can be traumatizing for a young civil society (Morocco in the 1950s and Algeria in the 1990s). It can even be fatal for a 'young democracy' (Tunisia). When the civil actors involved in the alliance are unable to impose their conditions, they cannot but submit, and hope for the best from a political messiah in whom they have no other choice but to place all their hopes.

Fifth

A hasty coalition is less dangerous for the future development of civil and political liberties if it coincides with a crisis of legitimacy of the state, a time when the cohesion of the ruling elite weakens and its need for minimal civil support thus emerges (Algeria).

One assumption underlies the five keys of this explanation: the need for conflictual relationships between civil and political actors. This assumption is not evident and needs explanation. In fact, one might object, along with Ilya Haryk,[1] that the development of civil society can start without the latter becoming politicized and deciding to assert its independence *vis-à-vis* the state. Actually, in Tunisia and Algeria there are thousands of organizations devoted to sports, religious thought, art and culture, the defence of women's rights and other freedoms. Surviving and growing in the protective shadow of the state, they are bearers of cultural and social change. What about the associative movement?

Is this not a civil society that develops along apolitical lines, with no differentiation from the state? Yes, this definitely is a society; but it is not *civil*, in the sense of an 'assemblage of citizens'. Those associations are committed to certain objectives they want to achieve without being aligned with any one of the actors in the political competition. However, their neutrality already places them on the political stage. Their apolitical attitude itself is a strategy of careful positioning in the political competition – a 'low profile' or 'duck's back' strategy that consists in making oneself as little menacing as possible *vis-à-vis* the central actor: the state. This strategy is, in fact, an act of reverence; the photograph of the head of state, displayed in the office, indicates to the dominant actor that he has nothing to fear from such and such an organization. This kind of apolitical attitude is basically an act of submission to the dominant political figure: the head of state, the army, or the party. Of little importance, therefore, are the specific reasons that justify the refusal of politicization: the initial act of access to citizenship consists at the same time in giving it up.

The apolitical attitude, when it is generalized and the associative movement has not yet broken into the political forum, or is no longer there (1987 Algeria, and Morocco until the 1980s with the exception of the organizations placed under the umbrella of the political parties), is concomitant with a scarcity of organizational resources; public leadership is replaced by networks of interpersonal contacts. Material resources, such as office buildings and subsidies, must be obtained in the form of state subsidy. Sometimes even the lists of members must be communicated to the authorities. In this situation of a low level of organizational development, the apolitical attitude makes the associative movement vulnerable to any form of political exploitation (whether it be the work of a political party or of the state).

For example, women's organizations in Algeria enthusiastically demonstrate against Islamism. However, until they denounce the violence committed against the female relatives of political dissidents, their commitment will only serve as a support for state authority – support that comes in handy to justify the repression in the eyes of international public opinion. One may recall the role of the Algerian women's delegation to the Fourth World Conference on Women held in Beijing in 1995; selected and sent with all expenses paid, the delegation included not a single Islamist woman, and its only message was to reaffirm the Islamist threat to women. As if the regime were the champion of women's emancipation! As if the Algerian Revolution and independence had brought women an equality that was then being threatened! In the context of an evolving civil society, the apolitical attitude can hardly be neutral; in the absence of the will to resist, it quickly turns into subjugation.

Such groups will not effectively enter the political arena until they are in a position to defend their objectives against anyone, whether it be the opposition or the government. Meanwhile, their social usefulness is certainly not unimportant: not only given what they offer to their immediate environment, or their contribution to the process of cultural and social change, but also because they serve as a training ground for state and civil actors and as a source of new blood in the public forum.

However, these apolitical groups are not civil actors. Society is not called 'civil' until there are organized groups of human beings capable of breaking into the political arena and fulfilling their role in it as responsible citizens. In the absence of this condition, the more or less complete closure of the public forum prevents external observers from decoding the state propaganda and identifying the real internal issues. In fact, interaction between the international forum and the national forums of locked dictatorships may either reinforce or weaken political locking.

The final outcome of this interaction depends, on the one hand, on the capacity of those in power to disseminate an exclusive propaganda and prevent dissident information from circulating across the borders, and, on the other hand, on the motivation of the international press to report the truth about what goes on. As a matter of fact, domestic failure of democratization processes does not mark the end of the story but rather its internationalization. We shall now see, in the second part of this book, the reason why the information presented in this first part might have seemed at times so unexpected but also how, inevitably, everything gets known and the fight for freedom can be resumed.

Note

1 Ilya Haryk, 'Pluralism in the Arab World', *Journal of Democracy*, 5 (3), 1994, pp. 44–50.

PART II

THE AFTERMATH OF DANGEROUS ALLIANCES
TRANSFORMATIONS AND CONTINUITIES
IN THE POLITICAL ARENA

Between Cries and Whispers

After the Tunisian dangerous alliance, Tunisia's civil actors can no longer engage, as they had been used to, in public discussions about political issues. Nothing is allowed any more except to applaud, and the slightest attempt at public expression is severely repressed. Yet in neighbouring Algeria, the ongoing massacres no longer prevent dissident voices from making themselves heard. These voices have even succeeded in obtaining backing from Paris, London, Washington and Montreal, though it took years and tens of thousands of deaths before the Algerian military were challenged in the international public forum. Still further to the west, Morocco enjoys a limited, yet undeniable freedom of expression; after King Hassan II's dark years, Moroccans have nevertheless been able to shout again, at home and abroad, Down with dictatorship!

Yet for a long time echoes from the strangled voices of the dissidents in the three countries were heard outside without the international public paying any serious attention. In the three cases, the world finally heard the calls for help issued by the freedom fighters. Why does international information fluctuate in this way, between cries and whispers? And how can it contribute to the reopening, albeit with much delay, of locked domestic forums?

Tunisia as well as Algeria and Morocco provides us with some answers to these questions.

7

HAPPY TUNISIA
THE AUTHORIZED ACCOUNT

Once it has closed down the public forum, following a fatal alliance with civil society, the totalitarian state cannot rule by force alone. It also needs a minimum internal consensus and some external support. This involves occupying the public forum that has been left empty and neutralizing the few discordant voices that will try to be heard. To this end, the Tunisian regime launched a public relations offensive, promoting the image of a small, happy country, having reconciled democracy with security, but persistently fragile against the danger of subversion. This offensive has been used to mislead the public on the nature of the clampdown, and to obtain the approval of Western countries.

A Dream for Tourists and Foreign Investors

The historiography of happiness begins with the coup: 'the news spreads like wildfire. The population heaves a sigh of relief. The citizens ... pour into the streets, applauding and cheering the man who brought about the change. Tunisia has truly been saved; hope is born, bringing renewed faith in the future', wrote Saddok Chaabane, Tunisia's then justice minister.[1]

The images of happy Tunisia that have circulated since the coup convey a euphoric representation of Tunisian reality: no poverty, no corruption. The European media constituted the main target of this charm offensive. Magazines such as *Afrique-Asie* and especially *Jeune Afrique*, but also, occasionally, major dailies such as *Libération*, proved to be avid hunters of exotic images, and sensitive to advertising dollars. To entertain their readers, they have disseminated the regime's barely concealed political publicity.

Here is one example (they look alike) of this coverage–publicity aimed at tourists thirsting for dreams and investors attracted by the prospects for profit in a peaceful country. In its November 1996 issue (no. 86, pp. 34–50), *Le Nouvel Afrique-Asie* published a report titled 'Culture and Modernity', which begins with a colour page announcing the annual programme of cultural activities in Tunisia (the Culture Minister's column, p. 40), and contains one full-colour page of advertising, paid for by Tunis Air. The general theme of the report is Tunisia's cultural and scientific development, on the occasion of the designation of Tunis by UNESCO as regional cultural capital in 1996. The opening article, 'Culture and Modernity', features a photo of the president, in a white laboratory coat, sitting at a table in front of a telecommunications console, spectacles on his nose (p. 36). The report concludes with a review of a speech addressed by the president to Tunisian journalists, calling on them to better inform the population. The length of the report (fifteen pages), its *clichés*, its exotic images, and especially its apologetic tone towards the regime, contrast with other articles in the same issue which are better documented with names of places, dates, and analyses that are quite tough on the US, Algeria, China, and so on.

This euphoric vision is factitious, but attractive to foreign visitors. The latter, accommodated in protected places (Hammamet, Jerba, Tozeur) and constantly surrounded by security forces, will be able to preserve their holiday dreams and, on their return, show their impressed relatives the exotic images (photographs, discography, books, local handicrafts) bought for hard currency. The euphoric image of happy Tunisia hides the corruption of those in power, the social tensions and recurring popular riots.

There are some blemishes, though. For example, a corruption scandal made the headlines in France while the Tunisian press kept silent. The president's brother, Moncef Ben Ali, was a prosperous businessman owning coffee shops, pizzerias, farm property and real estate, as well as import–export companies (computers and luxury cars). One day, the French drug squad, after two years of investigation, intercepted a group of traffickers at Orly. This happened on 27 February 1990. Among the traffickers was the president's brother. Within an hour, Moncef Ben Ali had received his diplomatic passport back from the Ambassador and taken the first flight to Tunis, with a suitcase that was not searched. An international arrest warrant was nevertheless issued by the French investigating magistrate, and Moncef Ben Ali was to be sentenced *in absentia* to ten years' imprisonment for his participation in this drug money laundering racket.

At first, the Tunisian authorities were caught off guard. Embarrassed, the state secretary for information denied any relationship between Moncef Ben Ali and the president. Then they came to their senses and the tone changed. 'It is certainly the Islamists who incited the traffickers to implicate the president's brother,' Moncef Ben Ali's lawyer declared to the press. In Tunisia, while local newspapers made vague references to the hateful pens of the French press manipulated by the 'fundamentalists', French newspapers were banned and France 2 was censored (the signal replaced by a black screen). A preliminary investigation in Tunis was launched, but was never heard of again.

A public trial could have made it possible to bring to light the possible implication of several Tunisian official bodies in the trafficking: the Customs, the central bank, and the ministries of Interior (the traffickers had Tunisian passports), Transport and the Economy, which had turned a blind eye to this traffic and the millions that it was generating. The president's brother died of a heart attack on 16 May 1996. Tunisian television announced the event in voice-over accompanied by a picture of the president reading the Koran. The funeral took place in private, and the body of the deceased was not shown in public.

Which sparked more rumours; this disappearance suited everybody: the president, whose image could have suffered as a result of the scandal, and France, who could forget about the international arrest warrant. Happy Tunisia will continue to attract tourists and investors. Never will the basic issue of the Tunisian government's involvement in the international drugs traffic be clarified; Tunisia is not supposed to be on that agenda.

Hence the image of Tunisia as a small, happy country where usually nothing happens remains uncontradicted. Except by a few news items in 1996: demonstrators burnt down and wreaked havoc in Gafsa, Sfax, Ghannouch. In Monastir, the beating to death of a young man sparked two riots, at which people were heard shouting: 'Where are you Bourguiba?' There were also several demonstrations in Tunis, more precisely in Bab Saadoun in front of the head office of the Tunisian General Union of Labour (UGTT), and in Bab Souika. In Ben Arous, the privatization programme led to dismissals, rumours about embezzlement and a demonstration. All these incidents managed to break into print in one or other of the European media, but in an anecdotal way and without analysis, reported as brief news items or minor setbacks, buried in the flood of happy images; Tunisia is not a problem.

The Security Mania

For it to remain credible and intact, the image of happy Tunisia must overcome an obstacle otherwise more important than hidden corruption and localized riots: the extent of police repression against the discontented. To justify this repression, the Tunisian official discourse must find for happy Tunisia a threat of the same dimension. So, it invented the 'danger' of 'fundamentalist' fanaticism, imported from abroad by an 'international subversion network' that allegedly hides its rear bases at its borders, in war-torn Algeria. The propaganda machine constructs this argument by fabricating events, by distorting the statements of adversaries now reduced to silence, and by claiming that Islamism is essentially violent. Sometimes, for more impact and persuasive power, the propaganda machine invokes contemporary sociology as well as public judgements in support of its way of seeing things. In addition, it uses scare tactics, multiplying alarming images against discordant voices from all political tendencies.

On every occasion, Tunisian government officials bring up the subjects of this propaganda. In a monotonous way, the president, the Tunisian External Communication Agency (ATCE) people, diplomats and other Tunisian public figures repeat them according to circumstances. Thus, the justice minister and university professor Saddok Chaabane elaborated upon them in his book, *Ben Ali et la voix du pluralisme* (*Ben Ali and the Voice of Pluralism*, see note 1). The book is a digest of doctrines, spread by a high-level spokesman and cloaked in scientific vestments.

Fabricating events

The violent image of Al-Nahdha (Rebirth – the banned Islamist party) that the official discourse projects is based on facts that are unverifiable or even downright false.

Thus, concerning the oath of loyalty that party members must take, Chaabane points to the secrecy requirement as proof of a violent clandestine structure existing in parallel with the official structure (p. 44). However, the secrecy required of Al-Nahdha members has a more simple reason; the movement being banned, to reveal its activities amounts to denouncing its members. 'During the 1989 elections, a number of innocent people were arrested and put in prison,' one leader told me, 'because we had not taken any precautions to protect their identity, and everything had been done publicly. It is not secrecy that we demand, but recognition as a political party, the right of free expression and public activity.' Its meetings and newspapers being banned, Al-Nahdha has to work in secrecy to protect its supporters. Under these conditions, secrecy can hardly be used in support of a charge of terrorism against Al-Nahdha.

Chaabane refers to the Soliman congress, in 1984, claiming that it served to establish a fanatical doctrinal line. The objective of this congress was, actually, to organize the leadership. The structures of the movement were set up and its representatives were elected with a mandate to prepare an action plan and set priorities for the next congress. As for the Sharia centre about which Chaabane talks, after reading the relevant documents it becomes obvious that this is not an organ for the violation of consciences, but simply an ulema council serving to advise Al-Nahdha on the conformity of its policies with Islamic law.

It could always be argued that this council constitutes an authoritarian structure, but then, how is it possible to avoid also saying that it is not dissimilar to those advisory councils with which Sunni Islam states surround themselves? In 1988, the Al-Nahdha council produced a doctrinal text to which every new member must adhere.[2] This was a condition of party membership only. That Al-Nahdha intends to apply it in an authoritarian manner to all citizens of a prospective Muslim state, as is claimed by Chaabane, is not in the doctrinal text, and appears to be sheer fabrication.

Likewise, the leaders whom I met deny having ever taken any stand on how to deal with the followers of the ruling party. If, as is claimed by Chaabane among others, someone in Tunisia has ever issued a fatwa calling for the murder of adversaries for being impious, that someone could be anyone. But Chaabane makes Al-Nahdha responsible for it by claiming that the movement heads all Islamist groups active in Tunisia. There is no evidence to support this assertion, despite the fact that the justice minister was well-positioned to unveil such evidence, if it really existed.

During the summer of 1987, right after the arrests in the ranks of the Islamists, a group of unidentified people planted a bomb in a hotel. Chaabane blamed the Islamist Ghannouchi for the attack, despite the latter being in prison, and so in no position to contact his supporters, who were at the same time themselves being spied on by the security services. Al-Nahdha and Ghannouchi, for their part, have condemned the attack and denied any involvement in it.[3]

In order to prove the violent nature of Islamism, Chaabane invokes the plot unveiled by the authorities in spring 1991, as well as the Bab

Souika affair. But the convictions were handed down by a legal system devoid of any credibility (see Chapter One).

There had none the less been violence in Tunisia, violence that was not always devoid of religious significance, and to which police provocation was bound to lead. Had it been orchestrated? And by whom? No one will ever know – the only possible exception being the plot to overthrow Bourguiba in 1987 – and the book written by Chaabane, even though he was justice minister when he wrote it, contains nothing but unwarranted accusations, without reference either to police files or trial records.

Nevertheless, the flow of accusations can still end up scaring the public, both domestic and international, without ever producing any evidence, by simply playing on unproven allegations, fear and words allegedly spoken by the adversary.

Distorting the statements of the adversary

Here, the allegations of the official discourse become openly tendentious. To Al-Nahdha's communiqués demanding the legalization of the party, free elections, pluralism and democracy, Chaabane ascribes ulterior motives: 'the fundamentalists have not accepted that the leadership should be snatched away from them' (p. 37 ff).

Chaabane (p. 38) also accuses Ghannouchi of double talk which sometimes approves of the terrorist operations of his supporters, and sometimes reproves them. But Ghannouchi never approved of those attacks; he only said he understood that some Islamists give in to government provocation. That does not amount to approval of violence, but at the very most attribution of the responsibility for it to police repression.

In fact, the writings of Ghannouchi and Al-Nahdha have repeatedly and unequivocally condemned violence. It is perhaps this that Chaabane calls double talk, as he alludes to secretly given terrorist directives that would indicate the true nature of the movement. But the justice minister has never been able to publish a single text that he allegedly had intercepted during his term.

And to avoid having to mention apparently imaginary calls to violence, Chaabane claims that there is a 'universal fundamentalist prototype' (p. 49), and that, by nature, political Islam cannot but be violent. Indeed, does it not go so far as to advocate 'the establishment of a totalitarian system that restricts the freedom of the individual, in the smallest details of his existence, and go as far as … making mandatory shaving one's head and wearing a beard' (p. 112)? (Among exiled Al-

Nahdha leaders whom I had the opportunity to meet, I don't remember anyone with a long beard and a shaven head.)

Pop sociology and the essentialist view of political Islam

It is rather from the sociological literature that Chaabane deduces that violence is essential to Islamism. 'The researchers', he claims, 'who have studied these movements from the inside have shown that religious movements cannot but become violent as soon as they get into politics: violence becomes indissociable from them' (pp. 39–40).' To support his contention he cites Bertrand Badie, Yadh Ben Achour, and several Tunisian academics, indistinctly described as field researchers. A correction would be in order here; Badie and Ben Achour are not field researchers. And, to my knowledge, none of them has studied these movements from the inside. As for the Tunisian researchers cited, all except one have published after 1990, that is, at a time when one could no longer write anything unless it was to the government's liking, while critical academics had chosen silence. These academics Chaabane is very careful not to cite, just as he forgets the works of Bruno Étienne and François Burgat, two experts on Islam who have analysed Islamist writings and interviewed Islamist leaders, but without concluding that political Islam is fundamentally violent and totalitarian.[4] To create the illusion of a scientific proof that does not exist, Chaabane sprinkles names and confuses terrorist violence with a blueprint for an Islamist society.

The terrifying images

The backing Chaabane claims for his views is not just scientific – it is political as well: the whole Tunisian population has rejected fundamentalism, Chaabane claims (p. 49), thus playing on an illusory consensus that exists nowhere but in the official discourse. Ben Ali is even transformed into an international leader who has been the first to sound the alarm abroad and to 'convince all governments to make it a top priority to nip [fundamentalism] in the bud' (p. 49).

Here, Chaabane's book magnifies Al-Nahdha's terrifying image by reproducing a myth that has been current for a long time, despite being based on nothing more than the speculations of the intelligence services: the belief in a worldwide 'fundamentalist' conspiracy. Playing on words, equating opposition, Islamism and terrorism, Chaabane evokes interstate consultative meetings on terrorism (Islamist or otherwise) to show that the whole international community testifies that Al-Nahdha belongs to a force that threatens world peace (p. 49).

The terrible suspicion, which was for a time entertained by diplomats against political Islam, was not unfounded; did not Khomeini's Iran state its desire to spread its influence to all 'oppressed peoples'? Yet, the United States, France and England have welcomed many Al-Nahdha dissidents to their territories, and the US State Department repeats each year that Tunisia persecutes its Islamist dissidents for their political opinions.

Moreover, and contrary to Chaabane's statement, the Tunisian Islamist movement has little in common with the Algerian or Egyptian terrorists; furthermore, the election of Islamists to the parliaments of Jordan and Turkey has not led to the renewal of violence or fanaticism that the author announces. Therefore, the direction that Islamist oppositions take, between violence and legality, seems to depend on the particular national context. The argument that political Islam is fundamentally violent is no longer valid.

However, when this unverifiable proposition is asserted by someone who is supposed to know better than anyone else (a sociologist and Tunisian government minister), fantasies about an opposition, Islamist or otherwise, that is unable to reply may accumulate. First, to those who wish to differentiate between moderate and extremist Islamists, Chaabane sends this warning: 'What escapes the West, is the fact that the moderates are so only in appearance and that every *djellaba* hides a dagger' (p. 43). The danger is, therefore, all the more serious in that it is invisible, impossible to detect. But then, since the daggers are invisible, they may be imagined to be everywhere. Second, to those who hope that moderate intellectuals within the Islamist movement might be able to contain violence, Chaabane prophesies, like Cassandra once did, that Al-Nahdha is 'a diabolical spiral that crushes ... anyone who tries to stop it' (p. 43). If there are 'terrorists' within Al-Nahdha, in the particular sense that Chaabane gives to this term, of promoters of a new moral order, then how should the official slogans of 'Change' and 'the New Era' be called?

In his fanciful assertion about the perils awaiting a transition that has not actually taken place, not the least of which is 'the coercive establishment of a totalitarian system that stifles the individual' (p. 15), the justice minister Chaabane apparently ignores the fact that the intolerance and totalitarianism then taking hold of the country were the doing of the regime, and not of the imprisoned or exiled Islamist opposition. Such is the ultimate objective of the political lie in the Tunisia of Ben Ali.

The Show Democracy: Arguments and Techniques of Stage-setting

The 'fundamentalist' peril thus blown out of all proportion finds its symbolic counterpart in the societal blueprint that underlies the regime's legitimacy: the rule of law and democracy, which cannot be established before the peril is overcome. In order to preserve the plausibility of the discourse of a happy and friendly-to-everybody Tunisia, peaceful and fragile, it is necessary to hide any facts that contradict it. It is necessary to conceal the subordination of the judicial system, to falsify history and to deny the social vacuum that exists, to pretend to establish democracy and human rights in a scientific manner. To ensure this, the official discourse reproduces a show with multiple dimensions: show law, show pluralism, and scientific democracy.

Show law

The Tunisian official discourse often takes its own sources for its actual practices, and draws from them arguments for its legitimacy discourse: an access to power in conformity with the Constitution, a 'progressive' democratic transition inaugurated by the abolition of the presidency for life, Tunisia's international commitments in relation to human rights, and the independence of the justice system. The official discourse disregards, however, the wide gap between text and practice. For example, the physicians who covered up Ben Ali's coup were summoned in the middle of the night, and signed Bourguiba's certificate of disability due to senility without having had the opportunity to examine their patient. Thus, what looked like a lawful succession was actually an in-house revolution. Another example is the abolition of the presidency for life, from 25 July 1988, seen as symbolically marking the beginning of the democratic reforms. There is one little fact that the official discourse has forgotten: the presidency for life, in the Constitution, was only for Bourguiba. Eliminating this personal privilege from the Constitution does no more than make final the fate of the toppled 'Supreme Warrior'. It does not have the effect of restoring the 'republican system's authentic significance' (p. 91) of popular sovereignty, but just of reintroducing an election mechanism that has everything to do with plebiscites (only one candidate and electoral outcomes exhibiting the '99 per cent syndrome'), and nothing to do with the electoral choice between several candidates.

Yet another example of the wide gap between government pronouncement and practice involved the ratification of the International

Convention against Torture (on 11 July 1988), and then of the Optional Protocol (of the Covenant on Civil and Political Liberties) allowing for states' and citizens' complaints to be heard (on 23 April 1993), as well as the periodic reports submitted by Tunisia to the United Nations (UN). These are invoked as good behaviour certificates, as if simply because the texts exist, torture and political repression have disappeared. On the contrary, the Tunisian ratification of the Convention and the Optional Protocol coincided with the beginning of the systematic violation of human rights in the country. Moreover, while it is true that the Tunisian legal system is, on paper, a model of equity, as we have seen in Chapter One, in practice these theoretical rules are distorted by the falsification of police records (in order to hide torture) and the sub-servience of the judiciary to the president's rule.

In this respect, one thing Chaabane wrote reveals the kind of freedom that judges enjoy *vis-à-vis* the government: 'It is the independence that Tunisian judges and lawyers enjoy, since the Change [*sic*], that has encouraged them to be the sincere defenders of the regime ... with regard to freedom and judicial guarantees' (p. 94). As long as the jurists are content to say only what is permitted and to express support for the regime, the latter can pretend that freedom of expression is in good shape. But what happens when judges dare to make unauthorized criticisms of the judicial system? After the meeting organized by the International Commission of Jurists, they were forced to retract their protest (see Chapter One). Independent in theory, the Tunisian judiciary is not so in practice. The texts are mere window-dressing.

Show pluralism

Ben Ali's regime legitimizes itself by another fiction, called 'Change,' sacralized by the capital letter, according to which Ben Ali has created, for the benefit of his people, the necessary conditions for the establishment of political pluralism. But this pluralism is said to be fragile as it is without historical roots, and has emerged out of the social and political vacuum that had allegedly characterized the old regime. Between rhetoric and reality, however, there is inversion of the terms of the change; it is the old regime that lived side by side with a dynamic labour movement, opposition parties, private newspapers that expressed themselves fairly freely, academics who had acquired an international scientific reputation (Chouikha, Ben Achour, etcetera) The real change took place not towards pluralism (pluralism existed under the old regime, even though it was sometimes violently controlled), but towards social vacuum.

That is why, paradoxically, the groups that play the game of the totalitarian policy of satellization are referred to by Chaabane as a 'sane' pluralistic opposition, whereas all those who dare to voice dissident viewpoints are accused of supporting fanaticism and threatening democracy. The latter are to be prevented from causing any harm, the former helped in 'developing competitive thinking *vis-à-vis* the ruling party' (p. 117), while both parties should be taught about democracy. But does democracy have to be taught by means of torture, police terror, denunciations, censorship, corruption and political lies?

Chaabane ignores this issue, and instead attributes to the parties themselves responsibility for their own weaknesses: he singles out for blame 'a mentality of dependence on the state', the lack of political objectives and alternatives to offer to the electorate, and the absence of a 'culture of competition, based on initiative, independence, the desire to distinguish oneself through the definition of programmes and the development of slogans' (p. 109). In the parties' defence, however, Chaabane invokes the immensity of the political genius of the president; the opposition parties were crushed, he claims, by the leadership of the ruling RCD, which 'adopted the core of the opposition's programmes and integrated it into a clear and comprehensive blueprint for society: that of Ben Ali' (p.123). But then, why promote a culture of competition and alternative objectives if the genius of Ben Ali is without equal?

The scientific democracy

The backing of science is used by minister Chaabane (who is also a social scientist and who should know better) to delude public opinion in a superficial and even fraudulent manner: multiplying sociological references (which sometimes contradict his statements), and negating the civil dynamism that preceded the regime by pretending to be filling a social vacuum that is in reality being created.

His book intends to prove that President Ben Ali rules Tunisia by methods that are approved by political sociology and taught at universities. The very personality of the head of state is said to call for such an attitude: his office being full of computers (why many?), his interest in experts' reports (p. 107), etcetera. Thus, Chaabane presents the world with 'progressive Change towards pluralism and democracy' as a viable solution, in contrast to violent democratic transitions, engaged in without proper preparation, against a background of social vacuum, and which fail because of that.

If we are to believe the results of the surveys conducted by Tunisia's Social Prospects Study Bureau, which Chaabane quotes in a rather unorthodox manner, we may say that the scientific method of Ben Ali has succeeded. To prove that a 'new atmosphere' (p. 50) has been created, Chaabane puts forward figures from a survey carried out in 1993: 51.3 per cent of those questioned said they preferred things 'as they are now', 76.1 per cent were optimistic about the future of their children, and 56.3 per cent believed that it was the state that best protected their interests. The problem is that in order to prove there is a new atmosphere, it would also be necessary to cite surveys conducted before the 'Change'. The sprinkling of figures means nothing, without this comparison between the before and the after. This is obvious, notwithstanding the distortions that mass surveillance cannot fail to produce in the answers of those interviewed.

Chaabane's conclusion that the people 'have regained their taste for participation and found renewed interest in taking part in the construction effort, after years of resignation and abstinence' is not based on any empirical evidence. What pretends to be a scientific discourse is in fact nothing more than political talk: the degeneration process of the Bourguibian state has been stopped, the 'fundamentalist' threat is of a militia ('terrorist') type and not just political, the mass of believers are moderate and Al-Nahdha members are extremists; the threat has been dealt with in the courts; government bodies responsible for the protection of human rights have increased in number; and opposition parties are in parliament. This discourse with its misleading images is enough to convince foreign observers who do not have the opportunity to hear other voices, while discontented Tunisians are excluded from the public forum as terrorist, fanatic and subversive elements, and their challenging discourses are banned and censored.

A happy country, nuisances turned into fanatic scarecrows, and a democratic project: this discourse, however, is not enough by itself for propaganda to be effective domestically. It is necessary to boost further the credibility of information that the people of the country know to be censored. To ensure this, Tunisian propaganda resorts to a special technique: mobilizing international support to convince the undecided and lukewarm.

The Quest for International Approval

The image of a 'neat and clean' change, without a drop of blood spilled, has remained undisputed in respect of the day of 7 November 1987 at least. This image led to rapid international recognition of the new regime, but later allowed thousands of citizens to be imprisoned, tortured and even assassinated.

Chaabane seems even to enjoy bringing up the affair over Kahlaoui, whose conviction was approved by the UN task force to which the matter was referred (p. 70–1). In so doing, Chaabane fails to mention also the more important resolution of the United Nations Commission on Human Rights in 1994 in Geneva, condemning Tunisia's policy as a whole, and not just over one particular case.[5]

By exaggerating the events that support its argument (the non-violent coup, the Kahlaoui affair, etcetera), and hiding the others, the propaganda machine creates, in the eyes of the domestic public, the illusion of international approval. But that cannot be enough, and the government endeavours to reinforce this illusion by multiplying publicity events: awards, festivals, competitions, etcetera. Conferences and cultural events are regularly organized around attractive and spectacular topics (obesity, women, etcetera), that are politically neutral in appearance only. Such are the 'Award of the President of the Republic for Human Rights,' and the postage stamp issued in honour of human rights. In the same vein was the news published by *Le Temps* (the French-language daily of the *Al-Sabah* group), on 21 December 1994, announcing that the president had received the Telamon Peace Prize. According to the article, he is the fourth recipient of this prize – awarded by the town of Agrigento in Sicily – after the German Chancellor Willy Brandt, King Juan Carlos of Spain, and the Swedish prime minister Olof Palme.

The visit of the Pope in the Autumn of 1996, and his praise of Tunisia as a 'land of tolerance and freedom'[6] in contrast with neighbouring Algeria, where seven monks had just been abducted and had not been heard of since,[7] was also used to support the image of the regime as a 'bulwark against intolerance'. Likewise, 'Tunisian Judaism Days' were held in Paris in December 1996, with openness and tolerance as their keynote.[8] These events took place during a period of rapprochement with Israel. On the cover page of the publicity leaflet for this event the following design appears: on a background of blue (Tunisia's emblematic colour), gemstones outline the Star of David and the Crescent, welded together and surmounted by a jasmine flower (symbol of Tunisian friendliness). Inside, on page 5, appears the ritual photograph of President Ben Ali, smiling and wearing a suit and tie, conversing this time with the Chief Rabbi of France. The exotic is the constant theme of the other illustrations: historic costumes, traditional musical instruments, carved wooden doors, the blue sea, fruits, palm trees, dunes, etcetera – images of a country where nothing changes. 'Yesterday, today and tomorrow', proclaims the cover-page slogan. Also noteworthy is the unusual advertisement for a fig brandy, honourably sitting next to an advert for a kosher restaurant.

The implicit message of these two publicity events is that there actually is a tolerant Islam: that of the regime. It is noteworthy that the celebrated tolerance is practised towards the Christians and the Jews who are not in politics, but not towards the Muslims who are.

Propaganda Achievements

As already noted, the approval of the West, as reported and amplified in the local press, is used to consolidate the image of the regime in the eyes of the domestic public. Abroad, Tunisian propaganda has apparently two objectives: to preserve the financial aid and trade relations that the regime needs and to neutralize objections to police repression.

In the beginning, Tunisian propaganda was quite effective both outside and inside the country. The Westernized elite became obsessed with fundamentalism and terrorism. Initially this elite, particularly Ben Ali, who made of the eradication of Islamism a doctrine called 'democratization', benefited from a favourable bias on the part of the Western governments, academics and media. This doctrine was used for a long time to divert attention from the real issues and to justify state violence, while businessmen traded with Tunisia, and the International Monetary Fund (IMF) produced its favourable reports. At the European Parliament, commercial interests and the desire to spare Tunisia because of its proximity to Algeria explain why, in spite of two narrowly passed votes of censure against Tunisia, the European Union trade agreement with the country has continued in existence.

To obtain this result with foreign governments and the international bodies, the regime has also relied on the doctrine that Tunisia is a small, fragile country, existing in a hostile environment (Libya and Algeria). The dependence of Ben Ali's regime on external aid makes it necessary that this artificial image is preserved abroad.[9] It has worked; governments have long been sensitive to the security discourse. During a visit to Tunis in October 1995, the French president, Jacques Chirac, described the official doctrine, 'democracy without the fundamentalists', as an acceptable democratic model, implicitly supporting the official government position that no one but the Islamists would be the target of repression. Mr Chirac's visit was taking place one month before the

Algerian presidential elections (from which the FIS was excluded). The Canadian justice minister, too, through his representatives in the courts, has endorsed the equation 'dissident = Islamist = terrorist'.[10]

The strategy has worked with academics as well. The security myth, as stated by the Tunisian official discourse, is thus taken up by Nicole Grimaud in her book *La Tunisie à la recherche de sa sécurité*. She asserts, a little too hastily, that the tense international context made necessary the repression of the 'fundamentalist' peril (pp. 195ff.) Because of a research strategy that was too narrowly based on authorized sources, she reproduced uncritically the official lies and half-lies. As a result, she subscribed too easily to the theory of a 'fundamentalist' contamination coming from Algeria, without noticing that in Tunisia there has been no trace of either systematic or significant imported violence – just, at most, two or three isolated incidents on the border.

Grimaud's book, containing a preface written by the vice-president of the Tunisian Association of International Studies, was published by a university publisher, the prestigious Presses Universitaires de France. Even scientists can be manipulated. Indeed, generally speaking, most of the academics I deal with have let themselves be taken in by the deceptions of politics. How come, they say to me, our own Tunisian students have only good things to say about their country? How can we believe you when we never hear anything about this? Of course, the students, terrorized by the fear of losing their scholarships or their passports, being aware that they are spying on one another, with few exceptions, do not dare to confide in their professors.

Censorship and propaganda have also made it possible to keep Tunisia off the media's agenda. Tunisia is of no interest to our readers, the French and British reporters that I met told me, because nothing happens there. Also, there are no critical books on Tunisian politics. Dozens are published on Morocco each year. As for Algeria, it is the subject of a new book each week in Paris. This paradox can in part be explained by the wall of silence that isolates real Tunisia from the external world: Tunisian academics cannot publish any critical analysis.

It can also be explained in part by the way in which the mainstream media approach international news; even when the truth about these locked dictatorships becomes known, it does not spread in the beginning beyond the narrow circles of diplomats and human rights organizations. Some newspapers with more select audiences (in France: *Libération, Le Monde diplomatique,* and *La Croix*) were for a long time the only media daring to publish critical analyses, but these were quickly buried in the flood of official good news coming from happy Tunisia.

The international press seems to react to Tunisian propaganda as it did to the Gulf War, Bosnia and Algeria: in the beginning, it fixes its attention on some danger that threatens humanity: the delusions of grandeur of the Iraqi dictator, the cruelty of the Serbs, the 'fundamentalist' threat, etcetera, and on spectacular and terrifying images that make it easy for the media to entertain its audience. Later, however, the international press may open its eyes to other issues that are brought to its attention by minority voices that have until then been silenced by the din of the propaganda drums. Let us now go back to the Algerian forum to see how the international press can thus evolve between propaganda and dissidence, and why, as a result, political locking may lose its effect over time.

Notes

1. Saddok Chaabane (1995) *Ben Ali et la voix du pluralisme,*Tunis: Cérès, p. 35.
2. It circulated in Arabic under a title translatable as 'The Ideological Line and Fundamental Way of the Tunisian Islamist Movement'.
3. As reported by Michel Deuré ('Responsibility for attacks on four hotels has not been claimed', 'The Tunisian Islamists on the carpet' and 'The attacks have provoked no panic among tourists', in *Le Monde*, 5 August 1987, pp. 5, 1 and 4 respectively) and Michel Deuré and Jean de la Guérivière's despatch of 28 August ('The trial of ninety Islamists has been deferred until 1 September', *Le Monde*, p. 8).
4. François Burgat (1988) *L'Islamisme au Maghreb: La Voix du sud*, Paris: Karthala, and (1996) *L'Islamisme en face*, Paris: La Découverte. Bruno Étienne (1987) *L'islamisme radical*, Paris: Hachette.
5. See the resolution adopted by the United Nations' Committee on Human Rights, 18–19 October 1994, Geneva, following Tunisia's fourth periodical report (M/CCPR/C/52/COM/TUN/3).
6. See, among others, *La Croix*, 16 April 1996, p. 7.
7. They were found murdered soon afterwards.
8. See Gabriel Kabla's editorial in the publicity leaflet that was released upon this event by an unknown organization, the Fédération des associations juives originaires de Tunisie.
9. Tunisia has benefited from French, Italian, German and US military co-operation. In 1987, training and equipment importation expenses led Ben Ali to ask to postpone the reimbursement of debt totalling US$500 billion (Nicole Grimaud [1995] *La Tunisie à la recherche de sa sécurité*, Paris: PUF, p. 190).
10. This is how the Nahdhaoui activist Mohamed Zrig was denied refugee status by Canada in 2000 on the sole grounds that Al-Nahdha was a terrorist organization and that, consequently, membership in Al-Nahdha had to be considered a crime against humanity. Among the evidence brought before the court were articles from *Paris-Match* (a sensationalist French magazine) and documentation from the Tunisian External Communication Agency (ATCE), the former official propaganda office in Tunis. Source: Canadian Immigration and Refugee Board, M92-10133, 27 January 2000.

8

THE INTERNATIONAL PRESS AND
THE ALGERIAN GUARDIANS OF DEMOCRACY

The setback to Algeria's democratic transition of the 1992 coup took place at the worst possible time for the army's public image – when the electorate was electing its representatives to the first pluralist parliament in Algerian history. This election had been organized in a climate of great civil ferment, after the fall of a totalitarian state that had torn the economy to shreds and brought oil revenues to the point of exhaustion. After the first ballot, three parties had acquired 80 per cent of the votes cast: the Islamic Salvation Front (FIS), the National Liberation Front (FLN), formerly the only lawful party in the country, and the Front of Socialist Forces (FFS). Subsequently, the putschists would suffer a serious lack of legitimacy as they had refused the popular verdict that dismissed them.

Three and a half years after the coup, the military mafia had not yet succeeded in convincing the Algerian public of their politics, as was evident from the civil war that had torn the country apart. In an attempt to solve the problem, the president installed by the military mafia, Liamine Zeroual, planned to hold presidential elections that were, in his eyes and those of his supporters, the first step toward the ending of the crisis. The strategy aimed at mobilizing massive participation in the vote and eliminating winners of the preceding election from the political forum.

The risks were high but the game was nevertheless efficiently played out in the absence of real opposition parties and independent newspapers capable of resisting official propaganda. The 1995 elections were staged as psychological warfare, whose aim was to produce the illusion of a truly pluralist ballot and a massive electoral victory. Among the propaganda devices deployed to mislead the public were censorship and control of the national media,[1] restriction of foreign media access to the country by the selective issuing of visas, by the accompanying of foreign journalists by security staff,[2] and by the banning of party meetings. All this made it easier for the official discourse to portray all dissidents as Islamists demons, to pretend that only residual terrorism still existed and that the military were saving peace and democracy, and to conceal the systematic exactions on civilians.

In general, international journalists have not critically analysed the official propaganda, paying little attention to the absence of credible monitoring of the presidential election. It was not until one year later that the international media started to listen to those dissidents who had been successfully silenced until then (see Chapter 4).

Why did the world's media take so much time to begin to challenge the Algerian military propaganda? The problem is not a new one in media studies. Why has it been necessary for the international public to wait for a book, *Notre ami le roi*, to discover the king of Morocco's secret gardens? Why did Western journalists collaborate with the Western military during the Gulf War? Why is it that, during the war in Bosnia, the media focused on the wicked Serbs and ignored the international nongovernmental organizations' reports of violence against unarmed civilians on all sides?[3] Why have states and intellectuals been struck so blindly by the exotic images of Happy Tunisia? The problem raises others: why does the media's naïveté fluctuate between trust and suspicion? Why do they always open their eyes, even if late in the game? And why can they not do so earlier?

The Algerian crisis will be taken here as a mere example of the ambiguous relationship of the military and the media in the international public forum. To illustrate how this relationship evolves from co-operation to conflict, I comment on the discourse found in two mainstream dailies, *Le Figaro* (Paris), *La Presse* (Montreal) and *Le Soir* (Brussels) during the year beginning with the Algerian electoral campaign of 1995.

The Rhetoric of Objectivity

To sell well, newspapers need their content to be both attractive (wars, crises, conflicts, etcetera) and believable (ideally, always right). The problem, in Algeria as in Bosnia and the Gulf War, comes from the press having to release available information without delay: in other words, without taking the time to verify it. Keeping up with the competition implies releasing unverified information without delay and commenting at length about undocumented matters.

Not having the time to distinguish the right from the wrong in the information they receive, newspapers have developed a rhetoric that gives the impression of objectivity. This rhetoric presents the news either as obvious facts (the obvious discourse of current prejudices, expertise, the-whole-world-knows-that, etcetera) or as yet unconfirmed information (the uncertainty discourse). Both discursive strategies, obviousness and uncertainty, serve to lead the reader to conclusions that the news anchor does not take the risk of asserting directly.[4] This rhetoric of objectivity gives an impression of high credibility that is so appealing to the readership.

The obviousness discourse

Amalgamation

A first rhetorical artifice, amalgamation, consists of reducing a heterogeneous, even contradictory, totality to a single person, a sole voice. The singular is sometimes used to further reinforce amalgamation, as with the 'Islamic veil', the 'Armed Islamic Group (GIA)', 'Islamist'. Is amalgamation a good selling argument? At the very least, shocking and terrifying images transmit current prejudices. The three newspapers analysed did indeed resort to amalgamation to project the spectacular and simplistic representation of a conflict between the forces of the good and evil.

Consensual argument

A consensual representation of the crisis and its solutions is a discursive shortcut that relieves journalists of discussing the asserted obviousness of released news. Thanks to anonymous pronouns such as 'one', 'it' and 'we', passive and intransitive verbs and nominal sentences, journalists can describe actions and processes without specifying which actors are actually involved. The argument likely to convince the reader is always implicitly present in the consensual argument. This argument may take the form of a call to conformity (conformity to the majority, reconciling the irreducible, common sense, etcetera) or to feelings being themselves portrayed as consensual (such as hope, fear, anger and sorrow). Whatever form it takes, the consensual argument is always read between the lines, as if opinion convergence between the readership and the journalist rendered an explicit statement unnecessary.

The quoting of expert sources
The stamp of expertise is another discursive tool serving to persuade the readership that a given piece of information is true not by discussing its substance but rather by reference to the personal credibility of the expert source discovered by the newspaper. The general problem here consists of how journalists choose their allegedly objective expert sources. In the coverage of the 1995 presidential election, the credibility of expert sources was weakened most of the time by one of two factors: either the expert was also a party to the Algerian crisis, or the expert source remained anonymous and unverifiable. Among the experts who were involved in the crisis were: Arezki Aït-Larbi, the Algerian correspondent of *La Presse* who was also an outstanding figure in the Berberist cultural movement; Mgr Teissier, a 'specialist' on Islam and Archbishop of Algiers;[5] Saïd Saadi, an expert close to one hard-line wing of the military mafia,[6] and leader of the Assembly for Culture and Democracy (RCD) (a political party which extols the eradication, either political or physical, of all Islamists, undistinctively qualified as fascists, without any possible exception); Hend Saadi, professor of mathematics at the University of Tizi-Ouzou and Saïd Saadi's brother;[7] the former minister Goumeziane and the political party leader Louisa Hanoun. It is not their sincerity I am questioning, but the fact that they are actors and, as such, cannot possibly qualify for the title of mere 'top-level witnesses'.[8]

In reports where the expert source remained anonymous, the 'commentators' were often referred to as 'generally well-informed sources/political circles', 'one independent observer', 'analysts and diplomats', 'a Western diplomat quoted by Reuters', 'anonymous observers', etcetera.

The expert sources chosen by the three newspapers included in the study did, in turn, use similar methods, which are none other than clever rhetorical dodges in the face of the impossible ethics of objectivity.

One such rhetorical device is that by reifying the people, their conflicts and sufferings into 'cases', 'problems' or 'issues', experts wipe their discourse clean from all antagonism, controversy and suffering. Their words sound neutral, but such experts are not. Mgr Teissier, for one, comments: 'We try to understand why we are targeted ... Is this a tentative public relations coup (by whom?)? Or real opposition to our living in Algeria?' In the prelate's passionless discourse, there is neither right nor wrong, but only the expert style of 'problems', 'questions', 'tensions', 'contradictions' and the like. His words are stamped with the following nobility: 'We want to share ... the tensions of the current world, especially those that notably led to ethnic cleansing of Bosnia. We stand up for the right of persons and communities to be different.' The role thus assigned to the Algerian Catholic Church by Mgr Teissier conceals tactical taboos. Does the prelate preach indiscriminate solidarity with everybody? Including the Islamists and the FIS? What about the Berbers? Does he condemn *all* forms of exclusion? Including the ban on a political party before it can be legally elected? Including the police sealing off the Diocese Centre of Berberian Documentation in Algiers?

An expert who does not know and yet refuses to hate or condemn may look very objective indeed. Nevertheless, is Mgr Teissier's humanitarian spirit limitless? Has the Algerian Catholic Church in any way denounced 'democratic cleansing' in Algeria? Nobody knows. What is more typical of the obviousness discourse in the press, on the other hand, is that the journalist does not ask Mgr Teissier this question. Furthermore, the latter is even presented as a 'specialist on Islam' at the beginning of the article.

Expert statements may also evade the need to present arguments in support of conclusions by proclaiming the fatality of a given situation. The following are examples of such fatalism: 'It is only that way that evil can prevail over good,'[9] and: 'Algerians wait in vain for the end of the tunnel to be reached ... The same old story has been repeated since independence.'[10]

Expert fatalism may even draw on historical facts:

There are moments when it is necessary to have the courage to admit that nothing else can be done ... Being thus caught between Scylla and Charybdis, France seems to have now understood that all choices are useless ... Algerian history has always been bloody and fragile, from the Arab colonization until the war of independence, from the Arab conquest in the eighth century to the French colonization of 1830. The tragedy goes on today ...[11]

A third rhetorical dodge is that the expert can spare journalists the trouble of presenting arguments by postponing any possible solution to the threshold of a utopian future that is left unclear in both its form and advent. Such was *La Presse*'s coverage of the 1995 elections: 'All dices have not been cast, however. The leadership should not commit the strategic error of interpreting the election results as support for its policy ... The actual political job of providing the country with well-suited governance will start afterwards.'[12]

The uncertainty discourse

To protect their image as neutral and competent media, newspapers can avoid taking a possibly controversial or non-neutral stand by feeding on institutional agendas and dominant discourse. They do so either by minimizing doubt to render a given piece of information more plausible or, in contrast, by insisting on the unconfirmed status of news. Both discursive processes allow the press to predict the worst and the best and to alternate fear and hope without taking the risk of expressing an opinion and being criticized later for being wrong. Both journalists and their chosen experts amply resort to the uncertainty discourse as a strategy for eliminating all risk of wrong predictions.

Making the uncertain likely

The uncertain made likely is a process that consists of attracting the attention of the public by using unverified sensational information, while leading the reader to believe that the source is credible, that the unconfirmed information is, nevertheless, plausible. Here are a few observed examples of the discursive process of making the uncertain likely:

- The argument of indicators: 'The Algerian government has already given signs … that it is ready to pay attention to the American arguments in favour of peace with the Islamists'.[13] 'Promising signs of the democratic tendency's approaching restoration … are increasingly visible.'[14] 'The participation seems [to whom?] to be massive.'[15]

- Recognition of likeliness: 'The Algerian president risks creating new divisions. Kabylia (meaning the Berber Cultural Movement), whose identitarian and linguistic claims have been ignored, is preparing for a noisy response.'[16] 'Zéroual wins … if the first estimations of yesterday's late-evening polls are to be trusted ….'[17] 'A policy of reform bound to fail? … Risky? Yes, hugely.'[18]

- Dodging behind others: 'Belkacem Guerrouari is angry: "A Muslim did that … Why do they target poor people?"'[19] 'The armed Islamists assassinate the civil population? So says Jafar.'[20] '"I vote against terrorist threat," explains a woman'. (Was this the sole person available for interview?)

- Reading between the lines: 'Recrimination motives … on the French side: the eternal instrumentalization of the crisis by the Algerian authorities'.[21] 'They issue a first statement, then nothing more can be learned. What, then, if the injured die?'[22] 'What if Nahnah prevented Zeroual from winning at the first poll?'[23]

- Suggestive juxtaposition of representations: 'The suspension of one Algiers daily, *The Forum*, will be followed by a charge of "profaning the national emblem",' announces Agence France-Presse. The French news agency does not comment explicitly on the event. Its wired news nevertheless combines it in a suggestive relationship with three other reports about press censorship: European journalists regret having been 'prevented by Algiers from attending a conference on press freedom'; the Algerian private press simultaneously publishes a similar denunciation; and a France-Presse communiqué states that 'Journalists continue to defy governmental censorship on terrorism.' The four events are juxtaposed under the news release title: 'Open conflict between the rulers and the press in Algiers'.[24]

Making the uncertain unlikely

This argument directs the reader toward a critical attitude which the journalist dares not explicitly suggest. It consists of subtly letting the reader guess that some given unconfirmed information should not be taken for granted. The uncertain is given a touch of unlikeliness by discursive techniques symmetrical to those of 'making the uncertain likely':

- The argument of lack of indicators: '[Zeroual] does not propose anything to solve Algeria's main problem, the incredible violence level.'[25] 'This does not prove that the country has turned democratic.'[26] 'Zeroual … will have to tackle illnesses that have plunged Algeria into chaos. Will [the power elite] let him do it, inasmuch as he wishes it? It is yet too early to discuss the matter. Alas! History does not suggest optimistic perspectives.'[27]

- Recognition of unlikeliness: 'Is it totally impossible that voters were pressured behind the scene? … This is too easily said.'[28] 'All the officials in Algiers attempted to convince us that terrorism … is a purely imported phenomenon.'[29] 'Some saw [in the truce call issued by FIS representatives in Algeria] manipulation by the Algerian rulers.'[30]

- Dodging behind others: quotation marks, question marks, etcetera. Examples of which are: 'uncontrolled (?) GIA killers'[31] 'supposedly "moderate" Islamists groups'[32] '[The government] once again announced … that the security situation had "greatly improved".'[33]

- Reading between the lines: 'One can question the reactions of the

Algerian press. While usually so prompt to denounce virulently the least French "inteference", it now sees in this visit to Algiers a sign of normalization.'[34] '[The government] once again announced [when will it be true?] that the security situation had "greatly improved".'[35] 'Zeroual already indicated his preference for reconciliation but his close relations' moves already indicate the limits of this "open-mindedness".'[36]

- Suggestive juxtaposition of contrasted representations: 'A "residual terrorism" which nevertheless killed sixty persons in the Algerian Mitidja.'[37] 'A certain foreign press that overestimates terrorism … After barely fifteen days, the dead toll … has reached 30 people.'[38] '[The government] has once more pretended that security had "greatly improved", a statement underlined by two attacks in Kabylia that killed six.'[39] (In this last sentence, the doubt is marked three times).

'Official news is news', said Ted Turner, the CNN boss, after the Gulf War.[40] Paraphrasing him, one may add to the practices of the international media: 'Unconfirmed news is still news.' Constrained by market pressures to announce without delay what has not yet been verified, aware of the fragility of its information and the gravity of events behind it, the diffuse international press resorts to the bland officialese mode of the uncertainty discourse.

Based on unverified information, the news, mainly manufactured by Algeria's military mafia in order to win the war, could be reproduced in the international press. But who complains about it? The rhetorical rituals of amalgamation, the consensual representation, the learned style and the uncertainty discourse daily entertain readers by providing suspense, exoticism and terrifying spectacles, the latest news, etcetera, without endangering the credibility of a product that sells well: newspapers. Such are the functions performed by the rhetoric of objectivity.

How the International Press Took Sides in the Algerian Conflict

An anguished international press had, until the coup of 1992, witnessed the rise of the FIS and assessed the dangers that Islamism represented for the young Algerian democracy. The press's point of view bore some relevance. However, only a very few journalists observed that the rise of the FIS was paralleled by an important development in Algerian civil society. Even fewer glimpsed the climate of civil war generated by the polarized controversy between Islamists and secularists. Most of the media heaved a sigh of embarrassed relief and, for a while, refrained from sounding the alarm when the elections were cancelled and the FIS was banned along with all its institutions. The interruption of the Algerian democratic transition was seen by the international media as necessary mischief, thus helping to justify the return of the military to the Algerian political forum. By the same token, the Algerian civil war proved to be an unexpected opportunity for the media, especially television, to broadcast daily spectacular and atrocious images of terrorism and to entertain a terrified public with drama.

The initial support of the international press for propaganda

Illusions about Algerian military propaganda had not yet dissipated in the international public forum when the Algerian presidential elections of November 1995 were announced to the world and the Algerian public as the only possible way to end the crisis.[41] The international press flew in *en masse* to attend the show live on the spot. The public relations dimension of the elections was noticeable, with international newspapers being sold in kiosks and the very visible presence of the international press. The international press was thus made use of to reinforce the election's credibility and influence voters into casting theirs ballots. Moreover, the international media contributed to the success of elections by amply and uncritically relaying propaganda images.

More precisely, the press saw in the election the only possible way out to peace, implicitly adhering to the policy of banning the FIS as an enemy of democracy and supporting the thesis that terrorist groups were the only existing security threat. The media faithfully reproduced the military show aiming at convincing the population that the situation was under control, and generally estimated that the elections were free and that the population would vote massively; they identified Zeroual as the favourite to win.

Thanks to the international media, the Algerian war propaganda resulted in an impressive participation by the population: 75 per cent of the electorate, according to the Ministry of the Interior (the FIS admitted only 37 per cent, which remains significant given the circumstances). An important swing of the electorate in favour of President Zeroual had, in fact, happened before the election. It is worth recalling here the opinion poll administered on the eve of the electoral campaign by the daily *Al-Watan* (The Nation), which did not expect Zeroual to receive more than 35 per cent of votes.

How, in a matter of weeks, could an estimate of 35 per cent evolve into a result of 65 per cent of the votes going to Zeroual? Through a statistical error in sampling? Manipulation of the results? Another explanation, a kind of bandwagon effect, should also be considered: the population, watching at all hours on the streets and each evening on television the cohorts of foreign journalist accompanied by police body-guards, might have adhered to the contagious hope then spreading from the international media. The presidential elections were aimed at legitimizing the president and, behind him, the military mafia that had co-opted him. Whatever the actual result of the ballot, both the FIS and the international press granted Zeroual a massive victory.

Meanwhile, the international press was fed strong images: the first pluralist election, victory over fundamentalism, veiled women, arms and uniforms. The Algerian army could maintain its institutional image as guardian of democracy. The day after the ballot, the army was withdrawn from the stage and terrorist violence came back. The manipulation had succeeded, thanks to the press (national and foreign). The Algerian presidential elections were thus a second Battle of Algiers in a war of images.

The spectacular nature of this terrorist violence became all the more newsworthy when the French and Christians were targeted the following summer. It is indeed from this violent summer (from March to August 1996), in contrast to the relative calm that had seemed to reign until the spring, that support for the government's propaganda began to all but disappear from newspapers: Zeroual could not restore peace while simultaneously undertaking military operations, maintaining the prohibition of opposition groups and negotiating with others.

From the spring of 1996, the international media increasingly released images of violence and protest discourse from both the dissidents and the authorized opposition. As fickle actors of the Algerian civil war, they had evolved within a matter of months from supporting a propaganda war to staging contention.

The Rebuilding of a Pluralistic Public Forum by the International Press

To question propaganda does not necessary mean following the ethics of objectivity. It can also be done through biased information, such as unconfirmed rumours, dissident information and minority voices, and through concealing the lack of rigour behind the rhetoric of objectivity. *La Presse, Le Figaro* and *Le Soir* chose the latter method, which gave them the opportunity to build an impressive agenda of controversy while protecting their credibility as neutral witnesses.

This may have little to do with the ethics of objectivity. However, in so doing, *La Presse, Le Figaro* and *Le Soir* contributed to the reopening of a public forum that the Algerian authorities had tried to silence, and helped to re-establish from abroad what had become impossible from within the country, namely public debates. *Le Soir*, especially, openly challenged Algerian government propaganda from the very beginning of the electoral campaign.

Thus, before even the election results were announced, the journalist Baudouin Loos undertook to assess the mechanisms of propaganda. After recalling that 'the 1992 elections had to be cancelled in order to ban the Islamists from power', Loos drew parallels between 'the attacks of Islamist activists' and 'the fierce reprisals from security forces'.[42] These reprisals had become known through public rumour and dissident information.[43] In the same article, Loos raised doubts about Zeroual's good intentions and his ability to implement his electoral programme. He also envisaged 'the possible staging of a show pluralism' and 'the muting of all peaceful opposition', seemingly quoting the dissident Algiers newspaper *La Nation*.

Despite the deceitful suggestion of his article's title, 'Algérie: quel président pour quelle politique?', Baudouin did not take the risk of prematurely announcing the result of the ballot. Rather, he speculated on the policy of the new president. Moreover, he protected himself from the accusation of taking sides, devoting a page to describing the election in suggestive but nuanced terms. The layout is particularly elegant, with a colour photograph covering one quarter of the centre-justified page. The author carelessly left out one detail: the possible manipulations of the ballot – this in spite of Henri Maxime's report in the same issue.[44]

Without dropping the illusion of massive participation in the election, in the days that followed Loos kept his distance from the propaganda. He trapped Zeroual by taking him at his word while announcing his probable failure: 'According to his declared intentions [doubt?], Liamine Zeroual will now [certainly?] … launch negotiations, in which the participants will gauge how serious he really is [doubt?] … it is far from sure that Zeroual's renewed legitimacy can put an end to terrorism … or rescue the economy.'[45]

Le Soir's more critical tone here is in no way new and it persists until the end of the show. Similarly, dissident voices and their unbalanced views – no actor is neutral – will appear increasingly in the headlines. Anonymous experts also help. A case in point is Philippe Regnier's article announcing a likely failure of the regime's industrial policy, the growth of underemployment and another wave of terrorism.[46]

In keeping with journalistic ethics, Regnier had, of course, interviewed the minister about his policy. To minimize the risk of an official Algerian reaction, Regnier did not take a personal stand but rather evoked a consensus among all observers. The hypothesis of economic bankruptcy was newsworthy enough for *Le Soir* to publish it, but awkwardly, Regnier had no statistics to quote, he made no economic analysis and apparently had not asked the minister about the methods and deadlines of his programme. His article easily cast doubt on the official Algerian optimism, designed to appeal to foreign investors. Would the European investors who read *Le Soir* complain about such interesting information?

The preceding month, on the occasion of the Bishop of Oran's assassination, also writing in *Le Soir*, Joëlle Meskens had commented on the regime's military failure: 'As for the Algerian rulers who thought to convince France that terrorism was under control, they have suffered a serious blow to their public image … The GIA have just demonstrated that, despite the death of their chief, Djamel Zitouni, the bloody inheritance has been … revived by other fearsome emirs.'[47]

Such a message can be made convincing merely by placing the spectacular assassination of a nonpolitical figure with highly moral credibility (a bishop) on the front page with a photograph. In this way, *Le Soir* improves the odds that the readership will see the teaser and read more about the event on the inside pages. Also, by suggesting an allegedly agreed condemnation of the GIA, the newspaper increases its sympathy, thus counterbalancing their emotional reluctance to admit that terrorist violence is more than 'residual' and that the GIA has not been defeated.

This is how, while protecting its credibility, *Le Soir* fed on both controversy and the spectacle of the civil war: having criticized the GIA, the Algerian rulers and French diplomacy, it thereby consolidated its public image of a neutral newspaper that never takes sides.

Le Figaro, by contrast, had put high hopes in the presidential election. Nevertheless, it finally found a way, although after much delay, to challenge Algerian propaganda with a different vision of the conflict. Thanks to Arezki Aït-Larbi, its new correspondent in Algeria, *Le Figaro* could give great prominence to a problem that had until then been neglected by the international press: the Berbers, whose identity and linguistic claims had been ignored, were preparing a noisy reaction to the new rules of the game established by Zeroual.[48] What were the demands of Kabylia, or, to be more exact, of one of its voices, Saïd Saadi, leader of the RCD party? An explicitly secular state, and the recognition of the Berber language Tamazight as a national language.

The choice of the Berberist activist Arezki Aït-Larbi as its correspondent in Algeria allowed *Le Figaro* to keep its distance from both the Algerian rulers and dissenters favouring negotiations with the FIS. This sudden sympathy for the Berber cause provided *Le Figaro* with a more credible editorial line. Had *Le Figaro* become neutral? How could Aït-Larbi be neutral while being actively committed to the defence of a persecuted minority? Due to the fact of this commitment in favour of the minority voice of the Kabyles, *Le Figaro* identifies a problem to which neither the military mafia nor its Islamist opponents had paid attention in the current crisis. *Le Figaro's* new vision, despite its acute partiality and indifference toward the fate of the illegally banned FIS, nevertheless contributed to balancing an international agenda that had ignored a minority voice that had been discriminated against.

The Montreal daily *La Presse* developed neither expertise nor an editorial position on the Algerian problem. By blindly alternating naïve comments and well-documented analysis, as well as pro-official positions and pro-Berber protest, it nevertheless succeeded in covering the Algerian crisis regularly, and more intensively (240 articles) than *Le Figaro* (182 articles) and *Le Soir* (101 articles).

Soon after the assassination of the monks, a poorly documented article in *La Presse* commented on the grim implications for Algeria's future and warned France against supporting the Algerian rulers. Robitaille's analysis, although written in the uncertainty style, provoked the Algerian ambassador to react.[49] Robitaille's rather sloppy article none the less issued a premonitory warning: 'Yet it is necessary to prevent another bloody ambush and leave no possible hostage on the terrain, to begin with Mgr Claverie …, an easy target for the fundamentalists if France ever decided to …'[50]

Interestingly, the journalist's basic errors, those concerning the opposition, went unnoticed by the ambassador. The latter, too happy to discredit as unreal the portrait of Algeria sketched by the journalist, also raised *ad hominem* arguments against Robitaille (the 'challenges' faced by the regime were 'not easily comprehended without sufficient knowledge of Algerian realities') along with hyperboles (a 'prosperous economy,' and 'civil society that is really mushrooming') and ambiguity (no figures, no economic analysis), while remaining silent on violence, the FIS, censorship, the increasing trade deficit, and so on. The ambassador's letter, coming after very unskilful and subjective criticism, could easily project another image of Algeria, pictured as 'a country whose institutions function and whose economy is in full expansion.'[51]

For the newspaper, the publication of such propaganda counterbalanced Robitaille's easy criticism, just as on the day of the election Agnès Gruda's very subtle analysis contrasted with Gilles Toupin's celebration of a victory for democracy. Gruda toned down the Algerian official optimism by recalling censorship, intimidation of voters by the administration, 'the absence of a believable and neutral control of the mechanics of the elections', etcetera. All these elements rendered the victory 'fragile', Gruda wrote, and warned against a hard-line regime and a new wave of violence. In Gruda's case, objectivity goes further than the mere ritual of alternative doubt. Gruda knows Algeria and her opinion was supported by evidence, which allowed her to give weak support to Algerian propaganda: 'Algerians are ready for a lesser evil,' she wrote, taking the important participation in the ballot as a 'sign of the decline' of radical Islamism.[52]

In the same issue, by contrast, the journalist Gilles Toupin reproduced a black-and-white vision of the conflict – of the army standing against terrorism, estimating that the vote 'would bring the rulers and their supporters the dividend of four years of a pitiless struggle against Islamism in arms'.[53] In writing this, Toupin paid no attention to the lack of public scrutiny of election procedures, media censorship, the rumours that there would be administrative reprisals against abstainers, or the possibility that the regime would harden once unanimously elected, all things mentioned by Gruda in the same issue.

From Robitaille to the Algerian ambassador and from Gruda to Toupin, La Presse compensated for its lack of expertise on the Algerian situation by alternating contradictory analyses. The absence of editorial line, the multiplication of competing viewpoints and the ample use of the rhetoric of uncertainty mark its particular position vis-à-vis the Algerian official discourse. Due to the Kabyle minority voice it has just discovered, in the long run La Presse will also drop the illusion of residual terrorism.[54]

It took longer for La Presse and Le Figaro to move away from propaganda than for Le Soir. La Presse and Le Figaro were, in fact, the victims of the ambiguous authorized opposition (RCD) to which they gave a voice, thus playing for a while on the side of propaganda. Because of their lack of interest in information from dissidents, they had to rely longer on official sources. Within this narrow but real margin, pluralism in the mainstream press will, over time, only widen the scope of ideas offered to the public.

However, there is more to it than that. In the long run, the international media will play another role that seems exclusive to them: they will gradually reopen, even if partially and from the outside, a local forum silenced by censorship and exclusion, provided that dissident information can reach those few journalists who, like Baudouin Loos, are willing to be the first to go off the beaten track and challenge fashionable ideas and viewpoints. These exceptional journalists will then be followed by others who, little by little, after serving up war propaganda, will turn to controversial statements against official sources. The role of the international media is never neutral, but rather fluctuates between the extremes, while their neutral image remains protected by the rhetoric of objectivity.

Notes

1. See, among others, the unpublished confidential communiqué from the Minister of the Interior of 7 June 1994 that orders the press not to publish anything other than official news about the crisis. Also with the communiqué came written advice to the press on how to treat official information (advice on terminology, importance on the agenda, ideological and patriotic symbols to relay to the public). These two documents were reproduced in the *Livre blanc sur la répression en Algérie*, three volumes under the anonymous signature of the 'Comité algérien des militants libres de la dignité humaine et des droits de l'homme' (1995) Plan-les-Ouattes, Geneva: Hoggar.
2. See, for further details, all issues of *La Lettre* (published by Reporters sans Frontières), *Le Monde diplomatique* and *Le Monde* during the Autumn of 1995.
3. This is commonly controversial among European sociologists and journalists. See, for instance, Dominique Wolton (1991) *War game*, Paris: Flammarion; *Télévision et pouvoir* (1996), Valence: CRAC; Jean-Marie Charron (1996) *Les journalistes et leurs qualifications*, Paris: CFPJ.
4. The two dimensions of the objectivity rhetoric – obviousness and uncertainty – were first observed by Simone Bonnafous. See that author's (1994) 'Parole médiatique en temps de crise: Étude de cas', *Études de communication*, Lille: Université de Lille III, pp. 113–30 and (June 1996) 'La Gestion de l'incertain par les médias contemporains dans la crise yougoslave', *Mots, ordinateurs, textes et société*, No. 47, pp. 7–22.
5. Can such an expert be considered neutral? How could any target of Islamist groups be so? Does he not have lives and interests to protect? How openly can he speak without either losing his supporters and allies in Algeria or provoking his enemies? Do his careful answers to Jean-Paul Rustan (*Le Figaro*, 8 August 1996)

and the questions he wisely evaded (about residual terrorism for instance) reflect an unbiased view or merely the fear of talking freely? Nobody can tell, but a more professional – objective – way would have consisted of finding a 'specialist on Islam' who was not a party to the Algerian crisis.

6. Baudouin Loos, 'Les attentats maintiennent le pays dans la peur: Le Cauchemar continue', *Le Soir*, 20 March 1996.
7. Was the professor of mathematics also a specialist in Algerian politics? The interview by Gilles Toupin took place just before his lecture in Montreal. See 'Crise algérienne: Le Pouvoir est impuissant', *La Presse*, 27 April 1996.
8. The expression is taken from Baudouin Loos, 'Oxfam a tenu son pari à Bruxelles: Quand acteurs et témoins mettent l'Algérie à nu', *Le Soir*, 8–9 October, 1996.
9. Franz-Olivier Giesbert, 'Réveille-toi Mahomet …', *Le Figaro*, 3–4 August 1996.
10. Baudouin Loos, 'Les attentats maintiennent le pays dans la peur: Le Cauchemar continue', *Le Soir*, 20 March 1996.
11. Louis B. Robitaille, 'La France face à la nuit algérienne', *La Presse*, 26 May 1996.
12. Gilles Toupin, 'Un vote pour la paix', *La Presse*, 17 November 1995.
13. Pierre Prier, 'Après la présidentielle: Les Américains retrouvent le chemin d'Alger', *Le Figaro*, 20 March 1996.
14. Gilles Toupin, 'Crise algérienne: Le Pouvoir est impuissant', *La Presse*, 27 April 1996.
15. Baudouin Loos 'Algérie: Quel président pour quelle politique?', *Le Soir*, 16 November 1995.
16. Arezki Aït-Larbi, 'Les Nouvelles règles du jeu de Zéroual', *Le Figaro*, 16 September 1996.
17. Reuters, 'Un Président politiquement vierge', as quoted in *La Presse*, 17 November.
18. Philippe Regnier, 'L'Explosion sociale guette l'Algérie', *Le Soir*, 13 November 1996.
19. Jean-Paul Rustan, 'Alger: Les Cafés, cibles des islamistes', *Le Figaro*, 9 August 1996.
20. Arezki Aït-Larbi, 'Kabylie: Le "triangle de la mort"', *Le Figaro*, 16 September 1995.
21. Patrick de Saint-Exupéry, 'Algérie: Charette renoue le dialogue', *Le Figaro*, 31 July 1996.
22. Jean-Paul Rustan, 'Alger: les cafés, cibles des islamistes', *Le Figaro*, 9 August 1996.
23. France-Presse, Reuter and Jérôme Strazulla, 'Nahnah, l'islamiste qui inquiète Zéroual', *Le Figaro*, 15 November 1995.
24. Agence France-Presse and Reuters from Algiers on 4 July 1996.
25. Baudouin Loos, 'Algérie: Liamine Zéroual cadenasse l'avenir', *Le Soir*, 16 October 1995.
26. Franz-Olivier Giesbert, 'Algérie: La Fin du prêt-à-penser', *Le Figaro*, 15 November 1995.
27. Baudouin Loos, 'Un Message clair, un avenir qui l'est moins', *Le Soir*, 27 November 1995.
28. Georges Suffert, 'L'Aveu imprévu', *Le Figaro*, 17 November 1995.
29. Philippe Regnier, 'L'Explosion sociale guette l'Algérie', *Le Soir*, 13 November 1996.
30. Agence France-Presse and Reuter, 'Algérie: un responsable du FIS appelle au dialogue', *Le Figaro*, 9 February 1996.
31. Louis B. Robitaille, 'La France face à la nuit algérienne', *La Presse*, 26 May 1996.
32. Baudouin Loos, 'Algérie: Liamine Zéroual cadenasse l'avenir', *Le Soir*, 16 October 1996.
33. Baudouin Loos, 'Les Attentats maintiennent le pays dans la peur: Le Cauchemar

algérien continue', *Le Soir*, 20 March 1996.
34. Patrick de Saint-Exupéry, 'Algérie: Charette renoue le dialogue', *Le Figaro*, 31 July 1996.
35. Baudouin Loos, 'Les Attentats maintiennent le pays dans la peur: Le Cauchemar algérien continue', *Le Soir*, 20 March 1996.
36. Baudouin Loos, 'Algérie: Quel président pour quelle politique?', *Le Soir*, 16 November 1995.
37. Baudouin Loos, 'Algérie: Liamine Zéroual cadenasse l'avenir', *Le Soir*, 16 October 1996.
38. Jean-Paul Rustan, 'Sous haute surveillance policière: L'Hommage d'Oran à Mgr Claverie', *Le Figaro*, 6 August 1996.
39. Baudouin Loos, 'Les Attentats maintiennent le pays dans la peur: Le Cauchemar algérien continue', *Le Soir*, 20 March 1996.
40. Ted Turner, as quoted by Christopher Young (1991), *Du rôle des médias dans les conflits internationaux* (Working Paper No. 38) Ottawa: Canadian Institute for International Peace and Security.
41. Another, tentative solution had been proposed by the Sant'Egidio group in early January 1995 but the international media had paid little attention to it (see Chapter 4).
42. Baudouin Loos, 'Algérie: Quel Président pour quelle politique?' *Le Soir*, 16 November 1995.
43. Dissident information first became known through books published by Hoggar (Plan-les-Ouattes, Geneva) and La Découverte (Paris) and the regular communiqués sent, from Spain, by the MAOL (Algerian Free Officers Movement).
44. Henri Maxime, 'La Capitale a vécu les élections au ralenti', *Le Soir*, 17 November 1995. Sent from Algiers, Maxime's article contradicted all the other news on the same page, as well as the predictions of massive participation, but nobody at his newspaper seemed to believe him.
45. Baudouin Loos, 'Rupture avec le système? Le Moment est opportun', *Le Soir*, 18–19 November 1995.
46. Philippe Regnier, 'L'Explosion sociale guette l'Algérie', *Le Soir*, 13 November 1996.
47. Joëlle Meskens, 'L'Évêque d'Oran tué: La France en émoi', *Le Soir*, 3–4 August 1996.
48. Arezki Aït-Larbi, 'Les Nouvelles règles du jeu de Zéroual', *Le Figaro*, 16 September 1996.
49. Abdesselem Bedrane, 'Le son de cloche algérien', *La Presse*, 3 July 1996.
50. Louis B. Robitaille, 'La France face à la nuit algérienne', *La Presse*, 26 May 1996. Was this a very astonishing coincidence or had Robitaille learned something in advance? If so, from whom? Could not Mgr Claverie's assassination have been prevented? This question and many others remain beyond the purpose of this book.
51. Abdesselem Bedrane, 'Le Son de cloche algérien', *La Presse*, 3 July 1996.
52. Agnès Gruda, 'Les Paris du Président', *La Presse*, 17 November 1995.
53. Gilles Toupin, 'Un vote pour la paix', *La Presse*, 17 November 1995.
54. Gilles Toupin, 'Crise algérienne: Le Pouvoir est impuissant', *La Presse*, 27 April 1996.

9

TUNISIAN DISSIDENT INFORMATION NETWORKS

After the fatal alliance, Tunisian civil society's networks of institutions and public figures capable of claiming popular sovereignty and civic rights in the public arena slowly dissolved into Tunisian muteness. The National Pact showed a consensus, which concealed the social vacuum artificially maintained by the police state. The dangerous alliance, involving both internationally famous leftist actors and the human rights movement overtly supporting the President, had a strong hallucinatory effect on the international media and the public. This explains why, compared to Algeria, international observers of the Tunisian political scene took much longer to decipher the official propaganda, and thus the realities of Tunisia long remained taboo in the international media. As in Algeria, however, relationships between the international press and Tunisian dissident sources have evolved. Images of Happy Tunisia have not prevented President Ben Ali's image from deteriorating in the long run in the international press. Similarly, dissident information has finally reached both the international and the domestic public despite the limits that the informational context imposes on the circulation of information and ideas.

The mechanisms of the dangerous alliance are ultimately reaching their limits. One limit comes from the capability of protest to survive in the form of underground dissidence. The second is slowly growing as exiled dissidents explain to an increasingly attentive audience the illusions of the Tunisian Plato's cave. In fact, exiles have gathered around a few prestigious figures. These are famous either for their role in Tunisian history, or the persecution they have endured, or their intellectual capacities and, sometimes, their writings. Thus exiles have managed to achieve abroad what has become impossible within Tunisia – a degree of influence for dissident information. The networks of dissidents tend to achieve two important roles: to wake up the international public and to support the isolated dissidents acting within the country.

It is worth mentioning that the Tunisian dissidents are actually acting in a much less favourable context than East European dissidents in the 1980s, which saw agitation in the civil societies of communist-ruled East Germany, Hungary, Poland and Czechoslovakia, where dissidence soon benefited from a large domestic social basis and the Cold War climate abroad, which helped to undermine the dictatorships' authority.[1]

The Tunisian dissidents are much more isolated than their East European counterparts, and internationally the public is too focused on the 'Islamist threat' to be able to see anything else. The Tunisian dissidents' situation has thus little to do with that of Sakharov and Solzhenitsyn who, in challenging Stalin's regime, benefited from a large international audience. However, in spite of the Tunisian dissidents' international isolation, their struggle has been marked by spectacular achievements. Their plight shows that Tunisian muteness, as engineered by the dangerous alliances, may not last forever. To understand how a pluralist public forum may be rebuilt in Tunisia, this chapter analyses the story of this isolated dissidence and its 'unarmed prophets'. They have already changed the future of Tunisia (see Chapter 11).

Unarmed Prophets

According to Machiavelli:

> It must be considered that there is nothing more difficult to carry out, nor more doubtful of success, nor more dangerous to handle, than to initiate a new order of things. For the reformer has enemies in all those who profit by the old order, and only lukewarm defenders in all those who would profit by the new order, this lukewarmness arising partly from fear of their adversaries, who have laws in their favour, and partly from the incredulity of mankind.... When [the reformers] can depend on their own strength and are able to use force, they rarely fail. Thus it comes about that all armed prophets have conquered and unarmed ones failed.[2]

Machiavelli was right about the reactions of enmity and incredulity that unarmed prophets provoke. His conclusion was, however, excessive: neither do all armed prophets win nor do all unarmed prophets lose. Since the invention of printing and the advent of the mass media, our era has been characterized by the idea of democracy and the consequent appearance of new actors in the public forum (the public, social movements, advocacy groups, etcetera) who challenge the armed prophets and threaten the future of dictatorships solely by their power of speech.

Has the evolution of the public forum provided ammunition to unarmed prophets such as Karl Marx, Henri Dunant, Gandhi or Pope John Paul II? Yes it has, by helping them to be heard loudly in the public forum. Unarmed prophets are far less impotent than Machiavelli suggested. Without mandate or armed forces, they can mobilize support for their ideas and alter the established law and order in favour of a new moral order and institutions. Without Solzhenitsyn, Sakharov and Pope John Paul II, for example, might not the history of the Soviet bloc have been different?[3] Without their messages of hope to populations trapped under dictatorial rule, would the downfall of communism and the destruction of the Berlin Wall have happened?

Similarly, there are a few Tunisian books that do not praise official propaganda. These exceptional books were written by Tunisian unarmed prophets such as Mohamed M'Zali, Ahmed Manaï and Moncef Marzouki. The lives of these three activist writers, the reprisals they underwent for promoting new institutions, their fierce resistance to an armed prophet, their role in the European and international public forums are the very characteristics of the Machiavellian conception of unarmed prophets.[4]

Mohamed M'Zali

Mohamed M'Zali is among the first Tunisian intellectuals who publicly questioned Ben Ali's regime. He holds a philosophy degree from the Sorbonne and was one of Bourguiba's comrades-in-arms in the liberation war. He also was appointed a Neo-Destour Party leader and was a militant in the Tunisian General Union of Labour (UGTT) before acting as a minister and then prime minister of Tunisia from 1980 to 1986. He has also been a member of the International Olympic Committee (IOC) since 1965.

One day in 1986, he heard the radio announce that he was dismissed from his position as prime minister. At the same time, a press campaign was launched accusing him of misappropriation of funds, for which he was supposedly going to be arrested very soon. After a moment of hesitation, the former soldier fled on foot to the Algerian border. Thanks to support from the IOC, and also to his reputation abroad, he was able to settle in Europe.

'I am an intellectual and cultivated person. I came to politics with a rather romantic mindset, dreaming of fulfilling ideals, out of love for the youth of my country,' M'Zali told me in a private interview in Paris in 1997. In line with the fashion of his generation, M'Zali was a patriot and a man of warm-hearted soul promoting the patrimonial vision of power and believing in the possibility of turning dictatorship into democracy from within the system. His political career was riddled with strategic mistakes from which he concluded that it is now necessary to continue the struggle using other means. 'As far as I am concerned, I subscribed to all the illusions of my generation … In spite of treason, … I have given up none of my beliefs …' This is why M'Zali engaged in a dissident's career, calling for 'true' Tunisian political pluralism away from 'swampy indistinction'. He further called for a political system 'capable of choosing among all political tendencies except violence'.[5] His 1991 book *Tunisie: quel avenir?* concludes with a call to civic action: 'May everyone come forward with a clear-cut programme in the face of an electorate released from its censors, in a climate of fair competition, not of proscription. May the best one win!'

On Bourguiba's dismissal on 7 November 1987, M'Zali did not send his congratulations to Ben Ali. Instead, he issued a four-line communiqué to the French press agency Agence France-Presse (AFP), saying that Ben Ali had to prove his good faith, by releasing all prisoners and returning sovereignty to the people, before he could be considered reliable. A few months after the release of his book, which was the first to criticize the 'new era', in 1992, his house in Tunis was seized and his relatives were harassed. European and Arab figures were concerned, but Ben Ali reassured them by pretending that M'Zali could come back to Tunisia at any time … without any mention, of course, of M'Zali's eventual loss of civic rights. Henceforth, M'Zali was regularly harassed by the Tunisian embassy's spies in Paris as well as regularly insulted and defamed by the Tunisian press, which called him a 'crook' and a 'fanatic' (see pages 160–6 below).

Why such relentlessness? M'Zali was never involved in the conflict between Ben Ali and Al-Nahdha; his writings disclose no taste for an eventual Islamic republic and he was dismissed before Ben Ali's takeover. As such, his position looked rather neutral. However, as a former prime minister, he also was a direct witness who had kept in contact with national figures and who knew the actors very well, including Ben Ali, whose career was started with the help of M'Zali. The former prime minister was thus an intruder. Moreover, this intruder had some influence abroad, especially on critical minds. He and Bourguiba are political symbols to be eliminated.

Moncef Marzouki

Moncef Marzouki has been a herald of freedom, human rights and civic duty in a world that has traditionally kept silent. In 1987, he published *Arabes, si vous parliez!* (Paris: Lieu Commun). He was chair of the Tunisian League of Human Rights (LTDH) at the time of its 'temporary' dissolution, and was eventually relieved of the LTDH leadership indefinitely in February 1994.

Soon afterwards, during the 1994 presidential election, while he was still a professor of medicine at Sousse University, he publicly announced in a handwritten communiqué his intention to run against the president. His writings and declarations were automatically censored by the Tunisian press and could only be published by the BBC from London and in the French daily *Le Monde*. After Ben Ali's re-election, Marzouki was arrested for having revealed to a Spanish newspaper information 'threatening public order and defaming the judiciary'. He spent four months in prison.

He has been continuously harassed by the regime since then, by means of telephone calls, the abolition of his Department of Medicine at Sousse University, shadowing by intelligence agents and being deprived of his passport. He none the less has kept on calling for general amnesty and for the return of public freedoms and has received invitations to attend international meetings of nongovernmental organizations.

Why does the regime not silence Marzouki once and for all? The reason may well be that he is acquainted with the more important international human rights organizations, such as the International Federation for Human Rights (IFHR), of which the LTDH is a member. His arrest in 1994 thus made the headlines of the international press. Marzouki's visibility in the international public forum has thus protected him. Understandably, the Tunisian authorities would rather let Marzouki go on campaigning in favour of democracy, civic rights and the release of prisoners of conscience than be condemned by its international partners, which are necessary to the regime for trade, economic and military co-operation as well as to conceal its repressive policies. In an interview granted to *La Voix de l'audace* after Marzouki's release from prison (No. 1, June–July 1995, pp. 10–11), he resumed his struggle thus: 'It may be stupid to try to change the world but it is criminal not to try. So I try.... Conflicts ... may be faced either by pretending they do not exist, which is tantamount to putting a lid on a volcano, or by resorting to the democratic way. ... Violence can be prevented only by fighting with words. ... It is because they have refused to acknowledge such evidence that our countries are so sick and have degenerated into violence. In my view, in light of the terrible Algerian and, to a lesser extent, the Egyptian examples, my struggle for democracy is a struggle for peace.'[6]

Ahmed Manaï

Ahmed Manaï took part in the 1989 election as an independent candidate. That was enough for him to deserve the title of 'Islamist plotter' granted to him by official Tunisian propaganda. In April 1991, a larger-scale reproduction of the 1987 repression just before Ben Ali's take-over took place. Ahmed Manaï, like many others, was arrested and tortured. He was actually arrested on 24 April, during the police inquiry on the Al-Nahdha plot to assassinate the president. After being released, apparently in exchange for a promise to never talk about his arrest, Ahmed fled abroad.

Directly after his first public statement the following October, his daughter Amira and son Bilel were arrested and charged with partici-pating in a banned organization. Their home was surrounded by the police and their mother Malika was threatened with sexual assault. Their time to leave had come and they all succeeded in secretly leaving their home and, the following night, crossing neighbouring Algeria's border after long hours of strenuous walking. By the same token, Ahmed had just reconquered his freedom of speech.

Manaï favours a pluralist Tunisia, in which all political tendencies peacefully cohabit: 'The Tunisian Islamists are not devils. We have to negotiate with them instead of eradicating them precisely because they call for peaceful and legal ways of conquering power and repudiate all violence' (private interview in Paris in 1996). By publishing the story of his torture in the Interior Ministry's building,[7] Ahmed Manaï revealed to the world the hidden reality of the 'Tunisian torment' and provided a detailed illustration of the damage done to the human soul by torture.

Since then, he has devoted himself to travelling all over Europe, giving conferences, writing to newspapers, giving radio interviews, etcetera. Manaï's efficient lobbying action was worth two violent attacks in Paris and a permanent denigration campaign in the Tunisian popular press.[8]

On 17 March 1997, as Manaï came home from a conference at the

Institut du monde arabe, he was assaulted by two men who beat him with baseball bats. The attack took place just a few days after Manaï had published a very harsh criticism of the Tunisian regime in *L'Audace*. Realizing what was going on, the janitor of the building started screaming in order to bring out neighbours, and thus probably saved Manaï's life. The two attackers immediately fled in a rented car driven by an accomplice, leaving Manaï lying unconscious on the sidewalk.

Covered with bruises, Manaï needed twelve stitches on his forehead and several days in hospital. He had lost his address book (containing precious information for intelligence services) and several documents – among which were a few pages of the manuscript of this book – while, strangely, his wallet and cheque book were left on the pavement.

This was the second attack on Manaï, who had been struck on the head the year before. Another opponent of the regime, Mondher Sfar, had already been scared after writing a letter to Pope John Paul II on the eve of the latter's 1995 visit to Tunis.

The second attack on Manaï did not go unnoticed. Both Manaï and Mondher Sfar filed assault charges against Ben Ali, accusing him of sponsoring the attacks. The mainstream media reported the event.[9] What could have been mere murder thus became a newsworthy affair discrediting Tunisian propaganda. This is how unarmed prophets, by their writings and their suffering, win fame, prestige and attention in the international public forum while the image of their persecutors continues to deteriorate.

In European Circles

The deterioration of the regime's image was manifested for the first time during the president's visit to Switzerland on 8 June 1995. In expectation of Ben Ali's arrival, Tunisian dissidents, including Manaï, worked to mobilize the Swiss public. The visit was taking place soon after the release of Manaï's book, *Le supplice tunisien*, and the Geneva Socialist Party, Maghrebian associations and the Muslim cultural centre denounced the visit. Protests became visible enough for Ben Ali not to go to Berne, where he had planned to meet the Swiss authorities. Likewise, he was not greeted by representatives of the canton of Geneva. Just before his meeting with the International Labour Organization, he spent a few hours at the Palais des Nations where he was greeted by an angry crowd of Tunisian opponents and activists of the Geneva Socialist Party. Ben Ali finally pretended that he had run short of time and did not attend the press conference organized for him by the Association of United Nations correspondents. The local press covered Ben Ali's visit mockingly.

The regime's image continued to worsen until 1996, when it became obvious that the public was turning against the regime. During that year the European Parliament for the first time condemned the regime for its poor human rights record. Ben Ali's visit to France had to be postponed several times, and the Belgian press had fun with accusations laid against the Tunisian dissident Walid Bennani by the Tunisian authorities, pretending that he was implicated in the Cools affair (see page 163). The same year, the US State Department published an unfavourable report about Tunisia for the second year in a row. Sixteen NGOs brought a petition against the regime before the United Nations Commission on Human Rights, and five others wrote an open letter to Ben Ali.[10]

The regime would have preferred to secure international recognition by seeing the head of state, Ben Ali, greeted with honours at the French national assembly, just as King Hassan II of Morocco had been. Having been announced to the French media several times, Ben Ali's visit was postponed first from March 1996 to September, after the condemnation of Moada, then to November, then to January 1997, and then again to May, probably for fear of the controversy that an official reception at the national assembly risked arousing. The announcement of a French legislative election came as one last pretext for Ben Ali to postpone his visit. The state's propaganda agency, the ATCE, was apparently held responsible for the deterioration of the regime's image and saw most of its foreign offices closed.

Finally, the following autumn, the French authorities gave only a sober welcome to the president, at the residence of the president of the national assembly, while the mainstream newspapers, such as *Le Monde, Libération* and *Le Figaro*, together with Amnesty International, the IFHR and the French Human Rights League used Ben Ali's presence to present publicly a realistic and nonindulgent portrait of the regime.

Such can be the impact of a dissident information network – unarmed prophets and other opponents in exile – that through humanitarian organizations and political parties patiently channels its message to the press and pressurizes governments. This is done without weapons, simply by the use of the universal values of dignity, justice and liberty, as recorded in international law.

The narrow circles of humanitarian organizations, diplomats, journalists, European left-wing political parties and intelligence services are becoming increasingly aware of repression in Tunisia. Dissident information networks in Europe have succeeded in weakening the influence of Tunisian official information, which is no longer well trusted in Europe.

Here is how the dissident information network works. At the first level, each exile tends to create his own mini-organization and to organize his communications channels (books, newspapers such as *L'Audace*, press relations etcetera) and lobbying activities (letters, petitions, briefings of the ruling elite, etcetera). This first-line involvement activates a 'two-step flow of influence'[11] at the level of non-governmental organizations and the media which, in turn, will put pressure on governments and the United Nations.

The story of the dissident newspaper *L'Audace* illustrates well how this 'multiple-step flow of influence' functions. *L'Audace* systematically reports withdrawals of passports, defamatory pamphlets and other persecution against the opponents in order to undermine the regime's propaganda. Its director, Slim Bagga, began his career as a journalist with the Tunisian weeklies *Le Maghreb* and *Réalités*. In 1994, in co-operation with Mezri Haddad, also a former Tunisian journalist and a political exile, Slim Bagga founded what they wanted to be a crossroads newspaper. 'In the first issue, I interviewed Haddad,' Slim Bagga told me. 'The President's Office telephoned me right away: "You are being questioned here. Why Haddad? Beware!" My first issue was nevertheless a very moderate one.' For the second issue, Slim Bagga had hoped for an interview with Mustapha Ben Jaafar. During the weekend, he sent questions by fax to Ben Jaafar in Tunis. No reaction came. After three or four more fax messages, Slim Bagga phoned Ben Jaafar the following Sunday, only to learn that Ben Jaafar had received none of them: his line had been diverted.

The second issue also commented on the elections. An article headlined 'La plume déchaînée' called Marzouki's arrest 'an offence'. 'The ATCE called me the following Monday,' Slim Bagga told me: 'Why Ben Jaafar?' – 'Ben Jaafar supports the law. He will not start the revolution, even if his words are disturbing ...' During the following days, Slim Bagga received insults and anonymous phone threats. He nevertheless published the third issue with an interview with M'Zali, and then the fourth with an interview with Salah Karker. Then came another phone call from the Ministry of the Interior: 'You know very well that the regime does not like Karker!'

Acts of intimidation against the editor then intensified in the form of insults, shadowing and vandalism to his home. Kiosks selling *L'Audace* in Aubervilliers and Paris (Saint-Michel and Belleville) were subjected to pressure tactics. After buying *L'Audace* on the street, Tunisians were shadowed by intelligence agents. *L'Audace* (which has a total circulation of 1,200 copies, of which 1,000 are sold in kiosks) is read not just by both opponents and Tunisian representatives, but also by French commercial partners of Tunisia, doctoral students and academics interested in related subjects. The dissenting newspaper thus serves as a communication link between the three influence levels: opponents, civil actors and media, and state agents. Let us specify that the direct target of dissent information is not Western states nor the United Nations, but civil organizations such as professional organizations (of jurists, physicists, psychiatrists), religious and human rights organizations. These in turn, by passing on and amplifying dissident information, draw media attention, which in turn pressures European states to take a moral stand on the issues. This is how the behind the scenes secrecy of totalitarian governance is finally displayed in the front window. The process can only accelerate with the granting of international honours such as the Human Rights Watch Prize awarded to Moncef Marzouki in 1994, publicly recognizing *in absentia* the merits of these unarmed prophets. In Marzouki's case, *Libération*, the Parisian daily, commented thus on his absence from the honours ceremony:

> An empty chair pointed out the absence of Moncef Marzouki, the only beneficiary prevented from travelling abroad 'because of his concern for human rights and democracy,' according to Human Rights Watch. A 'Tunisian authorized source' offered two excuses, the 'indispensable Marzouki's presence at the beginning of the academic year' and 'a common law conviction'.[12]

Civil organizations relay dissident information to several specific publics, such as the AVRE in Paris and the International Research Centre for the Victims of Torture in Copenhagen, who train physicians, psychiatrists, social workers, police staff and civil servants on how to deal with victims of torture. Similarly the London-based Article 19 sends its documentation to academics (libraries and professors), political parties, government officials and the press. Reporters sans frontières (RSF) releases information to the international press and mobilizes journalists. Each of these actors has, at one time or another, been refused entrance to Tunisia,[13] and Tunisian lecturers invited abroad have been deprived of their passports.

The mainstream media itself encounters problems with the Tunisian authorities that leave reporters staring in disbelief. While accompanying French President Jacques Chirac on a visit to Tunis in 1995, the special envoy of *Le Monde*, Jacques de Barrin, was kept waiting at the border. Incidentally, the event took place the day after de Barrin's article headlined 'Tunisian Happiness may not pass all tests'. The journalist's problems at the border provided *Libération* with the opportunity to remind its readership, the following day, that the public standing of the regime was weakened by an authoritarianism going far beyond the struggle against the Islamists. From then on, more and more critical analyses appeared in select periodicals such as *Le Courrier international*,[14] *Le Soir*,[15] *Le Monde diplomatique*,[16] *Le Courrier de Genève*,[17] and *Le Point*.[18] Copies of the latter were successively seized in Tunis while, on each occasion, the RSF took the opportunity to protest against censorship in Tunisia. The relationship between the European press and the regime therefore deteriorated rapidly. Consequently, in May 1996 the Tunisian Association of Newspaper Editors was suspended from membership in the World Association of Newspapers because of its passive attitude in face of the suppression of freedom of the press in Tunisia.

Similarly, the great newspapers have made increasing use of exiled Tunisian intellectuals. Kamel Jendoubi, spokesperson of the Committee for the Respect of Liberties in Tunisia, was able to write in *Le Monde*, 'Never has the country been subjected to so personal a governance as Mr Ben Ali's. Most decisions, even if only daily management is concerned, are made at the presidential level.'[19] Likewise, Mezri Haddad signed several articles in *Libération*, among which are his comments on the drug affair implicating the president's brother, under the title 'Reasons of State or Family' (23 December 1992) and, a few years later, another one, titled 'Totalitarian Temptation in Tunisia' (9 August 1996).[20]

Such prominence given to the exiles' discourse is useful to the internal audience, who can receive it via the internet as several web sites are consulted by academics and research centres. The radio can also be of some use. For example, it was through the voice of the BBC that, in the autumn of 1997, Tunisians learned about the deterioration of Ben Ali's international image. This new breach in the Tunisian Plato's cave could only contribute to shortcircuiting Tunisian press coverage of Ben Ali's ostensibly uncontested international prestige.

The exiles have, meanwhile, adopted the habit of faxing to Tunis press cuttings of material banned from kiosks as well as the declarations of dissidents. They did this at the time of Moncef affair (money laundering) and the four petitions that circulated inside Tunisia calling for democracy and denouncing the hijacking of the transition to democracy (that of 200 petitioners in 1993, that of 117 women in 1994, that supporting the electoral candidacy of Marzouki the same year, that of 202 anonymous intellectuals in 1997, etcetera).

Without the external opponents who boomerang these documents back into the country, nobody outside dissident circles in Tunisia would have heard of these petitions. As was explained to me by an exiled dissident, 'Addressees of this external underground information have, of course, the obligation to hand these messages over to the police — it is to be hoped they have read them. And we count on the public to spread by word of mouth what cannot appear in the newspapers.' Public rumour is thus already a mass opposition phenomenon. As such, it may possibly put an end to the isolation of those who dare not talk but none the less know that they are no longer the only ones to think in an unauthorized manner.

Internal Dissidence

Tunisian dissidence first appeared in 1994, in the form of a handful of isolated individuals gathering around Moncef Marzouki, who had just spent four months in prison after being ousted from the Tunisian League for Human Rights. In this informal group were Najib Hosni (Marzouki's lawyer) Hama Hammami (leader of the Tunisian Communist Labour Party [PCOT]) and his wife, the lawyer Radia Nasraoui, as well as several other citizens whose names would only become known because of petitions that they dared to sign in order to test freedom of expression.

The relative protection they obtain from their international supporters (mainly nongovernmental organizations and media) explain why they are not totally 'unarmed' in the face of the imposing administration and police apparatus. The authorities, understandably reluctant to expose disappearances and torture to international protest, can at least render the dissidents' daily lives extremely tedious by means of police and administrative harassment (passport seizures, telephone monitoring, intimidation and burglaries) and defamatory campaigns in the popular press. The cases of Najib Hosni, of Moada, of Alya and Khemaïs Chemmari illustrate how the international public sometimes serves to prevent reprisals against a vulnerable resistance. Meanwhile, the latter can only channel its messages through the public grapevine for want of real public debate.

Najib Hosni was thrown in prison on 15 June 1994, after being denounced by a widow for allegedly forging her late husband's signature in a land transaction. It must be recalled that the regime is reluctant to imprisons dissidents on political charges. The denunciation that sent Najib Hosni to prison was formally contradicted by the official who had supervised the transaction, by the husband's signature on other non-contested checks, and by the testimony of the husband's brothers. After two years in prison without trial, but not without being tortured, Hosni was condemned to eight years' imprisonment in January 1996. In the meantime, Human Rights Watch, the American Bar Association and the Lawyers' Committee for Human Rights held a counterinvestigation. They examined in detail the investigation file and concluded that a plot had been laid against Hosni. As a result of the ensuing support for Hosni in Europe and in the USA, the activist lawyer was granted an honorary doctorate by the University of Dixon, the International Human Rights Prize of the American Bar Association and the fourth Ludovic Trarieux Prize by the Human Rights Institute of the Bordeaux Bar Association (the first Prize had been accorded to Nelson Mandela in 1987). The 1996 Congress of the International Attorney Union was held in Madrid in the absence of its honorary guest, Najib Hosni.

Who really was Najib Hosni? A shady lawyer? An arms trafficker? The magnanimous President Ben Ali would none the less release Najib on parole, on 14 December 1996, two weeks before the liberation of Moada and Chemmari (on 31 December). The charge of firearms possession laid against him was dropped. The day Hosni left jail, he held a press conference announcing that his struggle for human rights and for prisoners of conscience would continue. He remained true to this pledge, and the regime continued to harass him.

A second dissident group emerged from the Socialist Democrats' Movement (Tunisia) (MDS) around the party leader Mohamed Moada and Khemaïs and Alya Chemmari. After the summer 1995 municipal elections in which the opposition won only 6 seats out of 4,090, Moada issued an open letter and a communiqué denouncing human rights violations (8 October). His letter was released in Europe just as the French president, Jacques Chirac, came to Tunis to eulogize Ben Ali. The public relation plan was upset by Le Monde's running of the headline: 'While the French head of state, who is on a two-day visit to the country, praises the "democratisation" of Tunisian politics, the opposition denounces the "hegemonic and dominating character of the regime"' (7 October 1995). The arrest of Moada on 9 October, just after Chirac's departure, did not go unnoticed by European newspapers such as Le Soir, the Financial Times, Libération and Le Figaro. Moada was nevertheless convicted and sentenced to eleven years in prison; under international pressure, however, he was freed on parole before the end of the year, just like Marzouki and Chemmari.

Khemaïs Chemmari was then a member of parliament. He and his wife, Alya, had been famous for some thirty years as defenders of human rights.[21] Both were implicated in the international campaign in favour of Moada. After declaring that Moada had been arrested solely from political motives, the Chemmari couple underwent unceasing harassment from the security services. Chemmari was deprived of his parliamentary immunity and charged with violating the secrecy of judicial investigation into the Moada affair. In reality, Chemmari had only violated the secrecy of Moada's open letter to the president by requesting a piece of evidence that could clear Moada. He was condemned to five years in prison in July 1996.

The MDS archives were then confiscated by the police and later given to a regime stooge, Smaïl Boulahya. He summoned an extraordinary MDS congress, in the absence of most of the party leaders (notably Moada and Chemmari, then under house arrest)[22] and was elected head of the MDS. Being banned from playing an active role in politics, Chemmari and Moada responded by becoming dissidents, while Boulhaya could declare: 'At the beginning of this historical transition, we cannot afford to think about alternation of power … Tunisia must follow its destiny under the command of President Ben Ali.'[23] Meanwhile, the LTDH alone continued to support dissidents. Its communiqués, never published in Tunisia, continued to sustain the campaigns of the IFHR and the RSF.

Dissident action has continued to expand. Within the UGTT, a third group appeared who demanded a real leadership congress such as the last one, held in 1991. Upon President Sahbani's complaint against them, the signatories were arrested and five of them were imprisoned.

As for the supporters of the Islamist movement Al-Nahdha, they probably developed internal resistance networks. Their exiled leaders' claims and the publishing in London of *Saout Tunis* (Voice of Tunis) imply that such is the case. Understandably, the Tunisian Islamists were more preoccupied with organizing the escape of persecuted activists and helping their families than with organizing resistance within the country.

All these groups seem to be able to communicate together and channel their declarations abroad. These declarations included the letters of 117 Tunisian women in support of democracy and liberties written shortly before the 1994 elections, the call for a general amnesty sounded by 126 activists by the end of 1995 and openly signed by Moncef Marzouki and Mustafa Ben Jaafar (another human rights activist who had tried in vain to found a political party), the April 1997 petition of the '202' directed to the president by Moncef Marzouki. The signatories of their latter included 13 academics, 11 physicians, 11 attorneys, 5 journalists, 17 teachers, 53 other professionals and managers, 22 LTDH representatives, 22 union activists, 39 activists of the General Union of Tunisian Students (UGET); all these resistance groups stem from civil institutions that existed before Ben Ali's take-over (see Chapter 2). The signatories, save Marzouki, have remained anonymous. A lot of names were nevertheless whispered in dissident circles abroad. The petition was even published in *Le Monde* at the end of April and in *L'Audace* (No. 28, May 1997), thus further dissolving the isolation of dissidents within Tunisia. That petition was soon followed by another, which was signed by 560 Tunisian exiles and was circu-lating in France at the time of the president's visit.

Discrediting Dissidents

In spite of censorship, and thanks to the dissident information networks, everything finally becomes known. Propaganda then can only conduct damage limitation and save the face of the regime by rendering embarrassing information trite and by discrediting those that reveal it to the public and the international media. Nevertheless, the regime did better in the international public forum with its early images of Happy Tunisia than with the later slander campaigns to which the international press no longer dares pay attention.

Routine slander

Has it become impossible to conceal state violence? This is not a problem for the authorities, who have found it more convenient not bluntly to deny it, but rather to present it as a blemish, an exception to the democratic rule, for which faulty official agents will normally be sanctioned. 'Charges of misuse of power are regularly and normally laid, without any fuss, against officials responsible for implementing the law,' wrote Chaabane.[24] This may be so, but the cases of unpunished mischief are legion. Chaabane admits having compiled some 302 cases from 1988 to 1995, 'among which five cases of forced confession and seven of unwarranted house search'. The president in person would have intervened (p. 54 and 64) in all 302 cases. The president's 302 personal interventions in the space of seven years is a lot for a state under the rule of law, but yet too little in comparison with the many cases of torture reported by Amnesty International.

Another argument, that progressive democratization is taking place in Tunisia in a context of the growth of Islamism, serves to conceal the reality of repression on the grounds that conditions that allow a healthy opposition to develop and to be involved in political competition are fragile and merit careful control. Thus political competition is not seen as a normal phenomenon of politics but as a fragile process, likely to become unstable at any moment like defective machinery. This political opposition is carefully controlled by the president's social engineering.

Discrediting opponents

Such an argument may influence the national public for a while, provided that challengers are isolated and discredited. Propaganda achieves this aim by playing with the public's sensitivity to the prestige of the courts, the threat of terrorism and mockery. The prestige of the courts makes it easier to hide the political motives behind the persecution of opponents by accusing them of common law offences. Thus Moncef Marzouki was accused of swindling after challenging Ben Ali during the 1994 elections. Najib Hosni, after defending Marzouki, was charged with falsifying documents and arms trafficking. Chemmari was charged with violating the secrecy of the judicial investigation into Hosni. The MDS leader, Moada, after publicly denouncing repression, was convicted of collaboration with Libya and currency trafficking and sentenced to eleven years in prison.

By contrast, propaganda does not always deny the opponents' political motivations but rather deforms and amplifies them by playing on the terrorism myth. Thus, the State Secretary of Information reacted to Manaï's book by calling him a mythomaniac Islamist extremist (as quoted from AFP's communiqué no. 41325 from Tunis, 8 March 1995).

Propaganda also feeds the general public with malicious gossip of all sorts against the dissidents. One favourite theme is the sexual morality of the Islamists: allegedly 80 per cent of them are AIDS-contaminated, and Ghannouchi's wife reportedly contracted a temporary marriage with the Sudanese Islamist thinker Hassan Al-Tourabi (*Al-Hadeth* [The Event], 28 February 1996, 1 May and 8 May 1996).

For the sake of efficiency, a set of discursive tactics combining the prestige of the law, the fear of terrorism and derision (by the invention of outrageous stories) can be mobilized against a single adversary. Thus the former prime minister, M'Zali, after his dismissal in 1986 and his escape abroad, was accused of an incredible series of offences making him out to be a crook, an international conspirator, an Islamist fanatic and a sexual maniac. 'Owning the United Islamist slaughterhouses in Amiens, he is again getting rich by selling mad cows to Algerians and Afghans, who as a result are dying by the hundreds' (*Al-Hadeth*, 28 February 1996).

On 6 May 1991, the Tunisian police invaded campuses and shot at students. M'Zali, Ben Salah and Ghannouchi signed an open letter of protest against the slaughter. From that moment on, M'Zali became, in the Tunisian press, the secret ally of the Islamists and a promoter of narrowmindedness. He was once even portrayed as an influential international agitator who, during the violent year of 1996 in Israel, allegedly ordered the Palestinian Hamas organization, the exiled Ghannouchi and Al-Tourabi (Sudan) to 'Fire!'[25]

When Iraq had invaded Kuwait on 2 August 1990, M'Zali declared to *Charq Al-Awsath* (The Middle East) and the *New Observer* that Iraq had committed a political misdeed, and warned against the disastrous consequences of a possible international confrontation. The Tunisian press commented that 'M'Zali has sold his conscience for a handful of dollars.' M'Zali became the archetypical traitor from then on.

As a member of the International Olympic Committee, M'Zali was detailed to award medals to the winners of the Atlanta games on 4 August 1996. The Tunisian boxer Fathi Messaoui was to receive a bronze medal. Upon a signal from the Tunisian ambassador, Messaoui disappeared before the end of the medals ceremony (as told to me by M'Zali in a private interview in Paris in 1996). In the Tunisian press's version on the following day, Messaoui refused a medal coming from blood-stained hands that had stolen, imprisoned and killed. The American audience was said to have applauded. In *Al-Hadeth* (7 August 1996, p. 2), the headline introducing a colour photograph and a cartoon taking up half a page read: 'After winning an Olympic medal, Messaoui gives M'Zali the KO.' *Al-Chourouk* (The Dawn) reproduced the same message using hardly more discreet terms: 'Messaoui refuses a bronze medal offered by a traitor to his country' (6 August 1996, p. 29).

A pornographic video featuring M'Zali circulated in Paris. According to *Al-Hadeth*, M'Zali, after consulting Swiss doctors and healers, was left without hope of recovering from AIDS, and turned to African quacks. He underwent facelifts in order to hide his extreme old age.

Another political exile was placed in an even more vulnerable position than M'Zali[26] when the libel campaign against him turned into a judicial affair that fed the Belgian press during a few months at the end of 1996. Walid Bennani, an Al-Nahdha leader, had applied for political asylum in Belgium after being condemned to life imprisonment in Tunisia in 1992, along with other convicts. An international warrant for his arrest had also been issued for possession of explosives. The Tunisian regime tried in vain twice to obtain his extradition, while the press in Tunis pretended that he was dealing in arms, drugs, prostitution, etcetera.

During the summer of 1996, Tunis arrested two Tunisians who supposedly confessed their involvement in the assassination of the former Belgian minister André Cools. One of the suspects was from Kasserine, Bennani's home town. Nothing more was necessary for a Tunisian magistrate to come to Belgium, accuse Bennani of the crime and ask the assistance of the Belgian police in a Tunisian judicial investigation. Neither the Belgian press nor the Belgian authorities were misled by the manoeuvre. The Belgian justice minister wrote to Bennani on 22 October: 'I wish to inform you that the Judiciary has no confirmation of your movement's participation in the Cools affair'. The Belgian press, being well informed by Tunisian dissident networks, described the affair as 'a frameup through which Tunisian officials hoped to consult the files on Islamists living in Belgium' and claimed that 'Tunis was trying to use the Cools affair against its Islamists' (*La Libre Belgique*, 6 and 8 October 1996). The Brussels daily *Le Soir* commented likewise: 'The Islamist connection is not a convincing argument in Belgium'; 'Cooperation with Tunisia will not be easy'; 'A refugee claims that the Tunisian regime wants to exploit the Cools affair against him' (a possible reflection of dissident campaigning); 'Cools: Tunis is after the Islamists'; 'Due to lack of evidence, the Islamist lead is dropped' (*Le Soir*, 6 [in two articles], 8, 23 and 26 October 1996).

While continuing to widen the breaches of Plato's cave in the eyes of the international public, exiled opponents have routinely been insulted by the popular press which attributes them with an incredible accumulation of offences, including arms or currency trading, prostitution, terrorism, collaboration with a hostile state, loose morals, swindling and assassination.

The man who knew too much

Among the dissidents to be neutralized, some have thorough experience with the regime and have kept contacts inside Tunisia.

These are the ones who feed dissident networks and governments with underground information concerning the Tunisian regime.

This was the direction in which Ahmed Ben Nour's fate was going to turn. A former minister of Bourguiba and State Secretary of National Defence and the Interior, he was about to finish his mandate as Tunisian ambassador to Italy in 1986. He was well aware of M'Zali's misfortune since the return of Ben Ali to the government, but was ready to go back home with his family when a press campaign was launched against him in Tunisia.

Ben Nour knew Ben Ali personally, having been his superior in Tunis. He also knew that a press campaign announced the inescapable downfall of the targeted person. Consequently, he did not hesitate to go into voluntarily exile in Paris where, from then on, French governmental and political officials used to ask him for advice. Little by little, he became friends with other exiled dissidents. By 1992, following his revelations concerning the money laundering affair and the president's brother, he had become a problem for the image of the regime.

The reaction came in June when the Tunisian government daily, *La Presse*, accused Ahmed Ben Nour of plotting with Islamist terrorists in order to discredit Tunisian political personalities by framing them using pornographic videocassettes. While warning its readership against the new lies that opponents would allegedly propagate to malign their country, the official newspaper referred to judicial prosecution initiatives in Paris against Ben Nour and his acolytes. However, I have found neither traces of such accusations filed in Paris (although lawsuits against opponents brought by the Tunisian authorities are frequent), nor any subsequent denial by *La Presse*.

During the subsequent months, *La Presse* and *Al-Chourouk* further accused Ben Nour of participating with the Israeli secret police Mossad in the assassination of Atef Bsissou, a Palestinian national, as well as in the attack on Hammam-Chott (Tunisia), in which the Palestinian leader Abu Iyad died. The gossip was reproduced in pamphlets apparently published from the RCD (the Tunisian ruling party) office in Paris and calling Ahmed Ben Nour a traitor to be eradicated. This designation, which in dissident circles in Paris was generally understood as a death threat, was issued at the same time as Bsissou's assassin was being held by the French police. Interestingly, the implicit call to murder Ben Nour was followed by similar threats against other dissidents, who would tentatively be threatened (Slim Bagga) and even gravely attacked (Sfar and Manaï), without the anonymous editors being concerned by possible repercussions from the French police.

The Ben Nour affair especially illustrates the tactical characteristics of the regime propaganda. After 24 September, the affair developed further with *Al-Chourouk* publishing a communiqué allegedly issued by the Palestinian Revolutionary Court in Beirut, announcing the sentencing to death of Ben Nour for co-operation with Mossad. The Associated Press office in Tunis released *Al-Chourouk*'s scoop on the wire the following day. Two days later, *La Presse* recycled the whole rumour as 'information published yesterday by international media'.

The Ben Nour affair is only one more case (see Chapter 6) of propaganda seeking to increase its credibility by means of the 'boomerang effect' of mobilizing support abroad: the Associated Press byline can indeed look more credible to readers than 'yellow' newspaper gossip. The tactics looked more deliberate on 24 and 26 September 1992: the official Palestinian agency, Wafa, denied these rumours but its communiqué never appeared in the Tunisian press. Likewise, the Palestinian representative's denial, transmitted to *Al-Hayat* (London) from Paris, was ignored by the Tunisian press.

Nevertheless, a rumour may run out of its authors' control when the media get hold of it. The Ben Nour affair was given an unwanted meaning when *Libération* noticed the strange coincidence between sudden developments in the Ben Nour affair in Tunis and developments in Paris concerning the money laundering scandal in which the president's brother was implicated.[27] The victim, Ahmed Ben Nour, elegantly described the report as 'disinformation recycling' (private interview, Paris, 1996).

'I am also a journalist'

The propaganda weakens under Western criticism. The invariable official reaction of the regime, accusing the accuser of being either dishonest or manipulated, is channelled either through the Tunisian press or through the indignant protests of unknown Tunisian groups. Thus communiqués, invariably insult-spangled but lacking evidence supporting their allegations, are issued by Pharmacists Without Frontiers, Young Physicians Without Frontiers, the Association of Tunisian Attorneys Without Frontiers, 'Communicator' Women (*sic*) and the Committee to Protect Tunisians Abroad.

Following the condemnation of Tunisia by the European Parliament, twelve of these mini-organizations sent to Agence France-Presse on 2 May 1996 a communiqué describing the decision of the European Parliament as 'obvious manipulation cleverly orchestrated by a handful of extremists'. Likewise, in the Najib Hosni affair, the Association of

Young Tunisian Attorneys and the Association of Tunisian Attorneys Without Frontiers raised protests against the International Committee for the Liberation of Najib Hosni, describing 'its members' evident and derisory lack of seriousness, in contrast with the legality and transparency of Tunisian justice'. In September 1996, ten Tunisian groups reacted to the open letter sent to Ben Ali by five international NGOs (see page 153). Under the signature of Nhri Mahfoud, the letter described the open letter as containing 'grotesque, ridiculous and delirious accusations' and accused the five signatories of representing a collusion of terrorist propaganda and personal corporatist interest.

Such letters may even be signed by an 'anonymous journalist'. Such was the case of a letter by a ruling party agent addressed to the *Wall Street Journal* following Barry Newman's report on Tunisia (see Chapter 3). Upon being uncovered, the agent justified his anonymous signature saying, 'I am also a journalist.'

The State of Tunisian Dissidence

The running down of the ATCE in 1997 (see page 153) confirmed the powerlessness of the strategy of, on the one hand, concealing totalitarian rule behind the smoke screen of a Happy Tunisia and, on the other, reacting to criticism by slander campaigns and letters of insult. As time has passed, numerous partners of the dangerous alliance have joined the resistance networks.

Rachid Ghannouchi assessed the Tunisian evolution thus: 'These people are intelligent and, I suppose, honest and sincere enough to draw the proper conclusions about past mistakes and not to fall in the same trap once again' (*L'Audace*, 27 March 1997, p. 11).

Ghannouchi is usually seen as a reactionary leader by Westerners who cannot read his Arabic-written books on democracy. However, he foresees possible democratic life in Tunisia as follows: 'If the Al-Nahdha movement took over some day, it would also misuse power in the absence of a strong civil society, institutions and political parties.' He therefore evokes Montesquieu: 'It is not for the state to grant more or fewer liberties, to strengthen or to decrease the weight of the opposition. Would it be so, liberties would no longer be rights but presents.'[28]

Given the powerlessness of propaganda that, against all likelihood, claims to represent a small, happy country where nothing should ever change, in the face of the growing frustrations among the Tunisian elite and the increasingly frequent manifestations of popular unrest, could

Tunisian civil society be reborn? Will a pluralist public forum be rebuilt or will totalitarian rule simply be renewed following another in-house revolution?

Notes

1. Jacques Semelin (1997), in *La Liberté au bout des ondes: Du coup de Prague à la chute du mur de Berlin* (Paris: Belfond), tells the history of the East European dissident movement before the downfall of communism and describes in detail its ability to mobilize popular support.
2. Niccolò Machiavelli (1908) *The Prince*, Toronto: J.M. Dent & Sons, pp. 21–2.
3. Marcel Merle (1994) 'Les Prophètes désarmés', in Michel Girard (ed.), *Les Individus dans la politique internationale*, Paris: Economica, pp. 181–97, and Jacques Semelin (1994) 'L'*Homo dissensus* et ses rapports avec l'Ouest – À travers les mémoires de Soljenitsyne, Sakharov et Boukovski' in ibid., pp. 199–215, were the first sociologists to define dissident writers as unarmed prophets.
4. Let me insist again: the term 'unarmed prophet' is not a morality certificate delivered to somebody but, rather, denotes a key role in dissident/challenger circles. To better illustrate this, let me recall that Marcel Merle suggested the examples of Theodor Herzl (the founding promoter of the Jewish state), Lugard and Lyautey (theoreticians of colonialism) as all playing the role of 'unarmed prophets' because their 'prophecies came true' – whether beneficial to mankind or not is another question.
5. Mohamed M'Zali (1991) *Tunisie: Quel avenir*, Paris, pp. 217 ff.
6. Marzuki's plight went on until he was deprived of all possibility of earning a living in Tunisia. After a vigorous international campaign, he was allowed to go into exile in France in Autumn 2001 and resumed his plea for freedoms from there.
7. Ahmed Manaï (1995) *Supplice tunisien: Le Jardin secret du général Ben Ali*, Paris: La Découverte.
8. *Al-Chourouk, Al-Hadeth* and *Les Annonces* have specialized in portraying the alleged treason and the 'Satanic pact' linking all the exiled dissidents.
9. But France will not bring the culprits before the court nor even investigate the affair.
10. Amnesty International, the International Federation of Human Rights, Human Rights Watch, the Lawyers Committee for Human Rights and Reporters Sans Frontières.
11. The expression 'two-step flow of influence' was coined by Elihu Katz and Paul Felix Lazarsfeld in *Personal Influence: The Part Played by the People in the Flow of Mass Communication*, Glencoe, IL: Free Press (1955, 1965).
12. 'Les gens', *Libération*, 7 December 1994.
13. Representatives of Amnesty International and the IFHR were turned back at the Tunisian border in the summer of 2000, not for the first time.
14. 'La Tunisie, sa croissance, ses hôtels et ses cachots', *Le Courrier international*, 25–31 January 1996, translated from *The Economist*.
15. Baudouin Loos, 'L'Opposition tunisienne sans illusion', *Le Soir*, 10–11 February 1996.
16. Ignacio Ramonet, 'Main de fer en Tunisie', *Le Monde diplomatique*, July 1996.

17. 'Au paradis des touristes, mieux vaut ne pas être opposant ou journaliste: La Tunisie, une si douce dictature, *Le Courrier de Genève*, 25 July 1996.
18. 'Tunisie, Crispation autoritaire', *Le Point*, 21 September 1996.
19. Kamel Jendoubi, 'Amère Tunisie', *Le Monde*, 7 November 1996.
20. Mezri Haddad's exile became too painful to support. In 2000, he went back to Tunisia, met with Ben Ali, and succumbed to the temptation of a dangerous alliance. This is how, sometimes, political roles shift, as an exiled opponent drops the posture of an 'unarmed prophet' and joins the choir lauding the 'armed prophet' Ben Ali.
21. Khemaïs Chemmari had served as vice-chair of the International Federation of Human Rights, vice-chair of the LTDH, founding board member of the Arab Institute of Human Rights, and adviser to the United Nations, the European Union, and the Agence de coopération culturelle et technique (a French interstate organization). His wife Alya is a lawyer and a women's rights activist.
22. According to *L'Audace*, only two out of ten members of the Political Bureau and fourteen out of approximately one hundred members of the National Council were present.
23. Interview in *Réalités*, as quoted by Laurent Guitter ('Chronique intérieure tunisienne', *Annuaire de l'Afrique du Nord*, Vol. XXXVI, 1997).
24. Saddok Chaabane (1995) *Ben Ali et la voix du pluralisme*, Tunis: Cérès, p. 54. Subsequent page references in the text are to this volume.
25. *Al-Hadeth*, 17 April 1996. The whole of page 5 was devoted to M'Zali's treachery.
26. M'Zali agreed to go back to his country in 2001. Unlike Haddad, he has remained silent since then.
27. 'Tunisie: Un opposant gênant', *Libération*, 29 September 1992, p. 20.
28. The last one was published in London in 1999 under the title (in Arabic) of *Approaches to Secularism and Civil Society*, by the Maghreb Centre for Research and Translation. This way, 'unarmed prophet' Ghannouchi may still have some influence on the course of democratization in Tunisia as long as his movement believes in his 'prophecies'.

10

ISLAM
DISMANTLING A CLICHÉ

The reader may still object that Islamism is incompatible with democracy. Even without Islamism, does not Islam dominate throughout the Muslim world, including political thought? Should not democratic civic culture therefore be unthinkable in the Maghreb?

The first objection, the view that Islamism is incompatible with democracy, is irrelevant for the purposes of this book. It should, rather, be discussed by the Maghrebi citizens, Muslim or not, Islamist or not, on the day when such a question can be debated openly and in a civilized manner. For the moment, it remains inappropriate to assess a movement, Islamism, that has not yet been authorized freely to define its electoral platforms anywhere in the Maghreb.

The second objection, based on the prevailing role of religion in Islamic culture, is worth discussing here, however. Islam is often portrayed by the orientalist literature as the basic structure of thought and discourse in the Arab Muslim world. As far as rules of governance are concerned, 'the decisive part played by Islam in the political dynamic' is said to be a specific feature of the Arab world.[1]

Such a contention is relevant to older Islamic writers such as the spiritual forefathers of contemporary radical Islam[2] (Al-Afghani, Mawdudi, Qutb, Abduh, Rida and Al-Banna), who merge *din* (religion), *dunyia* (the here below) and *dawla* (state) in a unitary vision of the world. Notwithstanding such learned knowledge, the necessary linkage, as seen by current prejudice, between religion and politics in the Muslim world stems from orientalist sociology which sees culture (religion) as an invariable factor, a dominant system of values, serving to explain the nature of all existing objects and give meaning to all aspects of social life. When applied to the contemporary Arab world by researchers such as Rodinson, Lewis and Vatin, this theory has resulted in an essentialist perception of Islam in which, supposedly, the Sharia (God's way), as it was revealed by Allah to the Prophet Muhammad, is the central principle organizing political life and regulating inter-individual and public relationships as much as man's relation to God.

However, the link between religion and politics has varied tremendously over history and throughout the Arab–Islamic world. Moreover, the essentialist vision of Islam keeps on puzzling local readers of contemporary literature and newspapers. As my Maghrebi students have told me, 'Before the rise of the Islamic Salvation Front [in Algeria] and Al-Nahdha [in Tunisia], Islam was never spoken of so much in the media and everywhere else.' Is their assessment correct? Is not Islam a universal view of the cosmos present everywhere in the Arab world? How does it relate to civic culture?

More precisely, what are the main representations of rights and liberty in the Maghrebi press? Do these representations contribute to a propitious climate for the development of liberty? Or is the Arab Muslim mentality inextricably bound to archaism, fanaticism and patrimonial authoritarianism?

In this respect, Maghrebi reality is little known. During the period when the Soviet bloc and Latin American dictatorships were crumbling and democratic transitions were taking place all over Africa and Asia, a visible democratic culture was flourishing in the Maghreb, where all public discourse used to focus on democracy and human rights.

However, the Western public is more used to hearing about the Maghreb as a land of wars, dictatorships and oppressed women. This is only one side of reality. On the other side are people starving and determinedly struggling for their lives, freedoms and dignity. This struggle is a central theme of contemporary Maghrebi literature, music and art, both in Arabic and in French.

In order to assess how Islamic values and symbols stand in the prevailing human rights agenda of the Maghrebi press, eight hundred articles involving human rights considerations, as defined in the Universal Declaration of Human Rights and the International Covenant on Civil and Political Rights,[3] were randomly selected from the main Maghrebi newspapers from 1989 to 1993.[4]

To better understand the findings of the study, a few preliminary remarks must be made about the Maghrebi press and its agenda. Any media account is but a reworking of the actual structure of events. The press does not create events. Of the articles I examined, only 7 per cent were produced and framed by the press without the apparent help of external sources.

The press's dependency on externally produced information is also manifested in newspapers' layout. Some 84 per cent of front-page news comes from external sources, whereas internally produced information is published on inside pages most of the time (91 per cent). Understandably, internally produced information is much less likely to cover international news (22 per cent) than is information from outside sources. Even in the case of national news, the Maghrebi press has less direct access to sensitive events pertaining to torture and violence (19 per cent of internally produced information) than its external sources (44 per cent of the news coming from outside sources).

It must be noted, first, that the Maghrebi press, so far as direct access to information is concerned, is in no worse a position than the mainstream Western press which also feeds on official, institutional sources. Thus, we should not conclude that the press is less independent in the developing countries than in Western societies.

A second remark has to be made regarding the ability of the Maghrebi press to keep state propaganda at some distance. In the coverage of human rights issues, the Maghrebi press takes only 30 per cent of its information from state sources, the remaining 70 per cent either coming from civil sources (63 per cent) or being created by the press itself (7 per cent). Above all, news sources are not the only indicator of press independence. Even in the worst possible situation, where 100 per cent of the news must be censorship-cleared, the press still has the possibility, at least in theory and notwithstanding the fear of reprisals or hidden interference, to set the priorities for the news agenda.

According to the American agenda-setting theory, the respective frequencies of appearances, especially in front-page headlines, gives readers a powerful hint on what should be considered more important or less important in the public forum. Yet 25 per cent of the articles on human rights issues appeared on the front page (43 per cent for the Moroccan press). Such was the importance that the Maghrebi press decided to attach to the issue of human rights during the period under observation.

Underlying my analysis is the methodological assumption that the meanings of religious symbols do not exist in isolation. They are, rather, slowly built by the way any given symbol is associated with or dissociated from others in a corpus.[5]

Proposition 1: Religion is a Marginal Theme in the Press

Only 10 per cent of the articles in the test sample explicitly disclose

Islamic values. This is very few in comparison with other values found, such as nationalism (35 per cent), democracy (22 per cent), national law (20 per cent) or modernity (18 per cent). That reference to Islam should be important in the human rights agenda would none the less have been no surprise. As a matter of fact, the human rights question has been used significantly in recent Islamic texts, culminating in the Universal Islamic Declaration of Human Rights,[6] in which, unsurprisingly, observance of human rights is considered not as positive law but as part of the believer's duties.

Proposition 2: Islam Is Not the Explanation for Everything

Islamic reference is, on the contrary, randomly distributed in the press discourse among many other themes. In no way does it structure meaning. Here are its most surprising failures of relevance.

1. Contrary to what prejudice may suggest, no association could be found between Islam and events such as the Israeli–Palestinian conflict or the second Gulf War, or the issue of women's rights.

2. In the media coverage of human rights, Islam, either threatened or proclaimed, bears no relation to political actors except, unsurprisingly, the Islamists.

3. In the semantic field of 'actions', only disinformation calls for Islam. Even state attributes such as normalization and constraint are unrelated to religion in the Maghrebi press.

4. In the semantic field of 'values', Islam appears irrelevant to nationalism and human rights, except in Morocco. See proposition 3 below.

Proposition 3: Culturally, Islam is also a Product of the Maghreb's Political Systems

In fact, Islam itself may be given instrumental meaning in political competition and thus may vary considerably according to contexts and actors. The neoculturalist theory must be recalled here. According to this theory, culture and systems of representations (among which is religion) are not invariable. Nor are they independent variables influencing social systems; instead, they are influenced by social actors and political systems.[7] This theoretical postulate perfectly fits our findings concerning the Maghreb: Islam is no abnormal phenomenon in the eyes of sociology. Here is why.

In the Maghrebi mainstream press, the religious variable seems to be marked with two traits having nothing to do with the Sunna or the Koran, being instead correlated with a contingent phenomenon, the growth of radical Islam in the Maghreb. The first trait is a common precarious status. As a rule, radical Islamist newspapers are banned. As for the authorized press, it is controlled either by the rulers or by sheltering political parties. Consequently, it discloses an Islamic vision that is either official or, at the very least, very cautious not to threaten the image of dominant actors. The second trait is common languages patterns. Its status being so fragile in the whole Maghreb, the religious variable produces a pattern that is common in Algeria, Morocco and Tunisia. In all three countries, the religious variable serves to discuss the growth of radical Islam, often portrayed as antithetical to 'authentic Islam'.

For the rest, the representations of Islam vary from one country to another.

Algerian particularities

Human rights were at the heart of any legitimacy discourse during our observation period. At the same time, the Algerian state went on proclaiming its right to protect 'authentic Islam' as an essential component of the national identity. This may explain why the Algerian press, unlike its Moroccan and Tunisian counterparts, rarely discussed human rights and Islam separately (Islam is overrepresented 4.8 times in the semantic field of human rights). Algeria was even the only Maghrebi country where Islam was overrepresented in one of the agenda's main topics. Interestingly, such intense cohabitation of two different value systems, one being religious and the other being a component of positive law, serves less to discuss the controversial compatibility of Islam and human rights than to stigmatize the radical type of Islam, precisely the type that is competing for power but whose party and newspapers have been banned. Meanwhile, the press keeps relatively silent about the state terrorizing its citizens: the role of the military in the massacres cannot be on the agenda.[8]

Besides this blatant self-censorship, the turgid prose of the Algerian press also stands out with the following four semantic patterns. First, references to Islam never appear in relation to governmental topics. Islam is never referred to when state agents (ministers, civil servants, judges, the military) are staged. This is how the press avoids evoking a state legitimacy crisis. Second, there is a constant dissociation of Islam and the people's right to build its future. When the latter appears, the other is absent and vice versa. It is worth noticing that in the Algerian press, the meaning of 'the people's right' differs considerably from the prescriptions of the Universal Declaration of Human Rights. While the latter refers to self-determination, through mechanisms such as referendums and elections, the Algerian sense is closer to the people's right to a better future. Moreover, Islam is never associated with electoral procedures but rather with an alleged popular will – presumably violated, usually by the Islamists – which the elite promotes and safeguards. This is in spite of the fact that the legislative election of 1991–92 was interrupted before the end of the process, when it became obvious that the FIS was about to win the race.

Understandably, the mere idea of the FIS winning the election, even if amply discussed in the press, cannot be associated with Islam. On the contrary, Islam appears and is overrepresented only when the press writes about terrorism (Islam is overrepresented 3.5 times) or FIS attacks (3.75 times).

The third characteristic is that religious references in the Algerian press seldom appear alone, but instead are usually accompanied by other values like nationalism, modernity, democracy and human rights. This is also an official technique by which Islam is dissociated from the real event (the coup, the state regulation, etcetera) but overvalued by its semantic linkage to vague qualifiers of political morality.

Fourth, contrary to what one may expect and contrary to the nationalist aspect of radical Islam,[9] any religious references challenging the official discourse of the rulers have been washed out of the press; these are now associated with European actors who support the regime: governments, advocacy organizations, the media, international economic organizations, portrayed no more as enemies of the Algerian nation but as emblematic figures of modernity, secularity and liberalism.

The religious references in the Algerian press, during the observation period at least, were strictly in line with the rulers' discourse.

Moroccan Islam

Morocco is more the realm of triumphant Islam. Religious values more seldom appear as threatened (1.7 per cent of the articles, in contrast with 10.8 per cent for Algeria and 14.5 per cent for Tunisia). They are randomly distributed in the Moroccan body of articles considered, and thus do not structure its meaning. Such a finding is not surprising in a country where the head of state is also a religious leader, *Amir Al-Mou'minin* (Commander of the Faithful), where the constitution forbids anyone to challenge Islam or the monarchy and where radical Islam is less visible than in Algeria and Tunisia.

Moroccan Islam is basically nationalist (Islam is overrepresented fifteen times in the vicinity of nationalist symbols). It does not need to be supported by other values, such as modernity and democracy, and it recurrently proclaims both its kinship with the Arab Muslim nation (as in Algeria) and the founding 'epic of independence'. Quotations from the Koran, ritual Islamic formulas, the duty of *jihad* (meaning both holy war and struggle for one's spiritual growth), war actions (*qital* or killing, armed resistance, sacrifice, struggle) and heroic virtues (genius, pride, nationalism, wisdom, greatness, heroism) appear frequently and in a rich, diversified style. Moroccan Islam, in the nationalist-warrior fashion, always defeated the 'crusades' (a commonly used term) launched by its external enemies: both the enemies of the Arab nation (Zionism and blasphemous Western Christianity) and the enemies of the Moroccan nation (colonialism). It has always protected its borders, both Moroccan (the Sahara issue) and pan-Arab (Palestine, Iraq, etcetera).

Like Algerian Islam, the Moroccan version also employs mental cliché. In the Moroccan press, however, cliché is manifested less by political taboos (that would be difficult in a pluralist and conflictual public forum like Morocco) than by allusive formulas (enemies, the coalition of colonizers) and the staging of mythical figures (Morocco of the future, Noble and Holy Jerusalem, the Eternal Nation deploying against its enemies) challenging mythical enemies ('Israel from the Euphrates to the Nile', 'Zionist networks', or any other invader).

As jointly manufactured by the monarchy and the national movement, the triumphal nationalist Islam of the Moroccan press also belongs to the realm of constitutional rule where it is forbidden to challenge the founding symbols of Morocco: the Throne, Islam and territorial integrity. Islam in the Moroccan press is thus the prevailing code of political communication, built upon ancient and recent wars in which Morocco participated. By the same token, it is a seduction discourse targeting a Muslim readership and serving to cultivate a good public image of the Moroccan political elite (both the Makhzen and the clientilist elite around the Throne and the national movement) for whom it is the *de jure* and *de facto* mouthpiece.

Such symbolic constructions already challenge common clichés about political Islam. Al-Afghani's vision of Islam, unfavourable to any segmentation of the community of believers, is incompatible with the idea of a nation state. In contrast, Algerian and Moroccan Islam, while challenging 'American imperialism' and 'French colonialism' in the name of the *Umma Al-Islamyia* (the Islamic Nation), also stem from a local nationalist reflex. The nation's borders being so inconsistent and identity so polysemic, both Al-Afghani and Burgat are correct.

Tunisia's intellectual poverty

Tunisian institutions may be more secular. Notwithstanding that, Ben Ali violently repressed radical Islam and civil society. Political violence was paralleled by a gradual impoverishment of the president's legitimacy discourse, while security was stealthily given priority over human rights in the Tunisian public forum. Such praetorian logic also marked the discourse of the press.

The Tunisian press correlates religious references with the agenda of 'subversion' and 'terrorism' (the attacks at Kebili, Kasserine, Bab Souika, the plot to down Ben Ali's plane with a Stinger missile) in order to denounce the project of a theocratic state, otherwise depicted as an 'imam state'. The language of the press is much more affected by the obsession with the community of all believers than in Morocco and Algeria. This is, first, because representations of radical Islam appear most of the time in conjunction with its symbolic opposite, 'liberating Islam', and, second, because Islam, in its liberating posture, is evoked more often (17.6 per cent of the articles) in the Tunisian press than in the Algerian (9.6 per cent) and Moroccan (7.7 per cent). Interestingly, Tunisian Islam absolutely *never* structures meaning in language. In the Tunisian press, Islam suffers from an obvious semantic poverty, which is unexpected in a Muslim country. Is it because of the more secularist tradition in Tunisia? Is it self-censorship imposed on the press by the authoritarianism? Is Islam the exclusive competence of the 'President of all the Tunisians'? Or is such semantic weakness the consequence of the prevailing intellectual poverty in a country where thinking has become a tricky game? Could all these hypotheses be at least partially true?

Conclusion

The answer to these questions is beyond the scope of this book. All we need to assess now is the fact that references to Islam do not have the same meaning in Morocco, Algeria and Tunisia. Our demonstration now comes to an end by validating the hypothesis with which this chapter started. Far from being unchangeable as a key factor in the Maghrebi press discourse, Islam is a pure product of political systems, each of them manipulating religion according to its own context. Is the phenomenon driven by relatively voluntary and spontaneous falsification? Or does it stem from a set of unconscious reflexes pertaining to press language and professional practices?

Without further discussion of that problem, we can at least conclude that the Maghrebi press contradicts the orientalist preconception of religion dominating politics in the Arab Muslim World. Upon reflection, this finding is in no way extraordinary: for many Muslims, as for many other human beings, there is a time for religious meditation and prayer, as there also is a time for public life. Faith in Allah may be important in the Islamic world but, for Maghrebi journalists, faith belongs in the private sphere.

What about political Islam, one might still object? In Muslim societies, does not consensus stem from Muslim peoples? Is not Islam the necessary reference in any power discourse? One American sociologist, Michael Hudson, first answered the objection by demonstrating that Islam can be a basis for legitimacy and an authoritarian resource on the one condition that it be deprived of any substantive meaning. In a way, this corresponds to a secularizing process, with the exception of two other manifestations of political Islam: the *Islam of challengers*, basically banned and claiming political power, and *scientific Islam*, about which narrow, learned circles of jurists, writers, philosophers and other highly cultivated actors have not yet agreed concerning whether Islam should be unitary (Mawdudi, Qutb, Al-Afghani, Al-Banna, etcetera) or pluralistic (Qaddafi, Abd-Al-Raziq, Al-Ashmawi, Zakaria, Al-Turabi, Al-Ghannouchi).[10]

Moreover, as we have seen, whether in its challenging or its learned posture, Islam is far from being a body of eternal and invariable doctrines.[11] As for day-to-day Islam in the public forum, that of the Maghrebi press for instance, we now know that it does not over-influence the political actors' behaviour. Thus, the orientalist prejudice, according to which Islam gives meaning to everything on Earth, is flawed. Of course, Islam sometimes does inspire political projects and law. It is also a tool in the struggle for power, varying according to the individual consciences of political actors as well as their respective strategies and the different contexts of political interaction.

Notes

1. Jean-Claude Vatin (1990) 'Les Partis (pris) démocratiques: Perceptions occidentales dans le monde arabe', *Démocratie et démocratisation dans le monde arabe*, Cairo: Cedej, p. 30.
2. It was Bruno Étienne who first coined the expression 'radical Islam'. See his (1978) *L'Islamisme radical*, Paris: Hachette.
3. Algeria, Morocco and Tunisia all ratified the Covenant. Thus they are bound by the international human rights texts, which has provided me with a useful and systematic analysis grid.
4. All the articles concerning human rights issues were chosen from the four front pages and four back pages of Morocco's *Al-Ittihad Al-Ishtiraki*, *Al-Bayane* (Arabic version), *L'Opinion* and *Le Matin* (four prominent dailies representing the main political forces), and Algeria's four largest dailies, *Al-Khabar*, *Liberté*, *Le Soir d'Algérie* and *Al-Watan*, while from Tunisia's poorly developed press, I had to use whole issues of all available newspapers. The period of observation comprises the years 1988 and 1993, plus a one-year period from July 1990 to June 1991. The content analysis focuses on variables such as information sources, polemical discourse, representation of the rulers and the ruled, values and agenda. The results shed light on the links between the political dynamics of each country, media coverage, and the civic culture. A detailed account of this analysis, its corpus, sampling techniques, variables, methodology and techniques of measurement, can be found in my article 'Marginalité et instrumentalité de l'Islam dans la presse du Maghreb Central', *Social Compass*. Vol. 44, No. 1, March 1977, pp. 55–70.
5. On association/dissociation, consider the following. Let A and B be two variables. There is association when A is overrepresented in articles where B is present with chi-square values of 0.01 or less. On the contrary, dissociation is when A is underrepresented in articles where B is present with chi-square values of 0.01 or less. (Chi-square is a statistical test measuring how strongly related two variables can be. The lower the chi-square value, the stronger the relationship.) Association and dissociation relationships between two variables were measured by indexes of overrepresentation and underrepresentation, as in the following example.

   Let A and B be either present (A_1, B_1) or absent (A_0, B_0) in the following frequency distribution:

	A_1	A_0	Total
B_1	75%	25%	100%
B_0	91%	9%	100%

   $$(A_1 B_1)/(A_0 B_1) = 75/91 = 0.82$$

   This equation discloses a relationship in which A is less likely to appear when B is present.

   In other words, A and B are dissociated when $(A_1,B_1) / (A_0,B_1) < 1$. The smaller the index value, the stronger the dissociation is. On the contrary, A and B are associated when $(A_1,B_1) / (A_0,B_1) > 1$. The higher the index value, the stronger the association. Finally, there is no semantic relation between A and B when the index value is close to 1.

6. As reproduced in, among others, Étienne (1978).
7. See Bertrand Badie and Guy Hermet (1990) *Politique comparée*, Paris: PUF, pp. 45–58.
8. This comment is anything but polemical, given the immensity of evidence brought by Youcef Bedjaoui, Abbas Aroua and Meziane Aït-Larbi (1999) in *An Inquiry into the Algerian Massacres*, Geneva: Hoggar (1,400 pages excluding the appendices).
9. The nationalist dimension of the Islamist movement was described by François Burgat (1988) *L'Islamisme au Maghreb: La Voix du Sud*, Paris: Karthala.
10. Bernard Lewis has only written about this learned Islam, using texts dating from the orthodox tradition until the fall of the Ottoman Empire in the early twentieth century. His belief that religion is ever-present in social life may be valid for such an ancient body of texts, but it becomes anachronistic when extrapolated to the dawn of the third millennium.
11. This view is contrary to what Hamid Ennayat proposes in (1982) *Modern Islamic Political Thought*, Austin: University of Texas Press, p. 135.

11

FREEDOM OR TYRANNY?
PERSPECTIVES IN THE MAGHREB

Tyranny cannot easily take root without willingness on the part of the victims or, at the very least, some of them. Weaker political elites in the Maghreb allowed themselves to be subdued in the hope of being granted a share in power. But contrary to their expectations they found themselves even further isolated and gagged as a result of these dangerous alliances, while civil institutions continued to lose the capability to inform the public freely and to challenge the regime. The ensuing state monopoly on public speech has served to produce an illusory consensus around a mock democracy and to keep the public in the dark as the totalitarian state tightened its grip.

Such was the drama that the twentieth century saw unfolding in the Maghreb's public forums. Although the days of ordeal are apparently far behind in still-authoritarian Morocco, the last chapter of the story has yet to be written for Algeria and Tunisia. Will tyranny or dissent win the upper hand?

Algeria

Over these twenty years of civil war, the Algerian government has almost never investigated murders, bombs, massacres and abductions. Those responsible for the deaths of hundreds of thousands of civilians are not only free but have been offered immunity from prosecution through President Bouteflika's *Concorde civile* programme.

Meanwhile, inside Algeria as well as abroad, rumours and testimonies have kept pointing the finger at the military, while NGOs have continued to call for an international commission of inquiry. In France, two books were best-sellers: *Qui a tué à Bentalha* (Who did the killing in

Bentalha?) by Nasroulah Yous and *La sale guerre* (The Dirty War) by
Habib Souaidia, an Algerian lieutenant exiled in France.[1] The hasty and
suspicious way in which General Khaled Nezzar slipped out of France
and headed home in spring 2001, after he had been charged with the
crime of torture, succeeded in transforming the military victory over
Islamist guerrillas into a political fiasco. High-profile members of the
Algerian parliament resigned in a movement of protest against the
regime's failure to contain violence and protect its citizens. A decision
issued by the International Court of Justice in The Hague later stated
that prosecuting a state representative while in office is illegal (14
February 2002).

This way, General Nezzar thought he had the opportunity to take
revenge on Souaidia and came back to France to sue the latter for libel.
General Nezzar lost his case after a well-publicized trial that served to
bring the military's secret role in the Algerian tragedy into the glare of
the media's spotlight and public scrutiny.[2]

Such events have become known to the Algerian people through
foreign media. For instance, the Qatari television station Al-Jazeerah on
29 May 2001 questioned impunity for crime in the Arab world generally
and, in particular, General Nezzar's shameful escape to Algiers.

Meanwhile, dissident circles such as the Algerian League for the
Defence of Human Rights (LADDH), the Algerian Gathering of Youth
(RAJ) and the Disappeared Citizens' Families Committee on the civilian
side, but also the Algerian Free Officers' Movement (MAOL) on the
army's side, have consolidated their information and lobbying networks. Can the dissidents become credible enough to pressure foreign
governments and international public opinion to stop supporting the
military? With an anonymous membership, the credibility of MAOL
has remained low. Nobody knows who they are. In contrast, the
LADDH, the RAI and the Disappeared Citizens' Families' Committee
have famous leaders who draw enough attention to gain occasionally
the front-page attention of the international press. Algerian dissident
circles have not achieved transborder solidarity links with international
actors, as have their Tunisian counterparts, however.

Tunisia

However uncertain the future may seem, political change has
obviously accelerated in Tunisia. As mentioned earlier, the National
Pact has disintegrated into a passive consensus of isolated actors, while
the international media and the domestic public were progressively fed

with dissident information, which mobilized international support for Tunisia's dissidents. In this way, social links started to be rebuilt, until overt resistance appeared with the foundation in December 1998 of the National Council for Freedoms in Tunisia (CNLT). The CNLT includes dissidents from the now-neutralized mainstream civil institutions like the Tunisian General Union of Labour (UGTT), the Socialist Democrats' Movement (Tunisia) (MDS) party, the Tunisian Women's Association for Democracy (ATFD) and the Tunisian League of Human Rights (LTDH). Although formally left outside of the CNLT, activists from the extreme left-wing Tunisian Communist Labour Party (PCOT) and the Rally for an Alternative International Development (RAID), which is affiliated to the anti-globalization movement ATTAC, also resorted to open dissent. Resistance has also spread to the Tunisian bar, of which Bechir Essid (see Chapter 1) was elected president in summer 2001.[3]

Outstanding public figures such as Omar Mestiri, Mustapha Ben Jaafar, Khemaïs Chammari, Moncef Marzouki, Khadidja Cherif and Radhia Nasraoui have been in the spotlights of the global human rights movement, and have released credible information and mobilized supporters through public campaigning not only in France but also in Belgium, Switzerland, the UK, Canada, Egypt and Morocco.

Meanwhile, international NGOs supporting them have been given opportunities to launch joint programmes and actions. In the year 2000, for instance, the United Nations Human Rights Commission decided to appoint a Secretary-General's Representative for the Defenders of Human Rights. In order to help the Secretary General's representative to perform his duties with efficiency, the International Federation for Human Rights (IFHR, in Paris) and the World Organization Against Torture (WOAT, in Geneva) jointly set up an 'Observatoire', or reporting centre, in charge of reporting to him all threats to human rights activists.

Similarly, the Euro-Mediterranean Human Rights Movement (EMHRN) was established in January 1997 on the initiative of North- and South-based human rights organizations, in response to the Barcelona Declaration issued by twenty-seven countries (including Algeria, Morocco and Tunisia) and the establishment of a Euro-Mediterranean partnership officially committed to democracy, human rights and the rule of law.

In these two latter cases, not only do international NGOs join in lobbying campaigns but they justify such action by new international agreements on human rights, in such a way that the signatories to these agreements are constantly reminded of their commitments.

One early spectacular achievement of this informal transnational network in the international public forum was the journalist Tawfik Ben Brik's hunger strike, which was publicised by Reporters sans Frontières and the Committee to Protect Journalists (in Washington) soon after the release of the book *Notre ami Ben Ali*.[4]

Under such circumstances, Ben Ali's regime has started to lose support even within the state apparatus. One late and blatant challenge to the rule of unanimity took place on 6 July 2001 when the French daily *Le Monde* published Judge Mokhtar Yahyaoui's open letter to Ben Ali:

> I am writing to you in protest at the dramatic situation of the Tunisian justice system. As a matter of fact, things have gone so far as to deprive the court and the judges of their constitutional powers as an independent institution of the Republic committed to justice.
>
> [...] The Tunisian judges are frustrated and irritated by being forced to reach decisions under the orders of the political authority.
>
> [...] Under constant harassment, the Tunisian judges are left without any resource to perform their duties … they must face intimidation and coercion to such a degree that they cannot express their wills and convictions.'[5]

While Judge Yahiaoui was writing to Ben Ali, the Tunisian Journalists' Association (AJT) suddenly recovered from its long silence and spoke out in support of Sihem Ben Sedrine, who had just been put in jail and claimed freedom of expression.[6]

Such news is rapidly spread among Tunisians by travellers coming back home. It is also broadcast by alternative Arabic television stations, such as Al-Jazeerah and Al-Mustakillah which put dissident figures on the world stage.

This is all taking place in an economic context that is summed up thus by Laurent Guiter: a high unemployment rate (15 per cent in 1997), insufficient private investment (1.5 per cent of the gross national product in 1999, mainly in the energy sector), sparse foreign investment, and a 20 per cent loss of jobs from 1989 to 1996.[7] This, added to growing discontent among workers and students and a continuous hunger strike movement inside prisons since spring 2000, does not help to sustain the image of Tunisia as being the 'African Dragon' (Ben Ali's slogan).

Since the beginning of 2001, the increasing challenges to the regime have provoked more open state violence, including beatings on the street, threats, harassment, torture and prison for student demonstrators and the main dissident figures.[8] This state violence has in turn given rise to more international campaigning.

In this spiralling process, Ben Ali is losing his legitimacy and his partners while maintaining the same propaganda scheme. Thus, after the September 11 attack in the USA, he launched a new programme of dialogue among civilizations and a new large-scale judicial campaign against his opponents, accusing them of being associated with terrorism abroad. Ben Ali's blatant incapacity to produce an alternative legitimation strategy after the previous one failed, as well as his outright denial of a terror politics that has become well known abroad, make the prospects for the regime to adapt to increasing demands for freedom appear insignificant.

The question is not so much how long President Ben Ali can stay in power before popular riots, or other challenges, trigger the downfall of his dictatorial regime, but rather what will happen then. The future of Tunisia may be called 'democratic transition' in public discourse but civil society networks (parties, newspapers, unions ...) may have been too deeply ravaged to be able to take over. Unless the international public, not only governments, significantly support the emerging dissident forces, another in-house revolution is likely, either with or without Ben Ali, and democratic reforms may thus be postponed once again.

Notes

1. Nasroulah Yous (2000), *Qui a tué a Bentalha? Chronique d'une massacre ou moncé*, Paris: La Découvert; Habib Souaidia (2001), *La sale guerre: le témiogroge d'un ancien officier des forces spéciales de l'armée algérienne*, Paris: La Découverte.
2. The proceedings of the trial were published as *La procès de la 'sale guerre'. Algérie: le général-major Khaled Nezzar contre le lieutenant Souaidia*, Paris, La Découverte, 2002, notes by François Gèze and Salima Mellah.
3. Up until the time of this book's publication, the banned Islamic movement Al-Nadha has kept silent. However, its activists are most likely to be active in Tunisia.
4. Jean-Pierre Tuquoi and Nicolas Beau (1999), *Notre ami Ben Ali: l'envers du miracle tunisien*, Paris: La Découverte, p. 227.
5. *Le Monde*, 6 July 2001, and the electronic bulletin of the Committee for the Defence of Liberties and Human Rights in Tunisia (CRLDHT) for 14 July.
6. In a communiqué sent to Agence France-Presse (AFP), 30 June 2001, and reproduced by Naros (http://naros.8m.net).
7. 'Laurent Guiter (1997, 1999) 'Tunisie: Chronique intérieure', *Annuaire de l'Afrique du Nord*, pp. 295–317.
8. Namely Najib Hosni, Moncef Marzouki, Mohammed Moada and Sihem Ben Sedrine, who were sent back to jail, and also Khadija Cherif and Radhia Nasraoui, who were assaulted in public by security representatives.

12

TOWARDS A SOCIOLOGY OF CITIZENSHIP IN A GLOBALIZING WORLD

As this comparative analysis of political change in the Maghreb is coming to an end, it is useful to broaden the scope of investigation in order to provide political science and political communication research with more efficient tools for understanding the universal drama of the confiscation and reconquest of freedom of speech and human dignity.

Globalization, as a matter of fact, has not always weakened state borders or induced greater freedom of speech for the individual, as we have seen in the Maghreb. Such was also the case in the former Soviet bloc, and it may be the lesson to be drawn from the vast series of dictatorship collapses and revivals that took place during the last two decades of the second millennium following Gorbachev's liberalization reforms in the USSR. At that moment, a wave of change swept around the world from Brazil to Mozambique and the Philippines. In this respect, the Maghrebi case provides an opportunity to sketch a sociology of citizenship in this globalizing era. At the beginning of this book, I proposed that the Tunisian 'Plato's cave', the mission of the Algerian 'guardians of democracy' and the Moroccan 'ordeal of Sisyphus' do no more than reproduce the archetypal story of humanity's destiny. Inasmuch as my proposal was correct, the scenarios taking place in the Maghrebi public forums should apply elsewhere as well.

From the episodes of democratic fervour of these two decades, two scenarios emerged that may contribute to the theory of democracy. In one of them, the rare one, the process has led to happy outcomes, as in Hungary, Slovakia, Poland and Germany (Semelin 1997 and Goban-Klas 1994). However, an adverse and more common scenario could also be observed as the USSR and Yugoslavia exploded into competing nations fighting wars of ethnic cleansing. Further south, in Algeria and Tunisia, other rationales of cleansing (religion, gender and politics) have followed the second scenario. In none of these countries has democracy been consolidated (contrary to what Diamond [1997] observed in several 'third-wave' democratic transitions), but the democratization process was instead halted and set back drastically without encountering serious civil resistance.

Such unhappy 'endings' of democratic transition took place in a globalizing context where transborder influences are far from insignificant. As we have seen, one first transborder effect of the prevailing civil submissive attitude consisted in the dissidents' initial isolation in the international public forum. Once the challenging dissident discourse had been muted, in the Maghreb, Africa and Central Asia likewise, new dictatorships could more easily neutralize public awareness of actual events (Downing 1996 and Semelin 1997).

By doing this, dictators did not only profit by civil submissiveness. There was also a second effect of transborder influence. In the international media as much as in the secret realms of diplomacy and international trade, new dictatorships found docile allies willing to relay disinformation to more developed democracies. In such a favourable conjuncture, new dictators could saturate the international public agenda with horror stories portraying new villains threatening law and order. This is how international public opinion long remained deaf to dissident information and, consequently, unaware of the revival of dictatorial rule following democratic transitions in Algeria, Tunisia and elsewhere. In the ensuing blindness and muteness spreading throughout the global forum, the new dictators had an important margin of manoeuvre for consolidating their legitimacy.[1]

Three questions now need to be reassessed if we are to understand better the phenomenon of setbacks to democratic transition. First, what causes the potential for civilian protest sometimes to drop close to zero in the political arena? Second, when such is the case, how is it that nobody seems to be aware that what is really going on is the pandemic spread of what we may call Tunisian muteness throughout the recently closed down public arena and a virulent 'spiralling silence' (Noelle-Neuman 1993) in the international arena? And third, what could possibly enable civil society to revive and reconquer freedom of speech and what role do transnational media and public opinion play in the process? These questions may become crucial issues in the development of the theory of political change.

The 'dangerous alliances' hypothesis has slowly emerged in this book as an answer to the first question. This answer contrasts with the hypothesis of O'Donnell and others who hold that 'covenants' are an efficient pathway for democratic transition because they serve to protect the right of all the political actors to survive in political deadlocks and crises (1986, 1991).[2] On the contrary, democratic transition may evolve into the dangerous alliances scenario whenever the weaker political actors feel incapable of negotiating the terms of their political survival. The latter then find no other solution than unconditional renunciation of freedom of speech in exchange for sheltering behind the shield of an almighty political saviour[3] in whom they see their only hope. These dangerous alliances will give way not to 'paradoxical democracy' (Ferrié and Santucci 2000), nor to 'mazes of democratic transition' (Mossadeq 2000), but to the Tunisian muteness syndrome, a social pathology that drastically aborts the democratic process.

As for the second troublesome problem, the lack of awareness of the international public in the face of muted public forums, Herman and Chomsky (1988) argue that the political economy of the media hinders them from disclosing the secrets of national diplomatic staff and international trade relations. However, Herman and Chomsky's explanation leaves one further question unanswered. As a matter of fact, the information self-censored by the mainstream media will finally become known. When that happens, how will the latter maintain their credibility in the eyes of their audience? As explained in Chapter 8, distortion in international information is the product of a complex system comprising marketing requirements, routine journalistic practices and a rhetoric of objectivity allowing journalists to speak amply about the unknown, before 'discovering' afterwards that the government had been lying. In the meantime, the media discourse will have blindly fed on propaganda sources, thus contributing to the 'spiralling silence' prevailing in the international public forum in the face of emerging dictatorships. Algeria is but one case among many.

Finally, days of ordeal do not last forever, and an answer to the third question is provided by recent developments in North Africa and the former Soviet Union. Free speech, after being lost, can be reconquered; specifically, the dissidents' connection with media networks can gradually isolate dictatorships in a hostile public forum. This scenario provides empirical evidence for my third hypothesis about the rising influence of unarmed prophets on international public opinion.

Underlying these three explanations – namely the prevalence of dangerous alliance between civil society and those in power, the distortions and limitations to the information that makes it into the international arena, and the nevertheless sometimes pervasive influence of 'unarmed prophets' on political change – is the classical assumption that only institutional counterweights or fragmentation/differentiation of political power can prevent tyranny. However, it is now necessary to develop further the classical vision of political science by adding to it the three dimensions of political change that have been traditionally neglected and whose importance has been illustrated in this book:

1. Public communication phenomena are central to democracy and democratization processes.

2. Political systems do not evolve in a vacuum. Rather, political change is influenced by transborder influences that either help dictatorial rule to extend its life span or trigger its downfall.

3. Nonstate actors' roles in this process are unpredictable, but decisive.

Owing to the lack of consideration of these three dimensions, the classical theory of democracy has long looked like a static and prescriptive model, aimed at defining what the democratic political system consists of, how it works, and practically nothing more. Such was the theory of checks and balances according to which the legislature, the judiciary and the executive had to be autonomous from each other. Such also was the idea that only a sovereign people can provide the legitimacy that representative government requires (from Montesquieu 1995 to Badie and Hermet 1984 and Leca and Grawitz 1985). The features of the opposite form of political system, totalitarianism, have likewise been established in the same static perspective (Arendt 1973), without considering the fact that any given form of political system (democracy, totalitarianism, etcetera) has to evolve from revolution to consolidation, followed by decadence and, possibly, disintegration. Accordingly, political scientists are sometimes led to say that neither ideal-type democracy (Zylberberg 1993) nor totalitarianism (Badie and Hermet 1984) exist.

It was not until the second half of the last millennium that the functionalist school of thought,[4] and the sociology of democracy[5] started to look more closely at the relationship between political systems and their environments (civil society, minorities, pluralism etcetera), opening the pathway to an understanding of political change. The sociology of democratizations[6] and the sociology of action (Touraine 1992) now see in civil society/social movements the decisive impulse toward democratization construction and/or destruction. In the face of this recent research work, the static and prescriptive model is not without value. However, it cannot, in its present form, explain why dictatorships fall and eventually revive and why republican government has proven so unstable (Ferrero 1942). It needs to be resketched in a more dynamic perspective.

Thus, after first discussing the political systems model and the classical model of democracy, I will attempt to reformulate the classical model into a dynamic one, integrating my three hypotheses into a model of the public communication process.

A Political Systems Model

The political system can be portrayed as a public forum where civil and state actors interact in alliance / conflict games. A first set of games takes place among the civil actors themselves as they produce and reproduce civil society and its institutions. A second set stems from the state actors' producing or reproducing of the state machinery. A third set of games is played out when civil / state interaction modifies the features of the public arena by either opening or closing it. All together, these three central variables, civil actors, state actors and the public arena, can be related in a strategic explanation of political change.

Above, I have defined civil society as a more or less cohesive network of institutional and individual actors, autonomous and functionally differentiated from one another and from the state machinery, and *capable of challenging not only the rulers but also the rules of governance.*[7] Such a definition is in line with the liberal postulate that tyranny can be neutralized by a balance of power between the executive, the legislature and the judiciary (Hobbes, Locke, Montesquieu and Tocqueville). My proposed variation of the classical theory states that civil society has to be considered as a possible fourth counterweight positioned outside the state apparatus and *capable of challenging not only the rulers who happen to be in power at a particular point in time but also the rules of governance.*

The key word here is 'differentiated'. Without functional differentiation, which totalitarian systems lack because society has been systematically domesticated by the state apparatus, the checks and balances influence of civil society on state organization is hardly observed at all.

State organization
In this model, the state organization is included as one variable of the political system which, as explained by Easton (1965a and 1965b), also comprises its environment. Among the outputs of the state organiza-

tion are the allocation of resources, the production of rules of governance, and consensus regulation in the public arena. According to the classical theory of checks and balances, each of the three state powers have to be limited by the two others. This prevents them from performing the natural function of ever consolidating and expanding their respective powers.

The public forum

The public forum is not a physical location like the agora in ancient Greece or the Maghrebi *djamaa*, but a virtual reality delimited by what is, or becomes, visible in politics through its various platforms: public rumour, the media, parliament and the judiciary. Political platforms are interconnected in such a way that what happens in any one of them is likely to be reported and discussed in the others. It is precisely through these interconnections that consensus building, the production of collective representations (values, myths, ideologies and language) and public debates take place.

Conventionally, the public forum is said to be democratic if the political actors can oppose one another in a peaceful and competitive struggle for ideas and power. This democratic quality is in turn manifested by opposing viewpoints and controversial issues being recurrently exchanged in the public arena without any form of censorship of the political actors.

The actors can exchange roles (civil/state) and status (opponent, challenger, dissident, state agent) in the public forum.

The Classical Democratic Model

In the classical perspective, a democratic forum cannot exist unless certain systemic prerequisites are met outside the conduct of public exchanges. These prerequisites are to be met in the framework of institutionalized relations between the state and civil actors that allow public debate to take place. A first prerequisite for democracy holds that civil society can peacefully discharge its leaders from office whenever it so wishes. This rule allows access to and removal from office to be openly driven by legitimization and consensus-building processes in the public forum. Logically, a second requirement of democracy is the opportunity bestowed upon any citizen to partake in electoral campaigns and public debates as a candidate, a voter and a contender. Understandably, these two conditions are most unlikely to be met unless a third has been achieved: the presence of an active and legal set of challengers and opposition parties that sustain ideas and programmes different from the rulers'.

Together, these three conditions, namely legitimacy / consensus-regulated hold of political power, free elections and political pluralism, are essential but not sufficient conditions of democracy. The despotic exercise of power is always prowling unless the magistracy is independent and immune to political pressures and an unobstructed flow of information is secured by a pluralist press. Without an independent court of justice and a pluralist press, how could civil society manage to keep state politics under its control and influence its course?

More specifically, without the free flow of information, how can a pluralist civil society wish to dismiss those in power if the competing political actors are unable to convey information to the people through the media network? Can there be any worthwhile debate on public issues if the public is poorly informed? The implicit answer to such questions is that the prescriptive model rests upon a pluralist public forum. Authoritarian politics, in contrast, requires major if not total 'domestication' of the public forum, its interconnected platforms and actors.

Two reasons explain why the static model of democracy can only be called prescriptive. First, the norms it provides for evaluating a given democratic system are anything but realistic. Second, the model ignores how a political system can evolve towards the seldom – if ever – completely achieved democratic form, and what objective social factors will bring it closer to or further away from the ideal norm.

A Dynamic Conflictual Model of Democracy

A significant advance in political theory was achieved when Dahl (1971) proposed a more realistic concept, polyarchy, which leaves room for imperfection and change. Generally speaking, polyarchy means imperfect modern democracy. In Dahl's vision, two conditions must be met for a given public forum to be called a polyarchy. First, a vast number of political (civil and state) actors can play a part on the stage (access is the quantitative dimension of polyarchy); and, second, most of the political spectrum of political opinion is visible (freedom of expression looks more like a qualitative dimension).

The concept of polyarchy, or imperfect democracy, makes room for change and improvement, contrary to the prescriptive classical concept of democracy. As a matter of fact, the objective conditions that make polyarchy possible were only partially explained by the classical theory of checks and balances among the three main branches of the state (Montesquieu, Toqueville, Locke). Dahl and after him modern political sociologists (Tilly 1983 and 2000, Graziano 1996) have therefore, through their shared concern with participation and opposition, added another dimension, an additional counterweight, to the classical vision of democracy.

As stated above, a functional differentiation of society is needed for the checks-and-balances effect of the fourth locus of power to operate effectively.[8] Otherwise, an undifferentiated society can do nothing but serve its rulers. The evolution of a given political system towards the polyarchic form can, thus, be portrayed as a differentiation process.

The development of civil society has been portrayed as a differentiation process (see, for instance, O'Donnell *et al.* [1986 and 1991]) through which civil institutions gain more and more autonomy from the state machinery. It has been too cautiously labelled the European model by Schmitter (Cansino 1997), as of course it also takes place elsewhere.[9] However, the differentiation process does not take place by magic. In the case of Morocco, I have explained it as follows.

Differentiation

Differentiation, as stated in Chapter 5, can be manifested empirically by the *established capacity* of a civil actor to exist without the help of the state, act without official authorization (or in spite of a formal ban), stand against state policies and publicly disagree with state authorities. *Established capacity* is proposed here as a key expression for defining the process and, as such, deserves a few observations:

1. The possibility of reversibility
A capacity that develops under certain conditions can reasonably start to decline in other circumstances. In other words, the differentiation process in society is theoretically reversible.

2. The postulate of minimal reciprocal dependency
Total differentiation has never been observed in any society. If sensible at all, the idea of total differentiation would imply a situation of permanent crisis leading to the disappearance of the political system; some degree of minimal reciprocal dependency between the state and civil society is necessary. Otherwise, the circulation of elites and their renewal within the power circles and civil participation in politics

would become inconceivable. This is why the state is sometimes defined as 'organized interdependence between rulers and ruled' (Boudon and Bourricaud 1982: 223).

3. Practical limits to the differentiation process
A practical problem of the differentiation process now needs to be raised: how far can the process go? At what point might the political system, torn between the competing strategies of state and civil actors, rupture? The problem of political stability is beyond the scope of this book but we can, none the less, recall that several systemic stabilizers (minimal agreements on political values, patterns of forming a consensus and, of course, the state's own organizational resources) in the Moroccan political development process have rendered such a rupture unlikely.

4. The methodological postulate of qualitative differentiation
Should differentiation be considered qualitative or quantitative in nature? Notwithstanding the problems of measurement, differentiation is best assessed by qualitative indicators being either present or absent, such as 'the capacity to act without official authorization' (which is by no means tantamount to 'always', 'seldom', or 'often' acting without official authorization). In other words, the recurrence of these qualitative indicators through different stages of historical evolution is needed in order to establish the civil actors' recurrent capacity to engage in autonomous action, from the initial unstable period to the stable phase of development of a polyarchy. What happens once may never happen again. So, recurrence over time of autonomous action is an essential component of the concept of differentiation. It indicates that civil autonomy is not merely conjunctural or, in other words, that polyarchy has advanced to the stage of stable institutionalization (Poland, Morocco, Egypt).

5. Two mutually exclusive categories?
One question could be raised here. Where does state organization start and civil society finish? The answer does not lie in the political actors themselves, as they can always decide to shift from a civil to a state role. As a matter of fact, such role shifts are frequent in the public forum. As for organic differentiation, it is not a valid indicator either, since state authority currently interferes with civilian private life on the one hand, and, on the other hand, it is far from being clear that one-party-system (non-polyarchic) mass organizations that are summoned and chaired

by state representatives are civil bodies. They may be composed of civilians but they are not civil. In other words, the only criterion of functional differentiation is the ability to act autonomously in the public forum. Furthermore, in a dynamic perspective, one must admit that the ever-changing and evolving phenomena of real life cannot be understood by merely suppressing their intrinsic ambiguity. If we are to understand political change at all, we will do it better by focusing on processes (merging/differentiation) than on clearcut (civil/state) typologies.

Conversely, and this is a second lesson to be drawn from the ambiguities of real life, it is not necessary for the development process to be fully accomplished, if completion is conceivable at all, for it to be qualified as 'stable'. Stability simply refers to an even balance of power in which the probabilities are remote that the development of a polyarchy be halted and set back. Such has not been the case in Tunisia, Algeria, and the several new states of Central Asia (Juviler 1998).

Input mobilization
Organizational inputs (such as economic resources, leadership, membership, legitimacy and appropriate organizational culture, information and communication channels) are to be mobilized by the civil actors in order to weaken their dependency on the state actors and thus strengthen their capability for autonomous action. Such a long-term process remains more or less predictable because it takes place in a complex and open system, the political system, where multiple actors produce ever-changing positioning strategies. This is why the development of polyarchy, even if successfully driven by civil institutions, can be nothing but slow, complex and unpredictable in the long run.

External solidarity
External solidarity is another ingredient of the process of social differentiation. How long can an isolated autonomous civil actor, however powerful and influential, resist being swallowed up by the state leviathan? As a matter of fact, the very concept of a civil society implies a relatively extensive network of institutional and individual actors, who will become more and more autonomous from the state as they develop their networks of external alliances and joint action. These networks also need time to prove trustworthy and efficient.

Perceived balance of power
Input mobilization, external solidarity and social differentiation have

been described, so far, as components of the polyarchy development process. Polyarchy development in turn must be explained as a process that does not happen mechanically but is driven by the subjective assessment each dominant actor may make of the balance of power. This assessment is, of course, largely inspired by previous experiences of power struggles: strategies that worked in the past are worth examining and, sometimes, repeating. Similarly, former failures are likely to supply lessons for the future. Political culture is moulded from history and tradition.

The necessity of civil pressure and unrest

As a given political system evolves towards the polyarchic form, conflictual but peaceful interactive games between the civil and state actors and the ensuing debates become increasingly intense and frequent. In academic circles, the prospects of polyarchy have been called into question by the controversies surrounding the relationship between civil society development and democratic reforms. Which should come first in order to support a favourable outcome for the other? Is it better that freedom be given or that it be struggled for? Haryk (1994), for one, argued that autocratic implementation of democratic institutions could succeed even while there was no strong network of civil institutions to promote and safeguard them. Unfortunately, the period he observed, only a few years of transition, was too short. In the long run, in Morocco for example, civic freedom has only been slowly won and consolidated through a differentiation process, being neither supported by democratic reforms nor totally destroyed by dangerous alliances. The former Soviet Union has followed a similar evolution (Downing 1996 and Goban-Klas 1994). The lesson to be drawn from comparative analysis in North Africa and the former Soviet Union is that public freedoms grow only under the pressure of public opinion. Without the latter, as in the cases of Algeria and Tunisia, democratic reforms are doomed. Political pluralism, as in Morocco and Poland, can none the less develop without democratic reforms if civil society can mobilize its organizational assets and allies. Polyarchy is then driven by a solid network of civil institutions that push the balance of power between civil and state actors to the point where the political cost of tyranny becomes unaffordable. The state actors then prefer to relinquish some of their coercive power in order to maintain political consensus around their incumbency. In no observed cases has democratic transition succeeded when simply implemented from above. From the experience of the late twentieth century, three cases, Gorbachev's *perestroika*, Algeria's short-lived democracy and President Ben Ali's New Era, invalidate the hypothesis of implemented-from-above democratic transition.

It must also be recalled that what matters most is not merely state/civil differentiation but the capability of each of the four powers to regulate the others. Accordingly, conflict and competition can take place between any spontaneous coalition of political actors. State organization does not react like a cohesive bloc under permanent civilian attack. In Italy, during the *Mani pulite* inquiry of winter 1993, for example, a judge (a judicial actor) and a handful of journalists (civil actors) challenged the corruption networks that were then permeating the political system. The government (the executive actor) was forced to resign as a result of their joint campaign.

Democratic transitions are reversible

In the light of the dynamic conflictual model described above, a stable unanimous consensus among all political actors concerning political ideology and discourse can be considered an unambiguous indicator of a closed public forum where only one role is possible: to applaud the author(s) of the present state of governance. No single case of spontaneous unanimity could be observed in any democratic transition. Likewise, in public forums of the former Soviet Union and of the Maghreb, once the civilian ability to protest had disappeared, only an artificial consensus could be manufactured, imposed through social anomie, censorship, corruption and political terror. Polyarchy regression is the exact opposite of the polyarchy development process. Polyarchy implies differentiation among the four powers, where unitary evolution means the merging of all political actors into a single role: serving the saviour.

In other words, democratic rule is reversible.

The Tunisian muteness syndrome

As described in this book, one practical example of unitary evolution is provided by the recent history of the Maghreb and the phenomenon of dangerous alliances that sometimes makes democratization veer off course. I have named this process the 'Tunisian muteness syndrome' not because it is Tunisian in nature, but merely because I observed it in Tunisia (just as the Ebola virus was so named after being first observed in Ebola although it is in no way restricted to the Ebola area). The Tunisian muteness syndrome differs from what Noelle-Neumann (1993) called the spiral of silence, a phenomenon driven by individuals' fear of social rejection. By contrast, the Tunisian syndrome is driven not by fear of rejection but by hopes of political promotion. Tunisian muteness is brought about in the 'dangerous alliances' scenario when democratic rule is given away by civil actors in exchange for power, or so they are led to believe.[10] This scenario unfolds through the following steps in the Maghreb.

Uncertainty
Unitary evolution can start during those insecure days that O'Donnell *et al.* (1986, 1991) call democratic transition. At such periods, as they correctly observe, uncertainty arises from two sources: power (what do the new rules actually mean? Will they, the rulers, really make it democratic?) and the rising star of opposition in the public forum (will it not destroy any hope for our political dreams and ambitions?).

Temptation
Being positioned between Scylla and Charybdis, the democracy-oriented actors can be offered what up until then has seemed beyond hope: their share of power, providing that they agree to join in a strategy of eradicating their common enemy. Such may be the proposal a new political saviour makes to them while looking for civilian support after a takeover.

Dangerous alliance
In such circumstances, some civil actors become less vigilant and demanding. They join in authoritarian, dangerous alliances with a political saviour in a desperate move to escape a worse outcome, thus giving their saviour sufficient authority and credibility slowly to implement tyranny. Due in good part to the high moral credibility of his new allies, the saviour will encounter little, if any, significant civilian resistance. At the same time and for similar reasons, the separation of powers in the state apparatus will be destroyed and their function will be merged into a single role: that of applauding the political saviour.

Together, uncertainty, temptation and dangerous alliances lead to the Tunisian muteness syndrome, a particular form of civil anomie, manifested by the notorious prevalence of a unanimous and infatuated adulation of the political saviour.

Such destruction of state-and-civil-society structures is in turn fatal to the polyarchic public forum because the relationships of checks and balances among the four powers are no longer possible when not only all differentiated roles have been eliminated, but also when civil society has lost its organizational autonomy and external solidarity links, when political actors have been isolated and silenced, and when the new political saviour has taken centre stage in the media, parliament and the judicial processes. What I have named the Tunisian muteness syndrome leaves civil society defenceless and voiceless, and the individual isolated in the face of the authoritarian tendency.

This is not, however, the end of the story, but only the starting point of its internationalization. Among the many people trapped inside a unitary political system, some will escape and some of the escaped will strive to reopen the closed public forum from outside the country. Beyond local borders, dissidents soon discover that the international public forum and the surrounding political systems can contribute to the survival of dictatorships. In turn, they develop lobbying networks and communication strategies initiating a radically different scenario: the reopening of the local public forum.

The International Media's Connivance with Dictatorship

Cultivation of the state's self-image abroad
The public relations strategy of a dictatorship's propaganda often consists first of convincing the international public and the media that the political saviour is supporting democracy (or people's power, or national independence) against dreadful political enemies. The spectrum of crypto-enemies has varied accordingly from international capitalism's plot against the working class to the threat of neocolonialist powers and, more recently, the fundamentalist movement in the Sunni Muslim world, all of which have served to legitimate 'temporary' lasting dictatorship.

Dissent having no international access
In such an unfavourable informational climate, exiled opponents have been forced into the posture of isolated dissidents strenuously fighting against the spiralling silence of the public forum. At this first stage, it is understandable that no one listens to these eccentric and unknown characters. For a long time, Soviet dissidents looked awkward and lacking in credibility under the spotlights of NATO's propaganda. Similarly, it took several years, if not decades, for the Maghrebi human rights activists of the 1980s and 1990s to mobilize major international support.

External connivance
Herman and Chomsky (1988), among others in the United States, built a strong case concerning the US foreign affairs establishment's connivance with dictatorships while the mainstream American media keep silent. In this instance, silence was a safe strategy for the media so long as public opinion remained indifferent to foreign policy. The same, I believe, is likely to apply to the foreign policies of other democracies. Let me just recall, as an example of this phenomenon, Canada's refusal to grant asylum to the victims of the Holocaust at a time when a powerful spiral of silence was imposing anti-Semitic attitudes on North American public opinion (Delisle 1998).

The political economy of media subjectivity
The hypothesis of the functional subjectivity of international information (as developed in Chapter 8) explains why a given political system may survive so long in spite of the 'stress' (in Easton's sense) put upon it by internal and external dissent until, at a later stage, an informational climate in favour of democratic reforms develops.

As a matter of fact, dissident and alternative information may provide evidence against a dictatorship's propaganda to the international public for a long time before the world's mainstream media put such information on its agenda. Such media partiality and deafness to muted voices feed upon the media's need to solve efficiently the following dilemma: credibility means that the news is never wrong or incomplete, but in a highly competitive context it is necessary to release news quickly, skipping the time-consuming task of verifying it.

The standard solution to this dilemma consists of routinely relying on the mainstream, ostensibly most authoritative sources, including official sources, and discarding alternative information. This is why even the international media can be so easily manipulated and tricked into publishing pure political fantasies (for example, the notion that the brave Algerian military are safeguarding democracy against the evil fundamentalists that came close to winning the 1992 free election).

In order to maintain their credibility in spite of their dangerous reliance on the official news sources reflecting their governments' standpoint, foreign correspondents have developed rhetorical devices consisting of presenting news as only possibly true but none the less coming from credible sources. This is how propaganda can be made to look so good and fills up the front pages of the world's newspapers over and over again until repetition makes it less newsworthy. It is only when the constant repetition of official propaganda makes it less newsworthy that the media start to shift their attention to dissident sources of information. The resulting creation of controversy has proved to be efficient marketing.

Media bias is also driven by the necessity for foreign journalists to preserve good relationships with their sources. Terror, censorship, the fear of being frozen out of potential stories, plus the cautious desire to be looked upon with favour by those in power and the consequent sense of privilege enjoyed (at the price of ignoring banned unofficial information) are the commonly noted motivations of journalists for co-operating with propaganda and censorship. Co-operation takes the form of reproducing the 'conventional wisdom of their host authorities, but in terms and images that have an ongoing purchase upon the public's mind' (Downing 1996: 236). The overwhelming lack of critical sense on the part of foreign correspondents is one more factor that con-tributes to the poor quality of international information.

It may be argued that the international mainstream media play a role in actually establishing dictatorial rule by reinforcing the unstable legit-imacy of authoritarian regimes through international recognition. This general phenomenon may explain why the international public is never provided, except maybe at the time of their collapse, with the true facts about dictatorships and why it is never given advanced signs of popular unrest and regime instability. Authoritarian rule cannot easily maintain security, economic growth or even political consensus with-out external connivance and blindness on the part of the international media.[11] In this respect, should not authoritarianism and totalitari-anism be considered typical of the globalization era? Would Nazi pro-paganda have been so influential in the international public arena without radio?

Reversing the Spiral of Silence

Is the public forum condemned to be helplessly muted whenever a determination develops to impose authoritarian rule, or spiralling silence, or both? Are most so-called democratic transitions bound to fail? Are dictatorships everlasting? Empirical evidence from the political transitions in the second half of the twentieth century, and more particularly those of North Africa, the former Soviet Union and Eastern Europe, illustrate how information can slowly leak out from a muted public forum within a country to dissident networks outside and be smuggled back in as underground information.

Unarmed prophets

For a better understanding of how authoritarian regimes decay, political science must shift attention from generalizations and overall tendencies to exceptions and, more specifically, to the role that individual nonstate actors can play in the process of reopening the public forum.

The expression 'unarmed prophets' was coined by Machiavelli to designate those individuals who dare challenge the rulers and promote new political institutions apparently without any significant means (no police, no army) to implement them. These nonviolent challengers, mockingly referred to by Machiavelli as 'unarmed prophets', can, however, sometimes get access to the international media, spread new ideas, and change the course of events. Here is how this admittedly uncommon occurrence seems to take place.

Even if they are in a minority, the unarmed prophets are by no means just eccentric individuals or abnormal phenomena. Rather, they are essentially products of their respective societies, whether this be in Eastern Europe, the USSR or North Africa. Public opinion may not have openly supported them, except on the eve of collapse of a dictatorship, but it seems to have shared the values invoked by the dissidents and reacted to propaganda accordingly. For instance, as Kubick (cited by Downing 1996: 57) argues, by turning the theme of 'the nation' into a taboo subject, the official media in communist Poland actually caused this silence to be perceived by Polish opinion as a refusal to address the key question of the Polish nation. Similarly, in countries such as Hungary, Poland and the USSR (Downing 1996: 74–5) and North Africa, a long tradition of revering books and writers has favoured the unarmed prophets.

However, resistance is a rather tricky game. For the majority, three attitudes – namely opportunism, fear, and belief in the regime's ideological discourse and promises of a better future – reinforce each other to produce the predominant submissive climate. Stiff penalties, for one, are imposed on those producing, circulating or simply reading banned information. Resistance is thus unlikely to start as a mass phenomenon, and very few individuals dare to challenge the political leadership. This explains the marginal position of the unarmed prophets at the inception of a regime's collapse. Their role is none the less central to the rebuilding of civil communication links, the mobilizing of international support, and at times to give dissident activism a significant place on the international agenda.

Let us look briefly at each of these three processes.

Rebuilding civil communication links

After the public forum has been closed to civil actors, political movements and activists often create their own alternative media in opposition to the indifference of the mainstream media.[12] Their strategy then consists of breaking through such indifference or bypassing censorship by establishing direct communication with the general public through *samizdat* (privately produced inside the country) and *tamizdat* (produced from abroad) bulletins.[13]

Either produced locally or smuggled in from the outside, banned information is none the less the stuff of rumours. Individuals who dare not take a stand finally learn that they are not the only ones thinking contrary to the official discourse. In the long run, alternative external and local media reinforce one another by letting their audiences know that the fight for freedom is gaining supporters inside the country and outside as well. By the same token, these media may contribute, as in the former Soviet Union and the former socialist Eastern Europe, to the slow rebuilding of communication ties in an anomic society, to subversion of the authoritarian/totalitarian political culture and to the production of a culture of protest. Thus on the eve of the regime's collapse, 'everybody knows and everybody knows that everybody knows', even inside the party, that political change is imminent. The first civil actor who then dares to challenge the authorities seems to send the signal for the start of rebellion – which then multiplies in a domino effect. In this way, Sanders (1992) argued that, after the cumulative spread of underground information, it was the Polish Solidarity strike that triggered the popular upheavals throughout the communist world.

Hannah Arendt views terror and ideology as the cornerstones of totalitarianism. Semelin claims that, conversely, resistance performs anti-fear and anti-propaganda functions (1997: p. 13), succeeding in slowly undermining the walls of totalitarianism and loosening the tongues even of official spokesmen. This is how a slow process – lasting thirty-five years (from 1955 to 1989) in the case of Poland, Hungary and Czechoslovakia, about the same span of time in the USSR and some twenty years in Morocco (from 1959 to the 1970s) – led to the gradual disintegration of monopolistic power in all these countries. A similar process seems to be at work in Tunisia and Algeria today. In this light, the creation of an alternative public forum by political activists and their media appears to lay the essential and long-term groundwork in opposition to the silencing of the mainstream media under dictatorial rule.

Mobilization of international support networks
In spite of the powerful obstacles to their claim for more freedom and
human dignity (in the sense provided by international law), dissidents
in Algeria and Tunisia have gradually tunnelled their way into the
same kinds of international networks (nongovernmental organizations,
political parties, alternative media and a few well-known journalists) of
political activism as their counterparts did in Eastern Europe and in the
USSR in the 1960s. This second wave of dissident networks has
performed similar functions – disclosing the dictatorial nature of their
respective regimes, and supporting internal dissidence – and, at times,
it has attained a high level of attention in the world's media.

The media as a target in the struggle over access and meaning
The long-term impact on the media of joint action by dissidents and
social movements is consistent with the teachings of the literature on
social movements. Van Zoonen, among others, explains that the
function of a social movement is to publicize existing conflicts and
produce a symbolic challenge to the dominant codes of society. The
communication of a movement's challenge is reconstructed by other
means of communication, with the mass media being among the most
powerful (Van Zoonen, as quoted by Downing 1996: 202). Understandably, a symbiotic relationship has developed between non-violent dissidents within a country and the international human rights movement, where support such as press releases, press conferences and
petitions can be found. The strategy of joint action aims at mobilizing
support, putting issues on the political agenda and boosting the morale
of participants (Downing 1996: 204).

The impact of dissidents combined with social movement activism
in the West has at times been increased by exceptional events such as
political trials in which the defendants pleaded not-guilty (for example,
the trials of Sinyavski and Daniel in the USSR in 1966), the brutal repression of popular uprisings (Budapest and Prague) or hunger strikes
(Taoufik Ben Brik's hunger strike in 2000 in Tunisia). It is noticeable that
international protest intensifies in consequence of such events.
International activist networks can also deploy a wide range of means,
from official protest to international prizes.[14] Such support for the dissidents' networks can be put on the media's agenda. It then becomes
good publicity not only for the NGOs, but also for the dissidents' cause.
This, in turn, pressures foreign states to take a stand and persuades dictatorships not to inflict serious harm on their dissidents. The rebuilding
of civil communication links, the mobilization of international support

204 THE AFTERMATH OF DANGEROUS ALLIANCES

and the gaining of a presence in the media gradually add to the unarmed prophets' influence in the public forum. The process goes on until their political weight becomes important enough to overcome the inertia of the spiralling silence. The unarmed prophets' open support of internal resistance in the international forum thus revives the social differentiation processes necessary for any stable transition to democracy and consolidation of a polyarchic political system.

Notes

1. The fear of the growing fundamentalist movement in the Maghreb rose to such a pitch that international public opinion became indifferent to the revival of dictatorial rule in Algeria and Tunisia. This widespread attitude bears similarities to the refusal of the international socialist movement to support dissidents of the Soviet bloc during the Cold War: better the mistakes of proletarian dictatorship than the domination of international capitalism.
2. In contrast to O'Donnell's hypothesis (O'Donnell *et al.* 1986 and 1991), Cutler observes that, after Stalin's death, his political heirs covenanted never again to resort to political violence in political competition (1980). In line with Cutler, I believe that neither regime downfall nor political covenant among political actors implies that democracy will ensue. Covenants are less democratization mechanisms than peaceful devices of transition from one rule of governance to another.
3. Given the catastrophic outcome of this Maghrebi scenario, one research priority should consist of identifying the conditions that induce political actors to join a dangerous alliance, as in Algeria, Morocco and Tunisia, as well as to investigate the objective circumstances under which political actors, such as those of Palestinian society, resist this fatal temptation.
4. With Easton (1965a and 1965b) and Merton (1968).
5. With Dahl (1971), Sartori (1987) and Graziano (1996).
6. See O'Donnell *et al.* (1986 and 1991), Tilly (1983 and 2000), McAdam *et al.* (1999), etcetera.
7. This definition intentionally ignores the possible, but controversial, link of the concept with economic powers.
8. The differentiation paradigm was also used to describe the erection of independent states (Leca and Grawitz 1985) and the rule of law. Such a vision, however interesting, is more relevant to a problematic of modernization than to one of democratization.
9. Schmitter's model of civil society (Cansino 1997) implies a society of groups that are independent of the state, legally recognized and capable of elaborating and promoting new social/political rules.
10. This is how in Algeria, during the war of independence, all the civil actors were induced to dismantle competing organizations and join the single party leadership of the National Liberation Front. Some thirty years later, political civilian actors repeated the same mistake by calling for, and thus legitimating, the military coup of 1992. Similarly, as we have seen in this book, the Tunisian National Pact and the alternation of power between left- and right-wing factions of the Istiqlal party in the late 1950s in Morocco were other examples of this sub-

missive strategy consisting of exchanging the civilian power to demand some share of state power.

11. State actors also help in the dictatorships' cultivation of an excellent international image, but this is beyond the scope of this book.

12. Alternative media may consist of anything from newspapers, leaflets, pamphlets and books to what Downing (1996: 76) calls 'everyday' protest media (songs, graffiti, street theatre, etc.).

13. The terms derive, of course, from the Russian dissident movement. However, Downing pleads (1996: 230) that the short-term impact of the alternative media should not be optimistically overemphasized, given both the divisibility of oppression, the corresponding fragmentation of resistance, and the ensuing propensity of excluded actors on either side for joint action, like starting a newspaper, which, in turn, becomes a target in an intra-elite struggle for ascendancy, while other media become colonized by the elite in power. I would like to add that the same restrictive tone should be used concerning post-socialist Algeria, where each military faction financially supports a private newspaper.

14. Solzhenitsyn received the Nobel Prize for literature in 1970 and Sakharov was granted the Nobel Peace Prize in 1975. Similarly, Najib Hosni, the Tunisian lawyer, received the International Human Rights Prize from the American Bar Association and several other international honours while he was being tortured in prison.

References

Arendt, Hannah (1973) *The Origins of Totalitarianism*, New York: Harcourt Brace Jovanovich.

Badie, Bertrand and Guy Hermet (eds) (1984) *Totalitarismes*, Paris: Economica.

Boudon and Bourricaud (1982) *Dictionnaire critique de la sociologie*, Paris: PUF.

Cansino, Cesar (1997) 'Una entrevista con Philippe Schmitter', *Este País*, No. 70, pp. 35–8.

Cutler, Robert M. (1980) 'Soviet Dissent Under Kruschev', *Comparative Politics*, Vol. 13, No. 1, pp. 15–35.

Dahl, Robert A. (1971) *Polyarchy: Participation and Opposition*, New Haven: Yale University Press.

Delisle, Esther (1998) *The Treator and the Jew: Antisemitism and the Delirium of Extremist Right-Wing Nationalism in French Canada from 1929 to 1939*, Montreal: Robert Davies Publishing.

Diamond, Larry Jay et al. (ed.) (1997), *Consolidating the Third Wave Democracies: Themes and Perspectives'*, Baltmore: Johns Hopkins University Press.

Downing, John (1996) *Internationalizing Media Theory — Transition, Power, Culture*, London: Sage.

Easton, David (1965a) *A Systems Analysis of Political Life*, New York: John Wiley & Sons.

Easton, David (1965b) *A Framework for Political Analysis*, Englewood Cliffs, NJ: Prentice-Hall.

Ferrero, Gugliemo (1942) *Pouvoir: Les Génies invisibles de la cité*, New York: Brentano's.

Ferrié, Jean-Noël and Jean-Claude Santucci (2000) 'La Démocratisation au Maroc et en Égypte: Regards croisés', unpublished research paper presented to the International Congress of Political Science in Quebec City in August.

Goban-Klas, Tomasz (1994) *The Orchestration of the Media: The Politics of Mass Communications in Communist Poland and the Aftermath*, Boulder, CO: Westview Press.

Graziano, Luigi (ed.) (1996) 'Tradition in Pluralist Thought', *International Political Science Review*, Vol. 17, No. 3, July.

Haryk, Ilya (1994) 'Pluralism in the Arab World', *Journal of Democracy*, Vol. 5, No. 3, pp. 43–56.

Herman, Edward S. and Noam Chomsky (1988) *Manufacturing Consent: The Political Economy of the Mass Media*, New York: Pantheon Books.

Juviler, Peter (1998) *Freedom's Ordeal for Human Rights and Democracy in Post-Soviet States*, Philadelphia: University of Pensylvania Press.

Leca, Jean and Madeleine Grawitz (1985) *Traité de science politique*, Paris: PUF.

Machiavelli, Niccolò (1908) *The Prince*, Toronto: J.M. Dent & Sons.

Merton, Robert K. (1968) *Social Theory and Social Structure*, New York : Free Press.

McAdam, Doug, Sidney Tarrow and Charles Tilly (1999) 'Contentious Processes in Democratization', 'Dynamics of Contention' (unpublished book).

Montesquieu, Charles Secondat de (1995) *L'Esprit des lois*, Paris: Gallimard.

El-Mossadeq, R'Kia (2000) 'Transition démocratique et labyrinthes de la transition démocratique'. Unpublished research paper presented to the International Congress of Political Science in Quebec City in August.

Noelle-Neumann, Elizabeth (1993) *The Spiral of Silence: Public Opinion — Our Social Skin*, Chicago: University of Chicago Press.

O'Donnell, Philip, Carl Schmitter *et al.* (eds) (1986 and 1991) *Transition from Authoritarian Rule*, 4 vols, Baltimore: Johns Hopkins University Press.

Sanders, Donald (1992) 'The Role of Mass Communication Processes in Producing Upheavals in the Soviet Union, Eastern Europe, and China', in Sarah Sandersen King and Donald P. Cushman (eds), *Political Communication*, Albany: State University of New York Press.

Sartori, Giovanni (1987) *The Theory of Democracy Revisited*, Chatham, NJ: Chatham House.

Semelin, Jacques (1997) *La Liberté au bout des ondes: Du coup de Prague à la chute du mur de Berlin*, Paris: Belfond.

Tilly, Charles. (1983) 'Speaking Your Mind Without Elections, Surveys, or Social Movements', *Public Opinion Quaterly*, Vol. 47, Winter, pp. 461–78.

Tilly, Charles (2000) 'Processes and Mechanisms of Democratization' in 'Struggle and Democratization' (unpublished manuscript).

Touraine, Alain (1992) *Critique de la modernité*, Paris: Fayard.

Zylberberg, Jacques (1993) *La Démocratie dans tous ces états*, Sainte-Foy: Presses de l'Université Laval.

Index

Freud, Sigmund, 5
Front of Socialist Forces, Algeria (FFS),
    64, 69-71, 78, 100, 129
'fundamentalism': label, 48; rejection of,
    119; threat creation/security myth,
    1, 116, 124, 127; Western obsession
    with, 126

Gandhi, Mahatma, 148
gender, equality promotion, 34
General Union of Algerian Workers
    (UGTA), 65
General Union of Moroccan Workers
    (UGTM), 84
General Union of Tunisian Students
    (UGET), 160
German Democratic Republic (GDR),
    73
Ghallab, Abdelkrim, 99
Ghannouchi Rachid Al-, 8, 27, 117-18,
    162, 166, 177
Ghazali, Salima, 77-8
globalization, 185
Gorbachev, Mikhail, 185, 195
Goumeziane, Smail, 132
Grawitz, Madeleine, 188
Graziano, Luigi, 192
Greater Maghreb, concept, 89
Greater Morocco, objective, 99
Grimaud, Nicole, 127
Gruda, Agnès, 142
Guiter, Laurent, 183
Gulf War, 35, 41, 43, 85, 94, 128, 130,
    136, 172

Hachani, Abdulkader, 68
Haddad, Mezri, 154, 156
Hamas, Palestinian, 162
Hamrouche, Mouloud, 61-2
Hani, Abderrahmane, 21
Hanoun, Louisa, 78, 132
happiness, Tunisian propaganda, 113
Harmel, Mohamed, 27
Haryk, Ilya, 108, 195
Hassan II, Morocco, 2, 81, 83, 87, 89-91,
    98-100, 102, 104, 111, 153
Herman, Edward S., 187, 199
Hermet, Guy, 188
Hidouci, Ghazi, 58, 61-2
Hobbes, Thomas, 189
Hoggar publishers, 78
Hosni, Najib, 16, 157, 161, 165
Hudson, Michael, 177

Human Rights Watch, 155, 158
human rights: international, 203; inter-
    national organizations, 96; legiti-
    macy discourse, 173; Moroccan
    organizations, 92; Moroccan
    reported abuses, 94; notion of, 34;
    politicized, 30; press coverage, 171-
    2; 'security' erosion, 176
Hussein, Saddam, 35

illiteracy, rates, 73, 96
Institute of Journalism and Information
    Sciences, 26, 40
International Association of Democratic
    Lawyers, 87
International Centre for the Victims of
    Torture, 155
International Commission of Jurists, 17
International Committee for the
    Liberation of Najib Hosni, 166
International Federation for Human
    Rights (IFHR), 7, 52, 100, 150, 153,
    159, 182
International Labour Organization, 152
international media: manipulation, 199;
    role, 143
International Monetary Fund (IMF),
    126
International Olympic Committee
    (IOC), 148, 162
international press, 113, 128, 137;
    Algeria coverage, 130, 132, 136-40;
    censorship, 49; failures, 186; motiva-
    tion, 109; Tunisian harassment of,
    50-2; Tunisian taboos, 146 internet,
    information, 77
Iran, 120; revolution, 27
Iraq, 12; Arab support for, 94
Islam: essentialist perception, 169;
    Maghreb press coverage, 171-7;
    Morocco, 176; nationalist concept, 99;
    pluralism, 176
Islamic Salvation Front (FIS), 2, 32, 56,
    64-9, 127, 129, 133, 136-8, 170, 174;
    banned, 62; internal divisions, 70;
    mass organisation, 61
Islamists: Algeria, 56, 61; demonization,
    116-20, 127, 30-2, 137, 161, 163, 169;
    warfare against, 66; Tunisia, 26-9,
    34; women against, 109
Israel, 162; -Palestinian conflict, 172
Istiqlal party, Morocco, 2, 81, 84-5, 88-
    91, 97-8, 100